The Real World of Poldark

Cornwall: 1783-1820

Bernard Deacon

Published by CoSERG, Redruth, Cornwall
https://bernarddeacon.com/

ISBN: 978-0-9513918-6-0

Printed by KDP

To Liz

Contents

Preface vii

Introduction.. 1

Chapter 1: The Mine 5

Chapter 2: The Counthouse 24

Chapter 3: The Cottage 41

Chapter 4: The Road 60

Chapter 5: The Sea.. 73

Chapter 6: The Chapel 92

Chapter 7: The Plain an Gwarry 106

Chapter 8: The Crowd... 123

Chapter 9: The Great House 141

Chapter 10: The Prison 156

Chapter 11: The Borough 176

Conclusion and reflections.. 188

Further reading and sources 192

Preface

Wozzon then, pard?

Ross Poldark 'ee say? Ess, I d'knaw the family well. Cousins of mine twice-removed over to Nampara, up beyond St Ann's. Not that I visit tha' often. Well, not at all, to tell 'ee the truth. Caan't spare the time y'see, what with teeling the taties, raring the pig and go'en down bal on evening core most weeks.

T'be 'onest with 'ee, I knaw'd his fayther Joshua better. Tha' wuz some boay, I tell 'ee. Always up for a popantowse, he wuz. And never said no to a drop, knaw what I d'mean, do 'ee? Mind 'ee, let that girt owld house fall into some staate, so I d'hear. Went to rack and ruin wi' Ross gone over t'Ameriky to scrap with they colonists. Bleddy daft idea tha' wuz too, most of us down Porthemmet were rootin' for they Amerikans.

Anyways, when Ross came back after owld Josh passed round land, well, there wuz 'ell up. They d'say he foun' they two 'alf-wit servants Prudie and Jud Paynter, 'ad drunk their way through owld Joshua's store of free traade brandy in record time. They wuz drunk as skunks when Ross 'appened 'ome middle of night. Some maazed 'ee were. You'd be too after spendin' a day cooped up in a coach from Snozzle, I tell 'ee. Threaten'd to thraw 'em out without a penny, 'ee did. Tho' dunno how serious tha' wuz as didden 'av a penny hisself at the time to taak on anyone else.

Anyways, all went quiet for a bit. Then we 'eard tell he'd stole some maid from over Illogan. Her people weren't too keen. Fayther and brothers stanked up Nampara to 'av it out with 'ee, But they forgot ee'd bin boxing champion at Trura School. Scat 'em all over the cloam. Went back Illogan and raised a pretty bunch of their maates. But 'twas all wind. Ran away when they thoft they saw a bucca on the cliffs. Or so they d'say.

Cut a long tale down fer 'ee, 'ventually Ross up and married that Demelza maid. That caused a few tongues t'start wagging, I'll tell 'ee. But the maid did fine. Raised several childern. Ran the farm like a Tartar. Wouldna' recognise the owld plaace.

Mind 'ee, she weren't so taken with Ross's feud with the Warleggans. Picked the wrong buggers there to wrassle with, if 'ee take my meaning. Owld Warleggan were a blacksmith out to Stithians. But he and his boay wuz lucky. Got in early on the copper traade. Made a mint. Then opened a bank and really started printing a passel of money til they owned 'alf of Cornwall.

Funny thing is, no matter 'ow many airs and graaces they put on, everybody laughs at they behind their backs. (Wudden do to do et to their faaces, tho'). On t'other 'and, Ross, who didden 'av nothen much, allus seemed to be proper gentry, knaw wot I mean? Blood will out, they d'say.

I'm told that people upcountry wants t'av a gake at we, knaw a bit more 'bout wot 'tis like down 'ere in these changen times. Caan't see why fer the life of me. But if it's news from owld Cornwall 'ee d'want then you've come to the right man. Here 'ee'll find a proper job, all sorts of traade about our plaace and the totalish folk that d'live 'ereabouts. 'Ritten by a boay 'oo knaws all 'bout these things. Or so 'ee sez. Not that I can be certan coz I caan't read too well meself. Never 'ad time, what with the taties, pigs and bal, y'see.

Best get along neaow tho', soaz. Feed the pig, then see whether th'owld woman's stopped nattering long enough to bake a pasty fer dinner and then a fuggan fer after.

Denzil Penberthy Poldark, Porthemmet, 1783.

Introduction

The *Poldark* novels of Winston Graham offer a picture of Cornwall from the 1780s to 1820. In these books, especially the first four, published between 1945 and 1953, Graham took real incidents that had occurred in Cornwall and wove them into his story. In so doing, he was advised in the late 1940s by a Cornish historian, Fred Harris, who headed Exeter University's Extra-Mural Department in Cornwall. Fred was a fund of knowledge on Cornwall's history in the period of the industrial revolution and Winston Graham quarried the insights of Fred and others to ensure his plots retained a connection to historical reality. This can be seen for example in the feud between the Bassets of Tehidy and the Boscawens of Tregothnan, which was based on actual disagreements between the families of those names. Moreover, some of his fictional creations closely reflected real life, as in the Warleggans who encapsulated the more general rise in Cornwall of merchant-banking families. With these characters stalking the background, he recounted the lives of the Poldarks, his more purely fictional invention.

In the mid-1970s a television adaptation of the early novels appeared while Winston Graham returned to the subject to add several more books to the series after a gap of 20 years. The first TV series was later followed by a second, aired in the 2010s. Critical analysis of the *Poldark* books and the television series based on them has generally been thin. An interesting exception is an article published in 2019. In this, Hannah Greig, who was the historical advisor to the recent TV series, provides a critical insight concerning the failure of the history in *Poldark* to make much impact and the importance of the audience's consumption of TV adaptations as much as the details of their production is an important one.

She agrees that Winston Graham, through the subtle and rich details and examples he used, showed a considerable grasp of the historical context of the times. But she goes further. She argues that Graham had 'created a deeply researched, revisionist historical world in his fiction', escaping the previous emphasis of eighteenth-century history on dukes and duchesses and the lives of the aristocracy. More than that, the *Poldark* books were 'innovative', anticipating the work of the 'new' British social history of the 1960s by a full twenty years.

Yet, this 'strikingly revisionist' account of eighteenth-century Cornwall has not been recognised as such at the point of consumption. When the initial TV adaptation appeared in the 1970s it was critically panned, not regarded as 'genre-defining' at all but as 'uncomplicated mainstream'. Furthermore, when the second series made its appearance, it was universally and simplistically packaged by the media as 'another Downton Abbey', despite the two histories being poles apart in their period setting and context. The meaning of the history in *Poldark* had somehow got lost in the transition from page to screen. As one of those producing the first TV series admitted, 'there was a bit of history but it was a romp'. The pull of the programme was not its historical innovation, which passed most people by, but the sexual tension around Ross Poldark's relationship with Demelza and the idealisation of Ross as hero. Precisely the same happened with the second series when the media fixated on the Ross Poldark/Aidan Turner character.

However, we can add another aspect to this critique. Audiences are not homogeneous. The TV series were consumed by people of different classes and genders who lived in different locations and had differing ethnic backgrounds. Most of the discussion of *Poldark* takes it for granted that the audience being addressed is one external to Cornwall. This is unsurprising given that the first series of the TV adaptation attracted as many as 12 million viewers, or around 28 times the entire population of Cornwall at the time.

In her article, Hannah Greig compared the opening title sequence of the second series of *Poldark* with that of *Downton Abbey*, noting that the 'turbulent Cornish coastline in the background roots the drama in its key location' of Cornwall. No doubt it did this for the majority of its audience, but coastlines and seascapes may not have the same meaning for a Cornish audience. For many native Cornish, particularly those brought up inland, the coastline is not the principal signifier of Cornwall. For them, it might be another well-known iconic place – Carn Brea, Brunel's bridge, St Michael's Mount for example - or it could equally well be the much more anonymous streets and lanes remembered from childhood, or an undistinguished yet cherished patch of woodland or countryside.

For insiders *Poldark* and the history within it may well take on different meanings. Some of these might not be positive. The reported 'Poldark effect', which seems to consist of even more tourists and congestion and a rise in long-distance enquiries at local estate agents about second homes for sale, might not be universally welcomed. Indeed, this effect may further serve to stifle any appreciation of the history in *Poldark*.

In this respect, the final season of the most recent TV series, which diverged from Graham's books, was a particular disappointment. The amount of eye candy provided by aerial shots of majestic cliffs and pounding surf grew exponentially. It began to seem as if everything in Cornwall took place on clifftops – chance meetings, suicide attempts, mining. Most ludicrously, even a school was built right next to a precipitous drop of a few hundred feet, which wouldn't have done too much for the local child mortality rate. Pretensions to historical reality dissolved in favour of a more straightforward romantic genre, Cornwall moving from centre stage to backdrop. The plot was more concerned to say something about the issues of twenty-first century Britain – racism, mental health, democracy and corruption in high places - than it was to explore those of Cornwall at the end of the eighteenth century.

With each episode the story became more improbable. By the last one, plot inconsistencies had reached absurd heights. Any resemblance to actual life in Cornwall at the end of the 1700s had been largely lost. It's not that the Cornish had become the butt of the usual tiresome and predictable stereotypes as in other TV programmes such as *Doc Martin*. Instead, they had entirely faded away. *Poldark* had ended up metaphorically leaving Cornwall by ignoring its people. Cornwall was now reduced to its familiar state of a mere picturesque backdrop for romantic fantasy, a safer and more comfortable reading preferred by the mass media and the marketing gurus of the tourist sector.

Some have proposed that the popularity of the *Poldark* books and their spin-offs is linked to a nostalgic yearning for a simpler past, felt especially at times of 'national' stress. As we saw above, it may be less profound than this and more simply be ascribed to the pull of the plot and the attraction of the main characters. Moreover, when using the words 'national stress', most commentators would have in mind, either consciously or sub-consciously, the English nation, or perhaps a fictitious 'British' nation. However, another nation shares these islands, one usually overlooked but nonetheless officially designated as a nation in 2014. If the popularity of *Poldark* is really linked to a nostalgic yearning at times of national crisis then one nation that might experience more than its fair share of that yearning is the Cornish one, for the Cornish face an even greater existential crisis. Rapid population growth and in-migration, urbanisation and gentrification and the relentless commodification of Cornwall driven by an insatiable tourist sector and central and local government policies have brought the Cornish nation to what some might argue are its final days. At such a time, when the future of Cornishness itself hangs in the balance, it's good to look back to a more optimistic period, a more confidently Cornish time, to refresh us for the struggles required in the present. That is what this book sets out to do.

My aim is not to assess whether Winston Graham was right or wrong in this or that historical detail. This is not a forensic examination of the accuracy of the wrecking episode on Hendrawna beach, or the riot in Truro or the raucous roistering that accompanied the election in Bodmin, all of which appear in his books. Although Winston Graham's history was ahead of its time, in *Poldark* reality is moulded to fit the narrative and enhance the plot. In this book, more prosaically, facts are used to build up a picture of what life was really like in the Cornwall of the *Poldark* saga, between 1783 and 1820.

Now that the *Poldark* series has ended and its last outing no more than an embarrassing memory, we might restore the Cornish dimension. To do this, we'll travel back in time to the real Cornwall and visit some of the main elements in the physical and social landscape of the times. Meanwhile, we'll not entirely lose sight of the fictional characters of Winston Graham's very readable books. However, the parallel fictional world of *Poldark* will be relegated to a place in the background. Instead, Cornwall and the lives of its people will move to the foreground. That does not mean the story of Cornwall in Poldark's times will be unremittingly dour, boring and unromantic. Quite the contrary; the period which saw Cornwall build on its early industrialisation was highly romantic. It was a time of staggering wealth and appalling squalor, of high days and hardship, ingenuity and invention, great power and grasping greed, righteous indignation and riotous outbursts, religious fervour and ferocious feuds, and all to a constant background noise of war and social change. It was fundamentally a time when the world began to turn on its axis and Cornwall for a brief spell found itself at the forefront of new ideas and a new world.

Bernard Deacon, Redruth, 2021

1
The Mine

In 1799 George Lipscomb, a 26-year old surgeon from Buckinghamshire, set out to explore the south west corner of the British Isles. Meandering on horseback across southern England, he finally reached the land west of the Tamar. Crossing the river, he rode slowly along the narrow lanes, up and down the hills and valleys of east Cornwall, seeing little to excite his imagination. Then, he reached Polgooth Mine, just to the west of St Austell in mid-Cornwall. Once there he:

> began to regret our having proceeded so slowly ... now
> we had arrived in a spot that was truly interesting, at
> the land of a new country of which we had previously
> formed no tolerable idea, and among a people whose
> customs and manners afforded us a subject worthy of
> rational reflection, as highly different from everything
> to which we had been accustomed.

Sadly, no sooner had this jaded traveller found something to jerk him out of his comfortable boredom than he had to turn his horse around and head back east. Lipscomb had encountered his first tin mine, but had not got anywhere near the busy, throbbing heart of Cornwall's industrial region. That lay several miles further west, where the district around Nampara, the fictional home of the Poldark family, marked its eastern boundary.

More intrepid visitors, or at least those not so pressed for time as George Lipscomb, did manage to venture as far as that precociously early industrial region. One, Thomas Preston from Norfolk, left his impression in his diary entries for 1821. As he journeyed into the west, Preston found 'the mines ... occupy the attention of the principal inhabitants'. At Truro, he noted that talk revolved around 'the value of shares of such and such a mine'. Eight miles further on, at Redruth 'it is the weight of a piece of ore or the quality of what was raised or dug up yesterday'. This neatly sums up the contrasting roles of these two towns in Poldark's time. Truro contained many of the merchants and middle classes who provided capital for the mines. It also hosted the town houses of the local gentry who owned the mineral rights. Redruth was more hands on. Its people were directly involved in the business of mining. When not themselves mining, they were making money from supplying the booming mining villages that had mushroomed during the 1700s and now clustered around this market town.

'the hollow jarring of the distant steam engines'

On television, we saw Ross Poldark galloping along the cliff tops, crystal clear in the sparkling sunlight. Back in 1795, an anonymous visitor was more concerned with the smoke that enveloped the mining district. Redruth was 'in a cloud of smoke ... which is the reason we did not breakfast'. Although he noted that Camborne was 'a small village delightfully free from smoke', the country between there and Penzance, 'is filled with smoke from the number of steam engines'. The smoke from the ponderous, creaking pumping engines, in addition to that from people's fireplaces, was striking evidence that west Cornwall was leading the way into the fossil-fuel driven industrialisation that has since revolutionised the world, perhaps rather too effectively for comfort. However, in the 1790s any such doubts lay well into the future. Other visitors too commented on the unusual level of air pollution in west Cornwall. In 1794 William Maton observed that the sand:

> blown about by every blast ... renders [the appearance
> of Hayle Towans] truly dismal, the immense volumes
> of smoke that roll over it, proceeding from the copper
> houses, increase its cheerless effect, while the hollow
> jarring of the distant steam engines remind us of the
> labours of the Cyclops in the entrails of Mount Etna.

Both the anonymous visitor and William Maton were also struck by the 'very few trees'. In west Cornwall the easily accessible woods had long since been cut down to make charcoal to smelt the tin dug up since Roman times or earlier. For visitors from the south east of England, fastidiously following the fashionable criteria for a 'good' landscape in 1800 – woods and water in proper proportion – these west Cornish landscapes were dreary, even 'horrid'. Later, in 1832, the *Quarterly Mining Review* described the mining district of Redruth. 'The country [has] a peculiarly naked and open appearance, this circumstance renders the villages, scattered cottages, engine houses, mine buildings, and machinery extremely conspicuous, even at a distance.' Our anonymous visitor of 1795 concluded that mining gave 'the country the appearance of a heap of ruins', with 'hills of rubbish ... brought up from the mines.'

Observing Francis Basset's estate of Tehidy, F.W.L. Stockdale wrote in 1824 that the 700-acre park with its 'extensive plantations', recently added in the late 1700s:

> appear like a well cultivated garden, in the midst of a
> sterile desert. Its spreading woods are beheld with
> additional delight, from the contrasted scenery of the
> surrounding country, where the face of nature has been
> robbed of all ornament, and the earth scattered over its
> surface in the pursuit of ore'.

Similarly, for the Reverend Richard Warner in 1808, the mining country was 'like a district filled with extinguished volcanoes, which, having exhausted their fury, could now only be traced in the universal desolation they had occasioned'. One of the most vivid descriptions of Cornwall's mining district was written by William Beckford, who visited Consolidated Mine in Gwennap in 1787:

> 'At every step one stumbles upon ladders that lead into
> utter darkness, or funnels that exhale warm copperous
> vapours. All around these openings the ore is piled up
> in heaps ready for purchasers. I saw it drawn reeking
> out of the mine by the help of a machine called a whim
> put in motion by mules, which in their turn are
> stimulated by impish children hanging over the poor
> brutes and flogging them without respite. This dismal
> scene of whims, suffering mules and hillocks of
> cinders extends for miles. Huge iron engines creaking
> and groaning invented by Watt, and tall chimneys
> smoking and flaming, that seem to belong to old
> Nicholas's abode, diversify the prospect. The miners
> who crawl out of the dark fissures are woeful figures in
> tattered garments with pickaxes on their shoulders.

For visitors, the scenes of industry and the spoil heaps, known in Cornwall as burrows, were a 'remarkable feature'. Cornwall between Truro and Penzance had been literally turned inside out, its innards dumped indiscriminately over fields and common land as mining operations extended in the 1700s. By the early 1800s, what greeted the traveller was the thump and hiss of steam engines, the clatter of the iron stamps crushing the ore, the sight of the smoking engine houses surrounded by their untidy scatter of mine buildings, cottages chaotically placed, lanes and footpaths winding from hamlet to mine, through all of which herds of goats roamed untethered.

a restless spirit of adventure reigned

As the landscape was disfigured, the ground beneath disgorged its riches for some and created work for many. Yet, writers at a distance had often not woken up to the fact that the cause of all this upheaval was not in fact the pursuit of tin. A long history of tin mining going back at least to the Roman period and probably before had spawned the ramshackle rules and regulations of the Stannaries by the thirteenth century. These were testament to the central role of tin mining in Cornish society and oversaw the closely policed and cumbersome process of coinages, where all smelted tin had, by law, to be assayed, weighed and stamped by Duchy of Cornwall officials. The lazy use of the word 'tinners' at this time to describe the crowds that, as we shall see later, periodically rioted at times of dearth and hardship further reinforced Cornwall's association with tin mining.

However, the main mineral propelling west Cornwall along a path to the age of modernity was not tin at all, but copper. The search for copper gained pace in the early 1700s as demand for this metal grew from the brass industry and from the growing use of copper in utensils, in armaments and not least for coins. While tin production was stable, copper production grew steadily during the 1700s. From half the value of tin in the 1720s, it was equal by the 1740s and four times greater by Poldark's time in the 1780s. Over the next 40 years it more than doubled again while the value of the tin extracted flatlined.

The tin mines were dispersed across Cornwall, at St Just and St Ives in West Penwith, in the parishes of Breage and Wendron near Helston, and in Poldark country at St Agnes. These were supplemented by mines like Polgooth and other smaller operations to the south and east of Bodmin Moor in east Cornwall. Copper production, on the other hand, was anything but dispersed. On the contrary, it was concentrated on a compact district between Hayle in the west and Chacewater in the east. Furthermore, before the 1800s the five most productive mines usually accounted for at least half of the copper ore mined. In the 1790s the largest mines were found in an incredibly constricted tract of country not much more than five miles in length, from Tincroft and Cooks Kitchen mines just east of Camborne, to Consolidated and United Mines, to the east of the villages of St Day and Carharrack. From this small district in 1798 came three quarters of the copper ore mined in Britain. By 1805, the re-opening of Dolcoath Mine, probably Cornwall's greatest mine, at Camborne, and the temporary upsurge of production at Wheal Alfred and Wheal Abraham between Camborne and Hayle had stretched this core mining district somewhat, but not greatly. The concentration of this mining district no doubt emphasised the striking impression it made on the visitors of the 1790s.

Within this confined zone, a restless spirit of adventure reigned. One example was seen in what became known as the 'Great County Adit', begun in 1748. This was a tunnel driven from Twelveheads in the Poldice Valley, which led south to the Fal estuary. The tunnel cut northwards with the original intention of helping to drain the mines of the St Day area. By 1793 it had reached far further, to Wheal Peevor, north east of Redruth. By 1819 the furthest branches of the adit extended five and a half miles from its portal at Twelveheads, draining 12 square miles. For its time, this was an instance of advanced construction techniques, although one completely invisible to the casual traveller above ground.

a 'considerable market town'

Cornwall's new copper mines demanded a growing number of workers. In 1799 the mining merchant and investor John Vivian estimated that over 10,000 men, women and children were directly employed by the copper mines. To feed the voracious appetite of the mines for labour, the population of Cornwall was at this time steadily rising. The estimated 135,000 of 1760 had become 160,000 by 1780. By 1801 the total population was to hit 200,000 and by 1821 over 260,000. This was population growth on a scale not seen again in Cornwall until the 1970s and 80s. Over the 40 years of the *Poldark* saga the Cornish population rose by 100,000, or over 60 per cent, a higher rate than east of the Tamar River.

A growing number of people meant new settlements. Cornwall's towns and villages were already dispersed, with no dominating large town as was usually found in English counties, and a large number of scattered hamlets. This inheritance from the time of Cornwall's days of Celtic independence was, if anything, sharpened as the industrial region emerged. Copper lodes were not neatly confined to a convenient central place but spread confusedly over a sprawling zone of mineralization. In consequence, mines were sprinkled over the countryside. New villages sprang up to house the labour they required. Later, these workers lived in the characteristic rows of small, stone cottages that began to be built in the first part of the 1800s. But that was after Poldark's time.

In his day new villages were more likely to contain a huddle of cob-walled cottages, hastily thrown up higgledly-piggledly. This process was seen with most clarity in the large parish of Gwennap, home to several of Cornwall's most productive copper mines in the 1790s. In Cornwall, those villages, hamlets or even the single farmsteads which were home to the parish church were known as churchtowns. At Gwennap, the churchtown in the south of the parish continued its sleepy existence, a handful of cottages nestling within easy reach of the medieval church. But to north and west, in the mining country, new villages – Lanner, Carharrack and St Day – were expanding fast, eventually to dwarf the old churchtown. Sometimes villages became towns. Hayle was a late eighteenth century straggling new town, its growth stimulated indirectly by the demands and produce of the mines. Camborne was a small churchtown with a mere seven houses in 1770. By 1800 it had grown to 120 houses and around 600 people and in 1802 a market was established. Buoyed by the wages paid at Dolcoath, in the 1800s Camborne began to rival its neighbour Redruth, just four miles away. By 1821 Stockdale could describe it as a 'considerable market town'.

Moreover, given the concentrated and uneven aspect of Cornwall's copper boom, its late eighteenth-century population growth was also unevenly distributed. Numbers grew fastest in the districts closest to the mines, especially before 1800. There was, in consequence, an ongoing shift in the balance of people, from the east to the west, towards the greedy labour demands of the western mines. But what did those working on and in those mines actually do?

'pick out the hard ore by the glimmering of a small candle'

Here's Reuben Clemow, in the first book of the *Poldark* saga, slouching back from his work down a mine. He's wearing an 'old hard hat with its candle stuck to the front by clay'. Candles were the sole source of illumination underground. He's also carrying some tools, including what's called a 'heavy iron jumper' in the book. This wasn't a cardigan, but a rod, usually called a borer, used for drilling holes in the rock. Earlier, his working day would have begun with the descent to his place of work. This was done by climbing down ladders from one 'level' of the mine to the next. Ladders weren't all vertical by any means, lying at various angles. Moreover, care had to be taken as they could be worn and slippery with rungs broken or missing. Once at his workplace, Reuben and his partner would take turns, one of them holding and twisting the borer, with the other wielding a hammer to beat the borer and drill it into the rock. When it was deep enough, gunpowder was packed into the hole, the powder tamped down and a fuse set and lit. The miners retired to what they trusted was a safe distance and waited for the resulting explosion to bring down some ore-bearing rock. Beating the borer and removing the ore and the waste rock were the two central tasks of the underground miner. Of course, there was a lot more to it than that. Expertise in knowing which way the lode of ore was trending and experience in setting the fuses in the days before the safety fuse had been invented (by a Cornishman) were all critical.

In 1794 the visitor William Maton went down a mine:

> accoutred in a flannel jacket and trousers, a cloth cap,
> an old, broad brimmed hat over the latter (to shelter the
> face from droppings) and a thick pair of shoes ... the
> flannel dress is worn close to the skin, in order to
> absorb the profuse perspiration which the closeness of
> the mine, or the labour of mounting the ladders may
> occasion.

Maton did not go into detail about what he saw underground but another visitor in 1791 did. At 80 fathoms (or 480 feet) depth he came across 'two sorry wretches [who] were busied in the process of their miserable employment. With hardly room to move their bodies, in sulphurous air, wet to the skin and buried in the solid rock, these poor devils ... pick out the hard ore by the glimmering of a small candle whose scattered rays will hardly penetrate the thick darkness'. This was not a place for the claustrophobic.

'they scarcely allow themselves time to eat and sleep'

Reuben Clemow would have been employed on one of two contracts, known as tribute and tutwork. Tribute contracts were used to extract the ore. The mine agents (captains) or the mine manager would divide the productive area of the mine into 'pitches', worked by groups of miners. These were called pares, although they would usually consist of more then two men. The pitches would be offered at a certain price, related to the value of the ore raised. If the mine's managers knew a pitch contained rich ore, the price might be low, with the miners receiving only a few shillings for every £ worth of ore they raised. In 1797 a tribute contract as low as four pence in the £ was agreed at Tincroft mine at a time when the adventurers (or shareholders) were taking £3,200 (or over £400,000 in today's money) a month. If, on the other hand, the pitch was a poor one, it might be offered at a high price. Pitches were accepted and contracts (or bargains) agreed at the setting days, which in the 1790s usually occurred every two months. Much was once made of the 'Dutch auction' aspect of these setting days, with groups of miners bidding against each other and offering a lower price to undercut their colleagues and win the pitch. It's now considered that this was rarer than formerly thought. If a pare of miners was established in a pitch, they were usually given the first chance to accept the price set by the mine management. Only if they rejected the bargain would the pitch then be thrown open to bids from other pares. Here's an example of a tribute contract from Briggan Mine at Redruth in 1793: 'a pitch from Nancarrow's shaft so far east as to join Amos Nicholl's pitch from the 55-fathom level as deep as the 61-fathom level'. This was taken by James Cocking and his partner for 13 shillings and four pence in the £.

As not even the most skilled mine captain could predict how exactly the pitch would turn out as it was worked, such contracts involved an element of luck. In 1804 two tributers had taken a poor pitch at 12 shillings in the £. They suddenly hit rich ore in relatively soft ground. According to William Jenkin, the Lanhydrock estate agent at Redruth, 'they scarcely allow themselves time to eat and sleep since they first discovered the ore' and were expected to receive £100 each (around £10,000 in modern terms) for two weeks work. The price of the pitch was also expected to fall to less than one shilling in the £ when the bargain ended. In 1802 Jenkin related how four tributers had tried to get out of a particularly bad contract after a month but were told that if they did so they would not be employed at the mine again. Afraid of losing their places, they continued reluctantly, broke into good ground and received £50 a man at the end of the contract. The ground could of course turn against the tributers and a lode of ore in what seemed a rich pitch peter out unexpectedly. In such circumstances the miners would be left with a disappointingly small income.

While tribute contracts were made to extract the ore, tutwork contracts were the means employed to drive new tunnels or shafts in unproductive ground. In these contracts pares of miners were paid a certain amount per distance developed, the amount depending on the difficulty of the ground being worked. A typical tutwork contract from Wheal Towan near Porthtowan in 1773 read: 'To Richard James and partners for driving adit at 40 shillings a fathom', a fathom being six feet. In a month they drove the adit 26 feet, or four and a bit fathoms.

Opinions on the tribute system varied. The Reverend Shaw in 1788 described it as 'the merest lottery ... thus we find the generality of these inhabitants wafted from time to time on the variable waves of prosperity and adversity'. Others were more sanguine. In 1809 Richard Warner wrote that the contracts usual in Cornish mining 'keeps their [the miners'] spirits in an agreeable agitation, renders their minds lively and alert, and prevents that dullness which generally characterises the English labourer.' While involving a degree of chance and introducing more uncertainty into miners' lives, tribute and tutwork contracts gave the miner a degree of autonomy rather than being employed directly by the hour or day. They were later seen as 'traditional' facets of Cornish mining, linking the nineteenth century miner back to the 'free, self-employed miner' of earlier centuries. In fact, they dated back no further than the early 1700s, replacing an earlier mix of employment types, including day labour.

Agreeably agitated or not, most underground miners, while hoping for a windfall bargain (known as a start or sturt) could spend a lot of their working lives struggling to keep their heads above water in the financial sense (and sometimes literally). Their supplies – candles, gunpowder, ropes, tools - had to be bought from the mine and sometimes the prices of these were not exactly the lowest. They also had to contract directly with surface workers and pay for the raising, dressing and preparing of the ore before it went to the smelter. The delay in payment while costs were being incurred meant that advances (or subsist) were often requested from the mine management. A poor month could well leave a tribute pare in debt to the mine.

'too much brandy drinking'

After digging out the ore or driving the adit miners had to get back to the surface. One of the most exhausting aspects of their daily toil was climbing back up the ladders. It was estimated that climbing 600 feet of the ladders at the end of a miner's shift (called a core in Cornish mining) took around an hour and a half. This climb had to be negotiated after several hours beating the borer and/or shifting rock and often in sopping wet clothes and considerable heat. By the 1790s some mines were as deep as 1,000 feet, which on this basis might have taken as long as two hours to negotiate.

Emerging into cooler, often wet, conditions above ground, the miner then had to walk home. There were few facilities for washing or changing clothes at the mines before the second quarter of the nineteenth century.

Things were ameliorated somewhat by a short working day. Before the 1810s most cores were six hours in length, although there was a growing tendency for this to be lengthened to eight in that decade as mine managements reacted to the periodic depressions which resulted from low ore prices. These, and the greater competition for work that they occasioned, allowed the mines to extend the length of the working day at a time when miners had little power to resist. Before that, in the 1790s, underground miners in Cornwall retained the strong leisure preference typical of pre-industrial workers. Why work once you had earned enough to live on? At a time of high prices and buoyant trade in 1793 William Jenkin reported from Redruth that 'many of them [the miners] refuse to work and have not gone underground for three weeks past'. This was the result of 'high wages' and 'the consequence has been too much brandy drinking'. The lawyer and mines investor Christopher Wallis at Helston was also grumbling in 1795 that 'the miners are uncommonly idle', not working 20 hours a week.

'unfortunately dropped a spark into a cask of gunpowder'

Such criticisms from their censorious 'betters' suggest that Cornish miners in Poldark's time were of an independent, indeed sometimes stubborn and truculent, character. Their independence was evident in the way they looked after themselves and their families, recognising that the unpredictability of their pay left them vulnerable to trade depressions or a run of bad bargains and potentially then dependent on either charity or the Poor Law. This was seen in the widespread membership of friendly and benefit societies among the Cornish miners. In 1803 in Illogan parish, in the centre of the mining district, an estimated 20 per cent of men were members of some kind of friendly society, a proportion that was at that time one of the highest in the UK. The miner realised the need for potential support not only because of the unpredictability of their pay but also because of the possibility of accidents or a long-term illness.

After nearly having his hands blown off when some gunpowder misfired, Mark Daniel sagely advised his young partner 'always d'use the powder wi' a greaterer care'. In those days, before the invention of the safety fuse, the primitive short fuses made from goose quills or reeds were a major hazard. Blinding was not uncommon, as a result of powder misfires. Mark had given good advice but constant working with gunpowder bred its inevitable casual familiarity. In 1792 the *Sherborne Mercury* reported a 'melancholy accident' at Poldice mine. 'Two of the labouring miners smoking their pipes in the fire (steam) engine house, unfortunately dropped a spark into a cask of gunpowder, which blew up and killed the two men dead on the spot, and wounded others in a very dangerous manner.'

Health and safety at work was not a particularly big thing in the 1790s. Other regular causes of accidents were being hit by falling rock. David Bussow perished in 1787 in a mine near Marazion when a stone fell from a kibble (bucket) and struck the unfortunate miner. There was a possibility of drowning in the perennially wet mines if miners broke through to flooded workings, or during a prolonged downpour of rain. Every day, the miners had to face the ladders. Slippery, wet or worn and broken staves (rungs) demanded care and concentration on the climb back up after an exhausting few hours of work. It comes as little surprise to find the parish registers in the mining parish of Wendron recording 13 deaths from mine accidents in the ten years from 1796 to 1806, an average of over one a year.

The lengthening hours of the cores did bring with them one benefit to the miners' general health, something regularly remarked upon in later commissions enquiring into conditions in the mining industry. In the 1800s and 1810s the practice of taking food down into the mines became commonplace. The food needed to be sturdy to withstand damage on the trip down. So what better than a pasty? The pasty, usually filled with potatoes and turnip and a little mutton or pork, became the food of choice for the working miner. If you were unable to get the ingredients for a pasty, then there was always the hobban. This was 'a coarse kind of cake, prepared by incorporating pieces of potato ... with a sheet of dough which is then rolled up and baked'. There was even a sweet version - the fuggan - which was a hobban with raisins, figs or plums added. Or the miner's sweet tooth – if he had any teeth left – could be assuaged by making one end of the pasty sweet while the other end was savoury. Most of the evidence for the diets of the miners at work comes from a generation after Poldark's days. However, we should imagine a gradual spread of pasty-eating in the mines after the 1790s. Any meat available would be reserved for the underground miners, with the surface workers more likely to have to make do with the less nutritious hobbans, although a piece of bacon could occasionally be added to these.

spalling, cobbing and bucking

Underground miners only made up a portion of the workforce. Dressing copper, making it ready for smelting, demanded considerably more labour than dressing tin. As a result, the demand for surface workers had soared. The majority of this workforce was comprised of young women and boys. As early as the 1750s gentry in the west were complaining of a shortage of servants as girls preferred to earn their living at the mine. For boys, surface work served as an introduction to underground mining for some, who were likely to be taken underground, usually by family members, around the age of ten. As an example, Samuel Drew, the noted contemporary historian and Methodist theologian, began his working life at the age of eight, albeit in a tin rather than a copper mine. In Drew's case he managed to escape the mine and within two years was apprenticed to a shoemaker.

Apprenticeship was not an option for most of the thousands of young girls who were flocking to the mines by the 1790s. Often, they had been eagerly pushed there as young as possible by their parents as their wages could make an extremely useful addition to the family income. Indeed, it might be the difference between poverty and, if not plenty, at least a comfortable day-to-day existence. Comfortable may not, however, be the best word to describe the working conditions of the bal maidens, even though they remained securely on the surface. In Cornish mines women never worked underground.

Once they were safely consigned to the history books bal maidens became the subject of a lot of saccharine romanticisation. We hear them in Winston Graham's books singing as they walked to work, 'their shrill, fresh voices as sweet and young as the morning'. True, once the Wesleys' hymns had gripped the Cornish imagination, there were accounts of miners, men as well as women, singing on their way to and from work. But we hear less about the work of the bal maiden, which was hard and physical. For the most part out in the open air and exposed to the frequent wind and rain of the Cornish weather, bal maidens basically broke up pieces of rock using hammers of various sizes. This hammering was sometimes done in a sitting position, sometimes standing. The youngest girls, from eight upwards, may have been trained to pick out worthless rock and older girls may have been 'griddling' the ore in a sieve, but from the age of 10 or 12 girls would be spalling, cobbing or bucking. These processes basically involved breaking down pieces of ore-bearing rock into smaller bits, gradually reducing them to tiny pebbles or powder. Considerable expertise was required and a degree of physical strength.

It was hard work and bred a feisty independence among the young women and girls employed to do it. Escape from this toil came with marriage. Married women would soon be busy enough coping with the steadily growing number of infants that inevitably followed marriage, often well within nine months as the legal act tended to follow rather than precede conception. Marriage ages were young among Cornish miners, as earnings could be maximised at a relatively early stage of the life cycle. In consequence, the likelihood of remaining a bal maiden decreased quite sharply after the age of 20. There was always the possibility of returning in later life, if a widow and childless and with no other support, but this was unusual. For most women in the mining districts work as a bal maiden provided a short rite of passage and period of independence in their teens and early twenties before the equally hard work and extra worries of married life took over.

'excellent men ... selected from among the working miners'

We have met the underground miner and encountered the bal maidens and boys hard at work up on the surface. However, Cornwall's mining population contained another set of men, a group that by the 1790s were taking on a strategic role in Cornish life. These were the mine captains, formally known as mine agents. Captains had a supervisory role and were the people with direct oversight of the working miners. Although in the larger mines answerable to the mine manager, the captain made decisions on tribute and tutwork contracts and had considerable autonomy. Captain Henshawe in Francis Poldark's Wheal Grambler and later in Ross's Wheal Leisure 'could neither read nor write'. He'd been down the mine since he was eight but 'was used to mixing with any class'. Yet Winston Graham may have overdrawn both the illiteracy and the social mobility of his fictional mine captain. In contrast, two captains at Dolcoath – James Thomas and William Petherick – whose working journal of 1822-23 has been analysed by the mining historian Allen Buckley, were far from illiterate.

Mine captains, it was stated in the *Quarterly Review* in 1827, were 'excellent men ... selected from among the working miners', although both Thomas and Petherick at Dolcoath were born into families of mine captains rather than rising through the ranks. But in the boom years of the eighteenth century becoming a mine captain had been one route to social respectability and, for a small minority, riches. While the two men who left the Dolcoath journal may not have been typical, their biographies give us a flavour of the captain's life.

James, or Jimmy, Thomas, was a nephew of the Thomas family who became the mine managers at Dolcoath in the 1800s. Although born in a thatched cottage at Bolenowe, near Camborne, in 1778, Jimmy's family leased a few acres of farmland and he inherited some of this in 1801/2. By then he had married Jane Penpraze at Crowan churchtown (in 1798). The couple had seven children. Five of them survived infancy and all four of his sons also became mine captains. At the age of 11 Jimmy had walked to Gwennap Pit to hear the last sermon preached there by John Wesley and at 22 become a lay preacher for the Wesleyans, a common role taken by mine captains. His working life as a junior mine captain began at the young age of 19 at the Cook's Kitchen mine. By 1815 he was a captain at Dolcoath, dealing with 'the day to day running of the mine underground ... [he] settled disputes, negotiated special payments and ensured the work was done properly and safely'. According to Allen Buckley, after his work Jimmy then walked two miles home to Bolenowe 'to lift his potatoes, carry his hay, or cut his furze'. Or perhaps Jane had done some of that in the meantime.

William Petherick was born in 1796 and brought up close to Dolcoath. He attended a dame school and there learnt to read and write. He was the nephew of John Rule, manager at Dolcoath from 1806 and this no doubt helped his advancement to mine captain in 1822 at the age of 25. Mine captains like William took their duties seriously and had a strong sense of their own importance. They could be hard. William was 'honest and expected the workforce to be likewise. He had no sympathy for malingerers, those who attempted fiddles and bal maidens who stole from the mine could expect no mercy from him'. William Petherick would no doubt have heartily approved of the punishment meted out to a miner at Dolcoath in 1788 who was caught stealing iron worth six pence. Committed to the quarter sessions, he was found guilty and sentenced to a year's hard labour in prison. At the end of this sentence he was to be 'conveyed to Dolcoath mine and be there stript naked from the middle upwards and whipt till his body be bloody'. He was one prisoner who may not have looked forward to the day of his release.

As a body of labourers, the Cornish miner generally tended to receive a complimentary press, both from visitors and insiders. Samuel Drew wrote in the early 1820s that 'though grossly improvident [the miners] are highly intelligent, compassionate, hospitable, industrious, speculative and brave. Among themselves they use the greatest familiarity, expressing their ideas without flattery or fear. On many occasions their language abounds with lively sallies of poignant wit, and their sarcasms are frequently keen and pointed, without being low and vulgar. To strangers they are civil in a high degree: being always ready to communicate the information they desire'. Although in earlier times there may have been some communication problems. William Pryce in 1778 observed that 'the idioms and terms of Cornish miners ... [were] not easily intelligible to gentlemen unaccustomed to mining, who may have occasion to converse or correspond with them'. Nonetheless, Joseph Farington, visiting Cornwall in 1810, 'found them civil and obliging and not all of the description supposed [as having 'something of the savage character']. Lord de Dunstanville (Francis Basset] had assured him that 'when assembled in bodies they are rough when moved by some occasion, but individually are sufficiently peaceable'.

'some bad ones (all of them love drinking too much)'

The mines, the underground miners, the surface workers and the mine captains who ensured things were running smoothly were all increasingly dependent on the improvements being made by engineers. They were responsible for the steam engines that were housed in the most immediately visible element of Cornish mining, both now and in Poldark's time – the distinctive Cornish engine houses that dot the landscape in the mining districts.

When Ross and Francis Poldark met Harris Pascoe to talk over the arrangements for re-opening Wheal Grace, Harris gave them a cryptic warning. They should be careful to avoid litigation over their decision not to use a steam engine supplied by the Birmingham firm of Boulton and Watt. The partnership of the Midlands industrialist Boulton and the Scottish scientist Watt had greatly improved the steam engine in 1775. Watt had invented an engine that could double the efficiency of existing engines. He entered into partnership with the Birmingham engineer Matthew Boulton and in 1775 the pair obtained a 25-year patent for their steam engine. Cornish mines were among the first and most eager customers to install their new engine.

Steam engines had been used in Cornwall since the first one was installed at the tin mine of Wheal Vor in 1710, but they were primitive and little more efficient than some of the ingenuous water wheels that still performed the bulk of the work draining the mines. However remarkable the Cornish miners' use of the power of running water to remove water was, as mines became progressively deeper, water power and deep drainage adits were just not enough. More power was required. But the steam engines at work in the mid-1770s were not performing that well, only 18 of the 40 installed on Cornish mines actually being worked.

Because of the high price they had to pay for coal, all of which had to be imported, the Cornish mines were an obvious market for Boulton and Watt's more efficient engines, the first of which was installed in 1777. This was followed by 40 or so more in the 1780s while a final total of 52 Boulton and Watt engines were at work in Cornwall by 1800. The pair charged a premium equal to a third of the value of the coal saved by using their engine. The historian of Cornwall's industrial revolution, John Rowe, estimated this was around £150 a year for each engine, a not inconsiderable amount more like £15,000 nowadays. Moreover, it did not take too many years for the premiums to exceed the value of the engine. As economic conditions deteriorated in the 1780s it was not surprising that adventurers began to look for cheaper alternatives, patent or no patent.

By this time, there were several talented engineers at work in Cornwall. Not all of these were home grown, notably the Hornblower family who had moved from Worcestershire at mid-century. Jonathan Hornblower senior wrote to Watt in 1776, telling him that 'there are very good engine smiths in Cornwall with some bad ones (all of them love drinking too much)'. Drunk or not, Cornish engine smiths were busy improving on Watt's engine. The response of Boulton and Watt was to threaten prosecution for infringing their patent and a slew of lawsuits duly followed in the 1790s. These proved to be inconclusive with the only people really gaining from them being lawyers. Nonetheless, Boulton and Watt were able to stop the engineer Edward Bull erecting engines in 1793, even though other mines were commissioning engines from the Hornblowers that were variations on (the Hornblowers argued different from) Watt's engine.

'the Cornish giant'

Into this blizzard of claims, counter claims and injunctions strode the not inconsiderably sized boots of Richard Trevithick, Cornwall's best known engineer of the time. Known affectionately as 'Cap'n Dick' or 'the Cornish giant', Trevithick has always had a special fascination for the Cornish. His reliance on practical experiment rather than theory, his physical strength – he was reputed to have hurled a sledgehammer clean over an engine house roof - his prickly independence and his financial hopelessness somehow resonated with the Cornish psyche. He was an inattentive schoolchild but managed to teach himself engineering and mechanics to an advanced level. By his twenties he was advising mine owners on their steam engines. In

1797 he married Jane Harvey, daughter of the founder of Harvey's Foundry at Hayle, a connection from which he curiously gained little advantage.

Trevithick's career with steam power was aided by Cornish mines adventurers' search to escape the payments they were making under Boulton and Watt's steam engine patent. Ultimately, it was Trevithick who was particularly associated with 'high-pressure steam'. His engines involved a more efficient use of steam and allowed for a smaller cylinder. This generally reduced the weight and size of engines. Eventually, it led to the 'Cornish engine' of 1812. Thereafter, Cornish steam engines achieved levels of efficiency that were deemed impossible by the scientific theory of the time.

It was a logical step to take this more efficient, lighter engine and mount it on wheels. From 1801 to 1808 Trevithick came up with at least five versions of a steam locomotive. The first trial run at Camborne gave rise to the song 'Going up Camborne Hill'. Unfortunately, this vehicle met a sorry end on the road to Tehidy, where Sir Francis Basset was eagerly waiting to see it. After breaking down, its attendants had retired to a convenient hostelry. Unwisely they left the fire burning. The boiler ran dry, overheated and the carriage was consumed in flames. Other attempts followed – in London, at Coalbrookdale in Shropshire, at Penydarren ironworks in south Wales and again in London. In the last three of these the engine ran on rails. The device worked although the rails buckled under the weight.

Trevithick spent many years adventuring and inventing in foreign parts. From 1808 to 1810 he was in London, involved in various schemes mainly connected to the river and the sea – a tunnel under the Thames, floating docks, a ship propelled by water jets, iron cargo containers, screw propellers and an early version of a turbine for example. None of these could be turned into lucrative money-spinners, however. After suffering from a bout of typhus and being declared bankrupt, he returned to Cornwall and to the steam engine.

In 1816 he left his seemingly incredibly patient wife and six children to sail to South America and Peru's silver mines. As was his tendency he soon fell out with his associates. Moreover, mining in South America was at this time severely disrupted by the wars of independence from Spanish rule. At one stage Trevithick served with the army of Simon Bolivar, the South American liberator. By 1822 he had left Peru and travelled through Central America to Costa Rica. On the journey he was almost drowned and narrowly escaped being bitten by an alligator. This Central American adventure also proved to be a disappointment and Trevithick found himself in 1827 penniless in Cartagena, Colombia. By an odd coincidence the railway engineer and inventor, and Trevithick's rival, Robert Stephenson, was also in that port. Stephenson lent Trevithick £50 for his voyage home. Late that year Trevithick finally re-joined his family after an absence of 11 years.

'cannot be exaggerated'

Boulton and Watt had finally managed to persuade someone to serve an injunction on Trevithick in 1796 to stop him 'improving' their engine, but he was still doing so at 19 mines a year later. Then, in one of those unpredictable twists that had so often marked Trevithick's life, he came to terms with the pair in 1797 and temporarily transferred his interests elsewhere. Not long after this Boulton and Watt's patent expired and Cornish engineers were free to tinker with their steam engines to their hearts' content.

They went about this with a will. By the 1810s the efficiency of Cornish steam engines was double that of Watt's first engine of 1775. This had doubled again by the 1820s, an impressive rate of efficiency growth that astonished contemporary scientists and which one historian of British steam technology has claimed 'cannot be exaggerated'. Although Trevithick's high-pressure steam engine of 1812 paved the way for later leaps in productivity, improvements were generally more the result of an army of working enginemen making small, incremental improvements to their engines, rather than spectacular, inventive breakthroughs by the likes of Trevithick. In this period too, steam engines were applied more regularly to activities beyond pumping. A whim was a winding engine, used to draw up the ore and waste from the mine and let down materials such as timber. In the 1780s a steam powered whim had been invented by William Murdoch, who was Boulton and Watt's agent at Redruth, but steam whim engines began to replace the previous horse-drawn or water-powered whims in greater numbers only after 1800. From 1813 steam technology was also applied to stamping the ore, crushing it into smaller fragments ready for dressing.

Overall, the Poldark era saw a remarkable transformation of steam engine technology, especially after the constraint of Boulton and Watt's patent was removed in 1800. The application of steam power was much more widespread in 1820 than in 1780, which no doubt did not do much for that air pollution problem in the mining districts, noted by the visitors of the 1790s. Yet, steam technology and air pollution were part and parcel of the growth of mining that drove the expansion of the eighteenth-century

Cornish economy. This created work for thousands and made a minority of people very rich indeed. However, a good proportion of that minority was more involved in the ancillary activities surrounding mining than in the mines themselves. They invested their time and cash in the banks that financed mining or the smelters who transformed the ore into metal, not to mention the other spin-off industries that flourished in the wake of the copper mining boom. It's time therefore to turn from the engine house to the counthouse.

2
The Counthouse

C opper mining did not just redraw the landscape of parts of west Cornwall or provide work. On the back of it, a few families were able to catapult up the social ladder. The Cornish historian Richard Polwhele wrote in 1806 that most of Cornwall's landed families owed their status either to the mine or the borough. We'll leave the borough to a later chapter, but copper mining provided a nice bounty for some of the older landed families. Principal among these beneficiaries were two families that appeared in the *Poldark* books. The Bassets, who could trace their ancestry back to the 1300s, were fortunate enough to sit right in the middle of the mining district and even luckier to own the mineral rights to a fair proportion of it. The Boscawens of Tregothnan, by this time Viscounts Falmouth, who had originally made their money trading in Tudor Truro, also saw their wealth greatly enhanced through ownership of these rights. Mineral rights meant companies leasing the right to mine had to pay an annual royalty to the owner based on the value of the ore raised, whether the mine was in profit or not. This windfall risk-free rent was not restricted to these two estates. Estates in Cornwall tended to be scattered, as were mineral rights. The Lanhydrock estate, although sited in mid-Cornwall, was still able to prosper from the mining boom in the west. Its accounts for 1805 and 1809 show that its income from mines was running at two or three times its income from rents.

As well as adding to the wealth of established families, mining financed the rise of new families. Even before the 1780s, the Lemons had shown in spectacular fashion how Cornwall's mines could provide a route into the landed class. In 1774 William Lemon's election as one of Cornwall's two 'county' Members of Parliament broke the hold of the traditional Cornish parliamentary gentry. Yet Lemon's grandfather, also named William, had come from a somewhat obscure 'humble' background. This had not prevented him getting a basic education and becoming an office clerk and then the manager of a tin smelting works near Penzance. William Lemon, later dubbed 'The Great Mr Lemon' nevertheless owed his rise to traditional means as well as intelligence. In 1724 he married and his wife – Isabella Vibert – brought with her sufficient capital for Lemon to invest in the tin mine Wheal Fortune between Marazion and Helston. This aptly named mine then made him his fortune, with over £10,000 in profits (more than £2 million nowadays). He then moved to Truro and from there invested in the Gwennap copper mines just as they were beginning to boom. Luck and marriage were clearly important components in his rise. Twice mayor of Truro, he bought his country estate at Carclew in 1749. His grandson William was in contrast educated at Oxford, did his Grand Tour of Europe and became an MP, to all intents and purposes indistinguishable from other gentry.

'rather sharp business practices'

The Lemons were already a part of the landed class by Poldark's time. So who was the inspiration for the Warleggans? Several other merchant dynasties followed hot on Lemon's heels and were active in Cornwall in the 1790s. One was the Daniells. In 1760 William Lemon passed on some of his business interests to his chief clerk Thomas Daniell of Truro. Daniell became head of a 'great Truro merchant dynasty', involved heavily in tin smelting in the district. His wealth enabled him to buy a country house at Trelissick on the verdant banks of the Fal estuary, well away from the fumes of his smelters. His son, Ralph Allen Daniell, added to the family fortunes from the lucrative, though short-lived, rise of Wheal Towan, near St Agnes, around 1800, then became an MP while also joining in establishing a copper smelting company at Llanelli in South Wales in 1805.

To the south of Trelissick, in Falmouth, was the Fox family. Moving west from Fowey in mid-Cornwall to the growing port of Falmouth in 1762, George Croker Fox at first made money from exporting pilchards and selling timber and other goods before getting involved in mining. The Foxes were involved in an intricate series of partnerships. They led a consortium in 1792 that built an iron foundry at Perranarworthal. In 1799 they were involved with Francis Basset in re-opening Dolcoath mine, while in 1809 they joined with Basset and the Williams family to finance the Poldice tramway, Cornwall's first railway. They were also heavily committed to Cornish mining with shares in several mines, while their interests extended beyond shareholding to supplying mines as merchants. The Foxes were also practicing Quakers and part of a wider Quaker business network giving them some valuable contacts in the other industrial regions of Britain.

Then there were the Bolithos, later described as the 'the merchant princes of Cornwall'. Like the Foxes the Bolithos had moved west in the 1700s, this time from Penryn to Penzance. It was Thomas Bolitho (1765-1858) who founded their business empire, expanding his tin smelting interests after 1800 and having business dealings in London and Liverpool. From smelting it was a short step to banking, the Bolithos opening their first banks in 1807. But the rise of the Bolithos was rather too late to serve as a convenient model for the Warleggans.

The final candidates for Winston Graham's Warleggans were the Williamses of Gwennap. Their business empire was built by John Williams (1753-1841). Not exactly a blacksmith like the Warleggan patriarch, his grandfather, another John, had nevertheless hailed from a family of tinners and smallholders. He had become manager of Lemon's Poldice Mine and made enough money to settle at Burncoose, on the fringes of the mining district. His grandson, 'Old John', followed him into mine management, building up a portfolio of management positions, with involvement in many of Cornwall's copper mines, including some of the most productive in the Gwennap district. The money from those allowed him to build Scorrier House in 1783. By the 1790s he had a reputation as a canny and effective mine manager. In the 1800s he branched out into infrastructure projects such as the Poldice tramway, mines in Ireland and in Calstock in east Cornwall, where he bought an estate in 1806. Involvement in banking followed in 1810 when Old John became a partner in the Cornish Bank. By this time, he was being helped by his sons, another John, or John Junior, and Michael.

While Old John was a staunch Methodist his son John Junior became a Quaker. This did not stop the family acquiring a reputation for what the most recent historian of Cornish banking has called a 'robust materialism'. When John Junior was being put forward as a partner in the Miners' Bank at Truro a series of letters flowed between James Willyams of Carnanton and the Reverend Henry Hawkins Tremayne of Heligan about his suitability. This correspondence emphasised 'his youth as well as his mining connections and influence, and his rather sharp business practices'. The Williamses, especially Old John, were 'hard men', even by the 'standards of a hard age', driven by individual charisma but building their empire through a series of partnerships, with the Foxes of Falmouth, with the Tweedys in the Cornish Bank and with the Harveys of Hayle.

'more like walking corpses than living beings'

At the time that Ross Poldark was thinking of doing the decent thing by marrying his scullery maid, Cornwall's merchants were tightening their grip on its economy. By 1800, this close-knit network, living within easy distance of each other, was linked together through business partnerships, joint projects and, increasingly, marriage. The buccaneering days of the eighteenth century now behind them, in the new century they began to merge into the older landed class, their money oiling the route to acceptance. Mining had underpinned the ease and comfort of that fortunate minority who owned the mineral rights and those lucky enough to possess shares in a lucrative mine. But the big money was more likely to be enjoyed not by those who depended directly on their involvement in mining but by those who controlled the transformation of the mineral ore into smelted metal. Not that this extended to those who laboured in the smelting works. Somewhat naively, Ross Poldark was shocked at the appearance of the workers at the copper smelting works he helped establish at Trevaunance. This was echoed in the real world by William Maton on visiting the copper smelting works at Copperhouse, Hayle, in 1794. He was horrified by 'the appearance which the workmen in the smelting houses exhibit'. Working in conditions of extreme heat and with the added peril of arsenic fumes, they were 'most emaciated figures.' 'Some of the poor wretches who were lading the liquid metal from the furnaces to the moulds looked more like walking corpses than living beings.' Maton was describing Cornwall's sole copper smelting works. Much more numerous were the tin smelting houses, partly because by Stannary law all Cornish tin had to be smelted in Cornwall, whereas copper smelting was already becoming concentrated around Swansea in South Wales.

Metal smelting was an old-established activity in Cornwall. For centuries tin ore (black tin) had been turned into white tin, the impurities of sulphur and other minerals removed by subjecting the tin ore to heat. Before the 1700s this occurred solely in blowing houses, small buildings where heat was applied directly by burning charcoal. In the early 1700s the reverberatory furnace was introduced to smelt tin. This applied heat indirectly and allowed the smelters to substitute coal as their fuel rather than the increasingly expensive charcoal. The number of smelting houses with reverberatory furnaces grew, although blowing houses were retained for the purest stream tin, when any possibility of pollution from the coal needed to be avoided. The smaller blowing houses had been scattered across Cornwall, but tin smelting houses tended to be more concentrated, near the ports of Penzance and Truro. The one at Calenick, on the banks of the Fal just south of Truro, was Truro's main tin smelter at this time, but others followed in 1810 and 1816 at Coosebean and Carvedras along the River Kenwyn to the north west of the town.

The switch to reverberatory furnaces and larger smelting houses concentrated smelting in fewer hands. This gave the smelters a leading role in tin mining. By the middle of the eighteenth century, according to one historian of Cornish tin mining, 'a small all-Cornish group completely controlled the smelting, financing and purchasing of tin'. They could do this because the mines needed cash to pay wages and buy supplies while the tin ore was being processed by the smelter ready for delivery at the next quarterly coinage. The smelters gave receipts to the mines, who then used them to raise ready money or sold them as bills of exchange, the metal at the coinage being owned by whoever held the bill. It was a short step from this to advancing credit and no surprise to find that tin smelters often became bankers.

Copper smelting was different, yet smelters still had the reputation of trying to fleece the miners if that was at all possible. In 1725 the institution of ticketing copper ore had been introduced in Cornwall in an attempt to prevent the smelters colluding among themselves and reducing the price offered to miners. At the monthly ticketings, mines would offer parcels of ore for sale. The various smelting companies would offer a sealed bid for each parcel, the parcel being sold to the highest bidder. There is a good description of this on page 112 of Winston Graham's *Demelza*.

By the 1790s all but one of the copper smelting companies were based in South Wales. The one exception was the Cornish Copper Company at Copperhouse, mentioned above. Here, copper was smelted from the 1750s until it closed in 1819. The 60 or so years of production at Copperhouse proved that copper could be smelted at a profit in Cornwall. The problem was the transport costs. Smelting copper required two to three times as much coal as did tin smelting. The coal had to be brought from South Wales, from the ports of Barry, Cardiff and Newport. Yet, what would the ships carry on their return trip? Going one way largely in ballast was clearly undesirable. Much more logical was to bring the coal for the mines' steam engines to Cornwall but then take the ore to Wales in return. Moreover, the Welsh smelters were closer to the main market for copper at Bristol and the English Midlands.

By the turn of the century, it was becoming plain that the future of copper smelting lay not in Cornwall but in Wales. That was where the larger profits would be made. Adventurers in Cornish mines realised this and began to move into Welsh smelting concerns. Pascoe Grenfell became the first to make the move to Wales in 1803. Born at Marazion near Penzance in 1761, Grenfell's father was a tin and copper merchant with offices in London. He was followed in 1805 by Ralph Allen Daniel who became a partner in a smelting works at Llanelli. Then John Vivian, a Truro merchant heavily involved in the mines, helped establish a copper works at Hafod. Within ten years this had become the second largest copper producer in Britain. During the later decades of the Poldark period the Cornish merchant dynasties were busy expanding their interests into Welsh smelting concerns. By 1820 the Williamses were poised to enter Welsh copper smelting. The Cornish takeover was complete, a remarkable example of the power of Cornish capital at this time.

induced to promise to go on taking the notes of the Cornish Bank

Cornwall's merchant dynasties were not just diversifying into copper smelting. They were also heavily involved in the first Cornish banks. In the *Poldark* books the independent banker Harris Pascoe valiantly competes with the resources of the Warleggans' bank. It wasn't quite like that in reality. Yes, this was the great age of the independent, pioneering banker and several banks were set up before 1800 – at Falmouth in 1782, Penzance in 1795, St Austell in 1793, Helston in 1788 and Bodmin in 1790. These country banks ensured that Cornwall was at the forefront of the development of provincial banking. Later, in 1807 Thomas and William Bolitho of Penzance established the Mount's Bay Commercial Bank there and in the same year the East Cornwall Bank at Liskeard. But in fact, the demands of the mining industry for credit had meant that banking partnerships had been a familiar part of the financial scene at a much earlier date in Cornwall than in many other regions.

In 1771 Cornwall saw not just its first bank, but two. They were both begun in the same year and in the same town – Truro. This was not so much a David and Goliath contest as in the *Poldark* saga but an equal struggle between two sets of gentry and merchants. The Miners' Bank, originally titled the Copper Miners' Bank, was specifically designed to service the needs of the mining industry. Just months after its formation some of the partners seceded to form the Cornish Bank. Political differences between William Lemon, supported by his brother-in-law John Buller of Morval at the Miners' Bank, and Sir William Molesworth of Pencarrow and Sir Humphrey Mackworth Praed at the Cornish Bank seem to have been at the root of this split. But there were also economic differences. The Miners' Bank partners tended to be more active shareholders in mines. Cornish Bank partners were much less so. The Cornish Bank was more of a landowners' bank, less inclined than the Miners' Bank to finance riskier speculation. That said, the differences became blurred, especially when Francis Basset joined the Cornish Bank in 1779 and definitely after 1810 when John Williams became a partner in that bank. Partnerships were initiated and dissolved with confusing frequency in these years as a changing mix of old families with canny investments in mining and new families with money from merchanting came and went over the half century from the 1770s.

Banking at this time could be risky. At one point in the *Poldark* story Demelza goes along to Harris Pascoe's bank in Truro and loudly declares her intention to deposit money in it. This was done to calm the fears of some of the bank's customers who were gathering to withdraw their savings. As banks always lend considerably more money than they hold in cash, if everyone wants to withdraw their deposits at the same time, a bank will go bust. These 'runs' on the banks were relatively commonplace in the 1800s. In 1825 Demelza's action was replicated in reality, and on a greater scale, when a declaration of confidence in the Cornish Bank was signed by Lord Falmouth and 'some brother landowners'. This succeeded in reassuring the townspeople and stopping a run on the Truro banks. The collapse of the Mevagissey Bank the previous year, in the midst of a more general financial crisis, had triggered this panic. Immediately after the Mevagissey Bank went under, 70 tradespeople in Truro had been induced to promise to go on taking the notes of the Cornish Bank. Meanwhile, merchants and traders at Penzance signed a public notice declaring their confidence in the local banks.

'the individual profit to be taken out of the general loss'

The growth of banking in these years was a sign of the increasingly vigorous circulation of money in a bigger and busier economy. But who commanded the lion's share of this extra cash? There were three ways of making money from mining. We've already met the first – the occasional windfall 'sturts' of the working miner. This often enabled the miner to take on the lease of a smallholding, build or rent a cottage and get married. But this was small beer when compared with the two other ways of profiting from mining. As we have seen, the easiest was to own the mineral royalties, passed on within landed families. You had to be lucky enough to be born into the right family. If you were then this was essentially a risk-free rent. In return for the right to mine, the mining adventurers would agree to pay a fixed proportion, usually six per cent, of the revenue from any ore sales – not of profits – to the owner of the mineral rights.

The second, riskier way to profit from the mines was to buy shares in them and, hopefully, a share in the profits. Some landowners did both. The fictional Ross Poldark was one; another was the real Francis Basset. It's been estimated that the Bassets had made £300,000 (or £34 million in modern terms) from mining royalties and dividends by 1796. Francis Basset and his father (also named Francis) were careful investors however, relying more on their royalties and limiting investment mainly to Dolcoath mine, the jewel in their crown, although shut down for a short space in the 1790s. The Bassets were also a constant presence in the various schemes more indirectly designed to benefit mining. These included the County Adit in the eighteenth century, new piers and harbours, the first tramroad in Cornwall in 1809, banking, and as we shall see below, the Cornish Metal Company. Others were less conservative, taking a riskier approach by investing in a portfolio of mines.

Contemporaries were in fact unsure whether mining provided an overall profit or not. The Redruth surgeon William Pryce, who wrote an account of Cornish mining in 1778, reported the 'popular opinion that no real surplusage beyond the charges ... do arise to the adventurers' even if the public in general were 'manifestly enriched' by the 'great trade and increase of money'. As the Poldarks' experience showed, mines could be fickle. Ross's father had prospered from Wheal Grace but was then ruined by its losses. His cousin Francis Poldark's Wheal Grambler had boosted the family fortunes but by 1783 was 'costing a fortune'. Wheal Leisure never made that much money but then the unexpected discovery of tin at Wheal Grace saved Ross from financial disaster.

Fickle they may have been, with poor years interspersed with good, but, with luck, an investor could also profit. Although sceptical about the overall profitability of mining Pryce admitted that 'many men have made opulent fortunes by their success in mining. Like national lotteries, the individual profit to be taken out of the general loss'. Sometimes, these profits were on a spectacular scale. Between 1792 and 1804 Wheal Unity and Poldice at Gwennap returned £53,000 in dividends to its shareholders. This was equivalent to over £6 million in modern terms. The short-lived prosperity of Wheal Towan at Porthtowan around 1800 had bestowed the nickname of 'guinea a minute Daniell' on its principal shareholder, Ralph Allen Daniell. On the other hand, Pryce estimated that even in good years only a third of

Cornish mines made a profit. More usually this was closer to one in six. But the mind-boggling profits of the few made up for the dismal performance of the majority.

'merrymaking which would have warmed the heart of Falstaff'

Adventurers in mines, the term 'adventurers' perhaps indicating a higher risk than the more prosaic word 'investors', bought shares in cost book companies. A mine company was usually divided into eighths or sixteenths or multiples of those. These shares then provided the mine with its working capital. Every month the income and expenditure was totted up by the mine purser who either declared a dividend, returning a surplus to the adventurers, or a loss, in which case a 'call' was made to the adventurers to put up more capital in order to keep the mine running. Cost book companies have often been regarded as an inefficient way of financing mining, resulting in a short-term quest for profit at the expense of long-term investment. Yet cost book companies managed to provide Cornish mines with sufficient working capital in their decades of growth to the early 1860s. The scepticism of some historians owed more to hindsight than analysis. In fact, cost book companies were a cross between a partnership and limited liability company. Although adventurers were personally liable for the debts of a mine, they could also forfeit their shares or sell them if they could find a buyer. Thus, in 1785 Christopher Wallis, a lawyer at Helston who dabbled heavily in mines, offered for sale one thirty-second share in Wheal Crenver.

Like Wallis, most of the adventurers in Cornish mines were locals. When Wheal Vor, near Helston, Cornwall's richest tin mine in the 1820s, was being reopened in the late 1810s, 74 per cent of its shareholders were Cornish. In the 1800s at least 72 per cent of the shares in Cooks Kitchen mine near Camborne were held by locals while three quarters or more of the shares in Ding Dong tin mine near Penzance and even the newly opened copper mines in the St Austell district were held by Cornish adventurers in the 1810s.

Those adventurers who lived close at hand were better placed to attend the monthly mine meetings. At these the purser, the man who acted as the financial manager of the mine, would report the state of the accounts. Pursers, usually one of the adventurers, were responsible for keeping the books, paying the bills, making calls for more capital and distributing dividends when in profit. Sometimes, the purser would even live at the mine, in the upstairs rooms of the counthouse, downstairs being used as offices for the mine clerks who kept the ledgers and pay books up to date.

Counthouses were the location for the regular setting days when pitches at the mine were re-allocated. They were also the venue for the counthouse dinners that normally followed the business meetings. A.K.Hamilton Jenkin painted a picture of these as fairly raucous occasions when large quantities of porter, ale, brandy, rum and gin might be finished off during and after a meal. They were, he wrote, 'the occasion of a scene of eating, drinking and merrymaking which would have warmed the heart of Falstaff'. Such dinners served to bond the local adventures even more tightly together. Within this interwoven group, merchants, sometimes known as in-adventurers because of their intimate connection with a mine to which they supplied goods, had a special place.

no proper accounting, overcharging for coal and a general lack of transparency in the cost book

William Pryce in 1778 pointed to the 'vast monthly charges' mines had to fork out for materials such as coal, timber, candles, gunpowder, leather and ropes. Merchants were in a position to profit from supplying this material, amounting to a value estimated at £100,000 (or over £11 million nowadays) a year in the 1790s. John Vivian stated at the end of that decade that he thought merchants with a direct interest in supplying the mine held 15 to 20 per cent of mining shares. While some mines, such as Dolcoath, did not allow merchants who had shares in the mine to tender for supplying material, in other mines these shares could give the merchants an inside route to obtain supply contracts. This meant that they could still profit even if the mine was making a loss. For this purpose, it was claimed that merchants often used their influence at adventurers' meetings to keep a losing mine open, at the expense of the other adventurers.

If merchants were able to exert their influence in this way, making use of their close local connections, it was claimed more broadly that the cosy groups of mainly local adventurers worked against the interests of outsiders, or 'out-adventurers'. During the depression of 1809 a number of shares in Cornish mines were bought by investors living outside Cornwall, but this soon ebbed away. Out-adventurers felt they were at a disadvantage, prone to manipulation by those nearer to the mines and unable to penetrate the arcane workings of the cost-book. In 1818 a group of London adventurers who held 40 of the 187 shares in United Mines at Gwennap brought an action against John and Michael Williams, the mine managers. This involved 18 complaints including mismanagement, no proper accounting, overcharging for coal and a general lack of transparency in the cost book.

They got little sympathy from the Stannary Court. Sixteen of their complaints were dismissed entirely.

Nevertheless, some outsiders succeeded in entering the closed world of the cost book companies. The classic example at the end of the *Poldark* period was John Taylor, from Norwich. Taylor relaunched Consolidated Mines at Gwennap in 1818 or 1819, after successfully running Wheal Friendship in Devon for a number of years and becoming involved in a number of other Cornish mines during the 1810s. He introduced some competition for the Williams family who had gradually expanded their involvement in mine management, so much so that by 1800 they controlled or managed between a third and a quarter of Cornish copper mines, including some of the most profitable.

'the adventurers in the mine have lost £70,000'

By that time Cornish mining had largely recovered from a serious depression suffered in the late 1770s and 1780s. Rising costs of production as mines were deepening coincided in those decades with growing competition from the copper mine at Parys Mountain on Ynys Môn, owned by Thomas Williams. Williams' mine, working shallow deposits, some by opencast methods, was cheaper to run than the deep Cornish mines and at its peak the output from Parys Mountain was almost equal to the total production from Cornwall. Unable to do anything about Williams, the Cornish mining interest blamed the old enemy – the copper smelters. They accused them of combining to suppress the price of copper ore. In fiction it was Ross Poldark who led the Carnmore Copper Company with the intention of purchasing copper directly from the mines and smelt it themselves. The leading lights in the real Cornish Metal Company were John Vivian and Sir Francis Basset, although there was never any plan to establish another smelting concern. In September 1785 they set up a cartel with the intention of buying all the copper ore produced in Cornwall over the following seven years and control its sale. Meanwhile, they agreed on a split of sales with Thomas Williams in Wales. The importance of the Cornish Metal Company cannot be understated. This was one of the most heavily capitalised ventures of eighteenth-century Britain and one funded almost wholly by Cornwall's gentry and its merchant dynasties.

Unfortunately, it didn't work. It was realised by 1787 that production had to be cut as the market was being swamped with copper and the company's stocks were ever growing. A series of crisis meetings resulted in an agreement to close some mines, including Dolcoath, while others suspended work temporarily because of the low prices. One was North Downs mine near Redruth, which was one of the biggest producers of the time. A temporary suspension there in 1787 had led to hundreds of miners marching on Truro, which unnerved the local gentry who put pressure on the North Downs adventurers to resume operations. But the inevitable was only postponed. In June 1788 the *Times* was reporting that:

> the great copper mine called North Downs in the parish
> of Redruth ... was shut up, by which 1,000 labourers
> are driven to the bitter alternative of begging or
> starving. The adventurers in the mine have lost
> £70,000, and yet its present state is so good, that even
> that large sum would have been reproduced in a short
> time.

The immediate crisis was eased by an agreement with Thomas Williams to limit production at Ynys Môn in return for a commission from the copper sales of the Cornish Metal Company. However, recovery had to await the 1790s when the stocks held by the Cornish Metal Company at last began to fall as copper prices rose. This was the result of a substantial deterioration in the quality of the Welsh ore as Parys Mountain began to be worked out, together with a rising demand. In 1792 the Cornish Metal Company was wound up, the *Sherborne Mercury* reporting that 'the present high price of tin and copper has caused a rage for mining in Cornwall, that no labourers can be found to work in the fields and the farmers are under serious apprehensions how they shall get in their harvest.'

Sometimes in these years, coins would be in short supply. This occurred for example in 1791 during the era of the Cornish Metal Company, and again in the years 1811 and 1812. At such times some mine owners produced their own copper coins or tokens, which they then used to pay their workers, while local traders agreed to accept the tokens as payment. In the second period of token production, when Sir Francis Basset and the Williams family produced their Dolcoath and Scorrier Pennies, the inevitable happened and counterfeit versions began to circulate. These soon undermined confidence in these home-made Cornish coins, which had to be withdrawn in 1813 and melted down. In 1817 the production of such tokens was forbidden by Parliament.

The shortage of coins in 1812 and 1813 heralded a major economic depression in 1815 when the long wars with France finally ended after 22 years. This post-war depression reminded Cornish mine adventurers that difficult years would still periodically recur. Wheal Alfred, between Camborne and Hayle, and a major copper producer in 1810, was forced to close in 1816. In November of the same year the *Times* reported that Chacewater Mine had shut, leaving 600 men, women and children looking for other work. But by this time new mines were also emerging as copper mining began to break out of its central heartland between Chacewater and Hayle. At Crinnis east of St Austell the adventurers made £120,000 (or almost £11 million now) in profit in the five years from 1811. The nearby Pembroke Mine had also entered the lists as one of the top five producing mines in Cornwall by 1820. By that year too, tin mining was on the verge of expansion with the reopening of Wheal Vor at Breage and hints that copper was beginning to give way to tin in the deepest levels of the mines of Camborne-Redruth. Consolidated Mines at Gwennap had also been restarted and soon reclaimed its position as one of Cornwall's major copper producers. Difficult years had again been survived and Cornish mining in 1820 in fact stood on the brink of a final generation of expansion.

'much trouble in getting the parts to fit together'

Mining spawned various spin-offs during the *Poldark* years. The most notable was engineering, feeding on the demand from the mines for engines and other iron machinery. In the 1770s Cornish foundries had been little more than machine shops or overgrown smithies. One of these was run by John Harvey, a blacksmith in the village of Carnhell Green between Camborne and Hayle. He moved to Hayle in 1779 and established a foundry there. His son Henry turned this into a modern foundry with separate departments for founding, forging, machining and fitting. Yet this was still fundamentally a jobbing foundry where parts were produced on demand. Precision could still be lacking. In 1800-01 the castings for Trevithick's steam carriage were made at Harvey's, where there was 'much trouble in getting the parts to fit together.' Meanwhile, more foundries had made their appearance, the most notable being Perran Foundry at Perranarworthal. This was financed in 1791 principally by the Foxes of Falmouth.

Other extractive industries were present in Cornwall. Growing quantities of granite were being shipped from Penryn and Falmouth, with an estimated 400 men employed in the quarries north of Penryn. Yet most of this granite, destined for big civil engineering works in London such as the Embankment, was still worked from 'moorstone', chunks of granite lying on the surface. Deeper quarries were not required until the 1840s. Meanwhile, some industries were in their infancy and on the verge of expansion. Only 4,000 tons of china clay was being shipped from Charlestown harbour in 1816, an amount that then increased fivefold over the next two decades. The St Austell area at the close of the *Poldark* years was still primarily tin and copper producing country rather than the clay country it later became. The production of slate from quarries, mainly in north Cornwall, continued apace, as it had done for hundreds of years. Again, major expansion had to await the coming of the railway. But the quarries at Delabole were well on their way to creating the biggest hole in Britain, if not in Europe.

surprised by the unexpected appearance of a wayward steam carriage
The advances in mining and other industries and the place of Cornwall at the leading edge of steam engine technology had also made it the location of choice for some of Britain's most inventive engineers. One was William Murdoch. Scottish born and raised, William had walked from Ayrshire to the English Midlands to seek employment at Boulton and Watt's engineering works and was taken on in 1777 to become a pattern maker and engine erector. In 1779 he was sent to Cornwall to oversee the installation and operation of Watt's engines. He based himself at Redruth, in the heart of Cornwall's mines, but Murdoch was no mere agent of Boulton and Watt.

Somewhat stubborn and short-tempered, he was also a prolific inventor and mechanical tinkerer. For instance, he improved steam engine design by inventing the 'sun and planet' gear in 1781. This enabled the up and down motion of the steam engine beam to be converted into circular motion, allowing engines to be used to wind material up and down a shaft. Around 1783-85 Murdoch was experimenting with models of steam carriages, frightening at least one Redruth resident who was surprised by the unexpected appearance of a wayward steam carriage in the lane from the town to the church. While Murdoch left that particular invention for Richard Trevithick to complete, he is best known as the inventor of gas lighting, succeeding in lighting his living room by this means in 1794.

After spending two decades in Cornwall, William Murdoch must have left with mixed emotions in 1798 or 1799. It had been a period of great creative energy for him but also personal tragedy. In 1785 he had married Anne Paynter, the daughter of a mine captain. However, their first children – twins – did not survive for more than a few days, while Anne died in 1790 after giving birth to another child. Moreover, at various times in the 1780s Murdoch was threatened with physical violence by crowds of miners who were encouraged to blame the depression of those years on Boulton and

Watt's demands for an excessive premium for their engines. Although Murdoch could presumably have taken care of himself as he was another six-footer like Richard Trevithick, with grumblings about Boulton and Watt's patent reaching a climax in the late 1790s he was no doubt relieved to depart.

But Cornwall wasn't just a place that attracted inventors and engineers like Murdoch and the Hornblower family. It also produced a string of home-grown gentleman-scientists in this period. These were playing an important role in advancing science on a British stage around the turn of the century.

almost killed himself by deliberately inhaling carbon monoxide

The statue of Penzance's most famous son looks east, down Market Jew Street, where Humphry Davy was born in 1778. But it also looks further east, past St Michael's Mount, across the Tamar and upcountry, where he made his name, and then across the sea to where he ended his days. His parents were not particularly well-off, although they could afford to send Humphry to Penzance Grammar School and then to Truro Grammar School. By all accounts Davy was an indifferent scholar and made little impression on his teachers. When his father died, he was apprenticed to a Penzance surgeon in 1795. There, he taught himself the rudiments of chemistry, as well as learning French, the language of the pre-eminent scientists of his day. More importantly, he made useful contacts, such as Davies Giddy (see below).

It was through Giddy that he came to the attention of Thomas Beddoes at Bristol. Beddoes invited Davy to join his Pneumatic Institute, which was investigating the use of gases in medicine. While at Bristol Davy experimented with nitrous oxide (laughing gas) and identified its possible use as an anaesthetic. He also almost killed himself by deliberately inhaling carbon monoxide to test its effects. As well as lacking much concern for health and safety, science in those days was less specialised and Davy counted among his friends at Bristol the poets Robert Southey and Samuel Taylor Coleridge, while writing some whimsical, romantic poetry himself.

In 1801, aged just 23, he was offered a post as assistant lecturer at the Royal Institution in London, established two years before. It was Davy's public lectures that brought him to wider attention. It secured invitations to all the best dinner parties, as well as a full lectureship within a year. A flood of discoveries followed thick and fast. Davy used electrolysis to isolate calcium, magnesium, potassium and sodium, proved that chlorine was an element and re-assessed the nature of heat. In 1804 he was invited to become a Fellow of the Royal Society, the main scientific institution of the time. In 1812 he was knighted and became a baronet in 1818. In 1813 Davy, accompanied by his wife and his assistant, Michael Faraday, even journeyed to France, which was still at war with Britain. He'd been invited by the French Government to receive a medal for his electro-chemical work. This accolade crowned a career largely spent demolishing the hitherto dominant French theories on heat.

Back from the continent Davy found time for his most well-known invention, the safety lamp. This ultimately saved many lives in coal mines, preventing the recurrence of disasters such as that at Felling Colliery near Newcastle in 1812, when 92 men lost their lives in a massive explosion. Davy was elected President of the Royal Society in 1820, but he never managed to reconcile the jealousies and feuds within it between the old gentleman-amateurs and the new professional academic scientists. His own manner, sometimes irritable and careless of etiquette, didn't help.

If Humphry Davy was primarily a scientist who became a gentleman, Davies Gilbert, or Giddy as he was known before 1817, was a gentleman who was also interested in science. Giddy was born at St Erth in 1767 and spent some of his schooldays at a mathematical school at Bristol, before studying at Oxford. He used his social status as a minor member of the landed class (whose family wealth again rested on successful speculation in mining ventures) to encourage Davy, 11 years his junior. Meanwhile, he used his aptitude for maths to give valuable advice to Jonathan Hornblower and Richard Trevithick on the efficiency of their engines.

But Giddy was also a politician. Spells as sheriff in 1792-93 and deputy lieutenant in 1795 were followed by a parliamentary career as MP for Helston and then Bodmin from 1804 to 1832. No idle backbench MP, Giddy chaired several committees and was active on a succession of practical issues, from roads and harbours to food supply to standardising weights and measures. From the 1790s his views drifted towards support for reaction. After 1815 he backed the Tory Government of post-war Britain and its policy of severely repressing those calling for change. As a result, in 1815 his house in London was attacked by a crowd because of his support for the new Corn Laws, widely seen as protecting the rents and income of the landed class at the expense of the labouring poor who would have to pay more for their bread.

Although invited to join the government, Giddy refused, preferring to work behind the scenes in committees and administration. Despite his later conservatism, he tended to steer a middle course and tried to avoid controversy, his biographer finding him 'indecisive and irresolute'. Yet, like Davy, he was an important figure in the development of Britain's scientific community, centrally involved in the Royal Society by 1820. By then he was known as Gilbert, having changed his name to that of his wife – Mary Gilbert – to ensure her succession to some estates in Sussex to which she was the heir. The couple had eight children, although four of them died before reaching the age of 18.

While Cornwall's gentlemanly amateurs were at the forefront of scientific endeavour in these decades their interests had been stimulated by Cornwall's broader role in industrialisation. In this the steam engine had been vital. But the astounding surge of productivity after 1810 was produced not by the scientists but by working engine men, tinkering with their engines, making small improvements here, changing the details there. Engine men were a skilled component of the broader class of labourers who worked in the mines and dug out the ore on which the wealth of the landed gentry and the leisure time of the inventors and scientists depended. It's time to return to those working miners and their families but move from their place of work into their homes.

3
The Cottage

I n the fictional universe of *Poldark*, Demelza had lived in a 'tiny, crowded cottage' before being whisked away by Ross. But exactly how rough and rudimentary were the cottages in which folk like Demelza and her family had to live? Fortunately, we possess several descriptions of the cottages of the labouring poor in these years. The home to which William Pryce, a mine doctor, took a victim of a mining accident in the 1770s does not sound too appealing. It was a 'hut', teeming with half-clothed children, 'destitute of all conveniences, and almost of all necessaries, the whole indeed is a scene of such complicated wretchedness and distress, as words have no power to describe'. This may have been especially bad, but William Jenkin at Redruth in 1799 also described miners' cottages as 'little huts', and in 1796 commented on the poor state of the bedding in miners' houses.

'semi-fluid accumulations of putrid slime'
At the end of our period Clement Carlyon, a Truro doctor, memorably described the cottages of the mining districts:

> wretchedly built and damp and dirty in the extreme. At their doors may be seen the usual mud-pools, which in winter overflow and render the approach to these inconvenient, whilst in summer these semi-fluid accumulations of putrid slime continue to exhale offensive and deleterious miasmata from their dark green surfaces.

This wasn't just the case in the mining districts. At St Keverne on the Lizard the cottages in 1806 also had 'their dung pits immediately before the doors; their beds are, in general, rotten and filthy, and they lie three, or four, together'. John Harris was actually brought up in one of these cottages near Camborne and later, when an established poet, recalled his childhood home of the 1820s. It was a 'boulder-built cottage, with reedy roof, bare rafters and clay floor'. There was:

> no back door, nor any windows looking northward,
> except one not a foot square in the little pantry, but on
> the south side it had four windows, a porch of
> primitive granite ... The woodwork of the roof was all
> visible, and sometimes the stars could be seen at night,
> there was no partition in the sleeping room, which ran
> from one end of the building to the other.

This sounds to have been one rung up from the two-roomed cottages, usually thatched and with cob walls, that the poorest inhabited. George Worgan in 1808 found the cottages in Cornwall to be 'very humble dwellings' with 'only two or three apartments, the upper one immediately under the thatch'. The sober assessment of a historian of industrial housing in Britain reinforces contemporary impressions. While from a distance the cottages, with their 'spruce gardens', sometimes set amidst verdant fields, looked 'charming', a closer inspection revealed a less romantic reality:

> The thick walls and comfortable looking thatch hid
> floors of beaten earth, or more usually a mixture of
> lime and ash which was little better than beaten earth,
> and continually damp. Moreover, these solid cob walls
> often suffered badly from damp and rats, there was
> rarely any trace of a damp proof course, and usually no
> proper foundations.

Even these basic habitations would, in normal times for the average family, contain hints of the consumer revolution that was introducing new delights to people in the eighteenth century, such as tea-drinking. By the end of the *Poldark* era, even a two-roomed dwelling might be expected to contain, in addition to the basic necessities of table and chairs, beds and bedding, plates and cutlery, a set of wine glasses, a tea tray and a mirror. Luxury! Those with more resources might aspire to a watch or a clock and a chest of drawers rather than a basic clothes box. Yet, a period of illness, unemployment or hardship could quickly plunge households from relative comfort into penury. In those circumstances the only option might be to sell some household possessions or find a cheaper and even more basic home to rent.

'makes one smell as if smoked like bacon'

None of the services we nowadays take for granted – power, water, sewage – were available to the cottage dweller in the villages of Sawle or Grambler. In 1808 Worgan reported that in east Cornwall wood and coal were the main fuels in use but in the west, although 'Welsh coal' would have been cheaper than in the east, turf and furze (gorse) still served as fuel. A hundred years earlier in 1698 Celia Fiennes had complained that burning turves produced 'an unpleasant smell, it makes one smell as if smoked like bacon'. This was another odour to be added to the already pungent mix in the cottage, not to mention the miasmata arising from the dung heap just outside the door.

Furze and turves had to be collected and dried. Obtaining fuel for the fire, the means of cooking as well as heating, was a constant chore, one carried out more often than not by women. They bred the women tough in those days. In the 1780s two women were earning four pence a day (about £2.50 now) 'loading dung' at St Agnes, while two others had been paid seven shillings and sixpence (£56) after carrying 900 faggots (bundles of sticks) on their backs. For women like these domestic chores such as collecting water was presumably child's play. The cottage might be lucky and possess or be near a well or a spring, but often, especially in towns, water had to be fetched from quite a distance. Later, in 1832, it was still being stated that 'great difficulty' was:

> experienced in procuring a sufficient supply of water
> for the ordinary purposes of life. It is not uncommon
> for water to be fetched from a distance of one or two
> miles – this is generally done in a small cask placed on
> a truck or barrow, forming no small additional labour
> to those individuals who are under the necessity of thus
> procuring it.

Water supplies in the mining districts were made more precarious by competition from the mines for water to power their engines and conversely by the mines pumping water out of the ground to keep them dry and thus lowering the water table. A lack of water combined with the presence of thatched roofs and open hearths meant that fires, once started, were difficult to extinguish. A bad fire in Kenwyn Street, Truro, led the *West Briton* in 1811 to point out the 'very great danger of allowing houses in the streets of a populous town to remain covered with thatch'. As slate roofs gradually replaced thatch this became less critical in the towns. In the villages it was another matter. In 1783 a fire destroyed six houses at Bohortha at St Anthony in Roseland while in 1812 there was a major fire at Crantock churchtown. A spark from a smithy accidentally set fire to a corn rick. In the prevailing dry weather, 1,000 bushels of wheat and barley were lost together with 50 tons of hay. Barns, stables, outhouses, and the smithy itself were consumed in the blaze, which at one time 'threatened to involve the whole village in one general ruin, as the houses are almost all thatched. Winnowing sheets were spread on the roofs, and these being kept constantly wet, gave time to extinguish the burning straw'. Less spectacular fires were quite common, sometimes resulting in deaths. For example, at Liskeard in 1823 a 13-year old girl was placing a pot on an open fire, came too close and her clothes caught fire. She died 36 hours later.

for every ten, one or two would not see their first birthday

That 13-year old may have been left in charge of younger children while her mother was out on an errand or earning some money. It was expected that the older girls would lend a hand helping to look after the younger, and there is usually assumed to be a considerable number of those. In the *Poldark* books Mrs Martin has eleven children. In reality, while such large families were not unknown, the number of children in a household at any one time would usually have been far fewer. The average size of a household at this time was actually between five and six persons. The households of young married couples and older people, whose children had left home, would have reduced the average. On the other hand, those households of farmers and the urban middle classes that contained servants would have increased it. That said, early marriage was the norm among the mining population. Twenty child-bearing years or more could easily allow for the possibility of equalling Mrs Martin's efforts and producing a double-digit number of offspring. But two factors qualified this in practice. First, there was the possibility of the mother dying in childbirth or either parent suffering an early death from accident or disease before their 40s. It's been estimated that a woman undergoing the average number of confinements in the pre-industrial period had a ten per cent chance of being killed by one of them. Second, infant and child mortality remained high. Babies might be born, but for every ten, one or two would not see their first birthday and another would die before the age of five.

Rather than focus on averages, it's probably a better idea to consider the life cycle of an average labouring family and the pressures that meant for cottage accommodation. On marriage the two-roomed cottage would be adequate, but children would quickly arrive and soon space would be at a premium. Ten years after marriage there may have been at least six births, with four children still alive. Another ten years might see the addition of another four. With the eldest by now 19 years old there might have been up to ten young adults and children sharing a potentially very overcrowded cottage. But by this time one or two of the older children would have left home, either working as an apprentice or servant away from home or be married. So, for most families the peak number of children living at home and fighting for space may have been around six or perhaps seven, and often fewer. However, as children began to earn from the age of ten, the family income would grow and there was a possibility of affording a bigger house at a higher rent.

'their complexions are soon spoilt by brandy-drinking'

Overcrowded or not, the average child was probably in a better position than those unfortunate enough to have been born out of wedlock. Mary Luke at Breage was committed in 1809 for refusing to name the father of an illegitimate child. She was thrown into Bodmin Jail for four years, during which she persistently refused to name the father. Unfortunately, the considerable sympathy her case aroused quickly evaporated when rumours surfaced that she had had four earlier children by four different fathers, while the fifth unnamed father was keeping her supplied with material comforts while she was in jail. Rather like today, a victim could quickly be relabelled as villain by the prejudices of popular opinion. Mary was hardly typical, however. The illegitimacy rate in Cornwall was lower than elsewhere, probably because slightly higher wages usually enabled marriage on pregnancy rather than any delay.

Sharing a small, two-roomed cottage may have led to other pressures in the days when divorce was unaffordable for anyone but the very rich and separation a major step for a woman without independent means. Desperate measures were sometimes resorted to. In 1820 at the Cornwall Assizes Sarah Polgrean of Ludgvan was put on trial for murder by administering arsenic to her husband. Several witnesses swore that Sarah, aged 37, had called her husband a 'jealous-hearted fellow' and wished him dead while a chemist confirmed she had bought some arsenic. She claimed the arsenic was to deal with rats, but an inspection of her house discovered no evidence of rats. She was found guilty of murder. and was executed on August 12, 1820. Her case might be contrasted with that of Robert Donnall, a 26-year old surgeon at Falmouth. Robert was accused of murdering his mother-in-law, by putting arsenic in her cocoa in 1816. He pleaded not guilty. But witnesses declared that at the time of her death he was in debt to the tune of £125 (over £12,000 now) and that his mother-in-law had left a considerable amount of money to her daughter and son-in-law in her will. More suspicious than this circumstantial evidence was the revelation that his mother-in-law had become sick two weeks previous to the death, with vomiting and stomach cramps, after a visit to her son-in-law's house. She had recovered from that episode, but then, again after a meal at her son-in-law's, had fallen ill with exactly the same symptoms. This time she died a day later. Despite the doctor who attended finding evidence of arsenic in her stomach contents, the jury found Donnall not guilty after a succession of respectable Falmouth residents attested to his upstanding character.

Death by arsenic poisoning was the exception. More familiar was the slow scything of the population through disease and illness. This was exacerbated by hard working conditions, a poor diet and appalling sanitation. Of course, there were always some who focused on other causes of bad health. The landlord and clergyman Richard Polwhele observed that in Cornwall, 'the girls are very pretty to the age of 13; after which their complexions are soon spoilt by brandy-drinking and their health impaired'. William Beckford, waiting at Falmouth in 1787 to board a packet boat, occupied his time with a visit to the mining district of Gwennap. He thought it 'a bleak desert, rendered still more doleful by the unhealthy appearance of its inhabitants'.

In Poldark's time, the working population was not only unhealthy in appearance; they were, to our eyes, short in stature. To illustrate this, we can turn to the newspaper, the *Sherborne Mercury*, which carried a series of notices in the 1780s requesting information on parish apprentices (their apprenticeship being paid by the parish) who had run away from their masters. These gave a description of their clothes – 'deep blue coat, black waistcoat, yellow cloth breeches', for example, plus any distinguishing features. Peter Prout, a 19-year old who had run away at Liskeard, had a speech impediment and was hard of hearing. The 13-year old Thomas Congdon at nearby St Neot had 'smallpox marks, disabilities and injured knees'. The descriptions also gave their heights. If we take all those young men aged 18 to 20 (and therefore fully grown) we find their median height was five foot, six and half inches, ranging from the shortest at five foot to the tallest at five foot, ten inches. The likes of Richard Trevithick and William Murdoch, both six foot in height, would have been rarities in Poldark's times, at least among the less well-off.

'a dish of pilchards chopt up with raw onions and salt'

Stunted growth reflected the common diet. In the *Poldark* books Paul Daniel goes home to a simple meal of barley bread and potatoes. These were, indeed, two of the three staples in the diet of labouring people at that time. But a third may have been even more central in the western parts. The Reverend Warner in 1809 thought that 'the fastidious epicure might shrink back with some abhorrence from a Cornish peasant's table, which rarely exhibits more than a dish of pilchards chopt up with raw onions and salt, diluted with cold water, eaten with the fingers, and accompanied by barley or oaten cakes.' The lack of cutlery may have been exaggerated by Warner, although folk rhymes might suggest fish was more likely to have been eaten with the fingers, leaving knives for meat. Contemporaries claimed that the cottager laid by around a thousand salted pilchards for winter, even though the space for their storage must have been limited.

Several other accounts reinforce the trinity of barley bread, potatoes and pilchards in the Cornish diet. William Jenkin at Redruth in 1800 claimed that a great number of the town's inhabitants never ate anything other than these three items. A letter from Penzance in 1795 observing the diet of the poor stated that 'barley and potatoes which articles with salt and tea (without milk or sugar) are the chief and almost their only support'. Later, in 1810, this was corroborated by Christopher Wallis at Helston, who described fish and potatoes as the 'usual fare' of the poor. William Lovett, the Chartist leader, had grown up in Penzance just after 1800. He remembered that 'our food consisted of barley bread, fish and potatoes, with a bit of pork on Sundays. In fact, barley bread was the common food in my boyhood, excepting that the fishermen mostly took a wheaten loaf to sea with them'.

Vegetables were not often mentioned, although those with a garden would no doubt have grown cabbages, onions, carrots and turnips to add some variety to their diet in spring and summer. If there was space, or even sometimes if there wasn't, a pig might be kept. George Worgan, writing on Cornish farming in 1808, provided a comprehensive account of the Cornish diet. He repeated the point that 'the most common' fare 'of the labouring class is barley bread with tea, and salted fish' stored in the autumn. They were eaten with potatoes at the meals of dinner and supper and as 'a relish' at breakfast and tea. Labourers with higher wages or smaller families might aspire to wheaten bread and more regular meat, while the slaughtered pig would add some pork and bacon. Rather oddly, chickens do not get a mention in contemporary accounts, although one would have thought that once their laying years were over, an old fowl would be a useful additional source of food. Despite the monotony of their diet however, Worgan concluded that 'the poor [in Cornwall] are in general better fed and clothed than in most other counties' which doesn't say much for those other places.

'discharge their filth from time to time direct into the street'

This diet was simple and humdrum but sustaining. However, the lack of variety in addition to damp houses and insufficient clothing made people susceptible to disease. Every year thousands, especially young children, were carried off by typhoid and typhus, dysentery, respiratory diseases and the childhood illnesses of measles, whooping cough and scarlet fever. The annual visits of these killers added to the worrisome burden of poor health. People's vulnerability to disease and early death was multiplied by the rudimentary sanitation, which encouraged the spread of diseases such as dysentery and typhus.

We have already met and steered well clear of the 'dung pits' at the doors of the cottages. In the countryside these were a nuisance but things were far worse in the towns of Poldark's times. In his days, the dung heaps and cesspools of the crowded courts behind the main streets awaited the scavengers who would buy their contents from the landowner and sell it on to farmers for manure. In addition, there were scores of unregulated slaughterhouses cheek by jowl with vegetable and fish markets plus the lack of a dependable water supply. Before the 1820s all this seems to have been taken for granted, or at least rarely commented on. A flavour of what it must have been like might be gleaned from a later report in 1849 from Penzance, triggered by panic over the arrival of cholera. By the harbour 'the filth from an upper storey is discharged by an open shoot into the court or passage below, others are without a convenience of any kind and discharge their filth from time to time direct into the street, or over the wall into the harbour above tide-level.'

'a profitable employment for their spare hours'

The more rural mining districts might have been spared this level of squalor, if only because cottages were further away from each other. Moreover, some miners who had been fortunate enough to gain a 'start' (windfall earnings from a profitable tribute bargain) used the money to rent a few acres of land. There were others whose family was already in possession of a smallholding on which they and their family could grow vegetables and keep a few animals. Indeed, it was the growing practice in the late 1700s for landlords in the west to grant leases to 'improve' unenclosed land. Sir Francis Basset in 1793 claimed that in the previous 30 years he and his father had enclosed 50 to 65 hectares (120-160 acres) in this way. In 1799 William Jenkin at Redruth presented a new batch of similar leases to his employer, saying 'some of them are new enclosures on Treloweth Common'. Jenkin thought they could go further. In 1802, to guard against miners spending their time in the alehouses, he called on landowners to do more to allot families a few acres for a small annual rent.

Such allotments or smallholdings, and indeed even the house and garden in the towns and villages, were usually let for three lives. The person taking the house would name three lives, the length of the lease being equal to the longest survivor. The initial cost, according to Worgan, was equal to 14 to 18 years' rent, although the annual rent was small, at around ten shillings (or less than a week's wages for a skilled tributer). At the end of one of the three lives, another might be added on paying a fine of three years' rent. However, this only happened if the landlord was willing. The trick was to name people who turned out to be long-lived. Normally, the practice was to use one or two of the three lives for the tenant and/or his wife, so that they were guaranteed security during their lifetime, and another for a teenage child – not an infant because of the danger of child mortality – to add possible security for the next generation.

If taking on a tract of open ground, once the three lives were named, the lease signed and the tenant in occupation, the family would be obliged to build a cottage on the smallholding. These cottages, any other farm buildings, hedges or other improvements would then revert to the landowner on the expiry of the lease. Worgan reported that 'there are dispersed over the wastes to the westwards of Truro ... many hundreds of cottages, and the wasteland about them is enclosed in small patches, and brought into good culture by a description of people of the labouring class, which may be called cottage leaseholders'. By means of the three-life leases or through inheritance, somewhere between a quarter and a half of families in the mining parishes in the 1700s had access to land of some kind. This, according to a historian of Cornwall writing in 1814, was a 'source of considerable advantage and comfort to the miners, while it affords them a profitable employment for their spare hours'. The *Poldark* saga includes a tale where Mark Daniel and his friends put up a cottage overnight in order to gain customary ownership of the cottage and the land on which it was built, claimed to be an 'old custom'. Strangely, this was not mentioned in any contemporary account and is either apocryphal or a folk myth built on the obligation to build a cottage, although not in 24 hours, on a smallholding.

While the open-ended duration of three-life leases added yet another unpredictable element to the cottagers' lives in Poldark's times, it also meant that a proportion of the workforce was insulated to some degree from the vicissitudes of the mining economy, with its short-term booms and sudden slumps, and the ever-present danger of unemployment. Moreover, even if without their own land, labourers could sometimes benefit from the allotment of a small piece of ground by farmers, on which they could grow potatoes, that 'blessing of the poor'. Those in the far west could also take advantage of the farmers' practice of renting out their cows:

> to labourers and poor people at £6 or £8 a cow, for
> seven or eight months; four, six, eight or ten cows to
> each person, the hirer pays his cow-rent by milk and
> butter ... These cow-renters have a piece of ground
> allotted them by the farmer, in which they grow
> potatoes. With these, and with the scalded milk which
> has yielded cream for the butter, they fatten a great
> many young porkers.

While the overnight cottage building was romanticised, there exist scarcely credible and far-fetched stories of super-human efforts by some labourers to convert unenclosed poor land into flourishing ground. The classic example came not from a mining district but from agricultural Landewednack, Cornwall's southernmost parish on the tip of the Lizard peninsula. There, a 50-year old labourer called William Pearce in 1785 set to work draining 12 acres of boggy land after the end of his daily stint as a farm labourer. From this land, by 1803, he was managing to produce 35 bushels of wheat, barley and oats, nine trusses of hay and had pasture for some cattle. This had been achieved on his own, 'with only an old mare to assist him in carrying manure from a considerable distance'. Not content to stop there, he 'also built his own dwelling-house and out-buildings, covered and furnished them himself'. Moreover, this was done mainly one-handed as 'he had a natural infirmity in one of his hands'. William Pearce was lauded by his betters as an example of 'patient labour and persevering industry', a hard-working example of Victorian self-help before the Victorians.

'paid for whipping two vagrants'

Not everyone had the fortitude, strength and self-discipline of a William Pearce and not everyone had the wherewithal to rent a smallholding. For those who, through economic disaster, incapacity, personal failings or sheer bad luck, fell on hard times, those times could be very hard indeed in Poldark's days. The able-bodied tramping poor were regarded with particular suspicion. The Penryn borough account books in 1789 record the five shillings 'paid for whipping two vagrants'. In 1819 vagrants at Bodmin were convicted of begging and flogged through the streets. In the same year of economic depression, the year of the 'Peterloo massacre' in Manchester, when the mounted Volunteers had cut down some of those protesting against conditions and several were killed in the melee, there were worried reports in the *West Briton* of an 'unusual' number of vagrants at Truro. On the other hand, if possessing valid papers, parish officers would help impecunious travellers on their way, probably relieved at getting them off their patch. In 1798 for example, the constable's account book at St Erme recorded that a shilling was 'paid on a pass for two travellers'.

Another traveller was less fortunate. In the depression year of 1817 a man 'with the appearance of a stream miner' had called at a farmer's house near Pelynt in search of employment. The farmer couldn't help but had sufficient charity to offer the man a free meal. However, the tramp declined the offer and left, looking, according to the farmer, 'dejected'. A few weeks later he was found in a field, half eaten by pigs, with his head torn from his body. Apparently, the unidentified man had taken a halter from a stable on leaving the farm and contrived to strangle himself with it. He had then lain there undetected for two or three weeks, while the pigs made a meal of him. This was sufficiently shocking to be reported in the London *Times*.

The most generalised distress in the *Poldark* period occurred not on the mainland at all but on the Isles of Scilly. The poverty at Scilly was described as 'truly distressing' in the winter of 1811/12 when the inhabitants were unable to buy salt to cure their fish. The Government was finally persuaded to deliver some salt to be sold to the poor without the much-detested salt duty. Six years later, things had not improved. On the contrary, when war ended in 1815 smuggling, an important source of income for the islanders, was suppressed more energetically. On top of that, in 1818 it was reported that the potato crop on the islands had failed. An official report looked into the case but brusquely concluded that conditions were no worse than on the mainland, adding that in any case aid 'would tend to check industry' and set a bad example.

By the end of the following winter however, even the hard-faced gentry who were refusing aid had to admit that things had become a lot worse. By then there were reports of families on the smaller off-islands living solely on limpets amidst levels of distress not seen in 50 years. 'Almost everything [had been] sold for bread' while people were going to work, collecting seaweed, on 'one slice of bread, hot water and limpets'. A public meeting was called – in London – to consider the distress and offer possible remedies. A number of causes were listed. There had been a failure of fishing for a few years, smuggling had been suppressed, the transition to peace had reduced the number of visits by Royal Navy vessels, the salt duties made it too expensive to cure fish and the use of short leases by the Duchy of Cornwall did not encourage improvements. No spectacular solutions were offered however, and the islanders were essentially left to recover by themselves.

'women perform a large share of the rural labour, particularly the harvest work'

Over on the mainland things never got quite so bad as they did on Scilly. Nonetheless, the words 'the poor' could easily apply to the majority of the working population, even in better times. Although the fascination in Cornwall was with the mines, and the glittering profits they sometimes brought, many more families remained dependent on farming than on mining. This was especially the case east of Truro before the 1810s. For most folk in Poldark's days toiling in the fields was the common experience. Fortunately, Robert Fraser's *General View of the Agriculture of the County of Cornwall*, first published in 1794 and revised and added to by George Worgan in 1808, provides a convenient snapshot of Cornish farming and the conditions of both farmers and their labourers at just this point in time.

Farm labourers were at work from six in the morning to six in the evening in summer, from daybreak to dusk in winter. The busiest time of the year would be during the harvest, when hours could be much longer. While Poldark preferred to scythe his fields with his shirt off, most Cornish harvesters of the time would have kept theirs on. In fact, they preferred a coarse shirt with trousers made from duck, a heavy cotton canvas. In cooler weather they would also have donned a duck smock and when wet this might have been overlain by a shawl made of old sacks.

Hay crops were cut with a scythe in early summer. Wheat was harvested in July and early August and the main grain crop – barley – followed in September. Some of the grain may still have been cut with a sickle. In 'earlier times' according to A.K.Hamilton Jenkin, this was mainly done by women. When the heavier scythe took over, so did men. They were now followed along the field by the women whose job was to pick up the cut grain and bind it into sheaves. The sheaves were then carried off to be placed in shocks and sometimes in 'arrish mows'. These were carefully laid piles of shocks, left to dry. The corn was later taken to the farmyard and ricks built on frames of boards laid over 'steads'. Steads were foundations, usually of stone, which raised the ricks three or four feet off the ground. They were then protected from any rats on the ground below, while the effect of rain and wind above was moderated by the addition of reed or rush thatch, tied over the rick with straw ropes.

During the labour-intensive process of harvesting, men, women and boys would receive their meat and drink, including the necessary amounts of beer and cider, over and above their wages. The scythe-men might receive up to three shillings and six pence an acre cut. A skilled man was reckoned to be able to cut a couple of acres a day. That implies possible daily earnings of the equivalent of £15 to £21 nowadays, which would have been a veritable bonanza, given the normal daily wage of a labourer of the time, which was between a shilling and 18 pence. That was around nine to twelve shillings for a full week, or £45-65 in today's money. Harvesting done and the rick finished, there would be the ceremony of 'crying the neck', announcing the safe harvesting of the last neck of corn. This was accompanied by more drinking and then a harvest supper supplied by the farmer.

Harvesting was the high point of the farming year but throughout the rest the mundane jobs of ploughing, sowing, keeping the weeds down and the animals tended all had to go on. Much of this was done by women, paid around six to eight pence a day (equal to around £2 to £2.60 now). George Worgan reported that women 'perform a large share of the rural labour, particularly the harvest work, weeding the corn (in spring), hoeing turnips, potatoes etc., attending the thrashing machines'. These latter had only been recently introduced when Worgan was writing in 1808. Women may have begun work a little later than men, usually around 8am, but before and after work would have had other domestic tasks in an endless round of labour. This is not to mention looking after children, although any child over the age of seven was likely to be in the fields helping with the work and getting a princely three to four pence a day for it (or just over £1 in today's reckoning).

'coarse household work'

Jud and Prudie, Ross's occasionally drunken, often lazy farm servants, were not typical. For a start most farm servants were a lot younger. At an early point in their teens some boys and girls would be taken into farm service, living on the farm. Farm service was more common in east than west Cornwall, where the farms were 'very small indeed', with few over 50 acres in extent. In Cornwall's small farm economy, a generation later in 1851 as many as 44 per cent of farmers relied solely on their own family's labour, while 33 per cent only employed one or two labourers. Yet farm service, with its minimal wages, was still an attractive option for many small farmers.

Girls were tasked to assist the farmer's wife around the farmhouse but also attend to the pigs, poultry and calves. Remembering her childhood in the 1820s a woman at Mullion on the Lizard recounted the work of the female farm servant – bringing in the furze (for fuel), feeding the pigs, boiling potatoes, rearing calves, working in the fields at harvest time, helping with the milking, weeding corn, picking stones, winnowing. Then there was the 'coarse household work', and making bread, mending stockings and in winter washing wool and carding it. This farm servant would also get two evenings off. Farmers' daughters would be expected to help with some of these jobs and in the small farms there would be a rough equality, all sitting down to a meal at the same table. This was something that marked the farmer off from the gentleman. Even an impecunious gentleman such as Ross would not have contemplated Jud and Prudie sharing his meal.

For all this, female farm servants were paid £3 to £4 a year (around £200-£320 now) in addition to their board. Boys might get double that. They would find one of their main jobs was to drive the oxen widely used in Poldark's Cornwall to pull a plough and draw carts and waggons. This was done with a goad, plus verbal encouragement. Several visitors commented on the rhythmic chanting of the farm boys calling out to their oxen as they plodded through the fields and lanes of Cornwall, an aural peculiarity now long lost. Oxen were docile and patient and good at driving a straight furrow when ploughing. On the other hand, they were slow – four oxen being needed to do the work of two horses - and were later replaced by the latter. But not in Poldark's days.

'a good best parlour'

Farmhouses could be rudimentary, often not a great improvement on the cottages of the labourers. Worgan described 'old farmhouses', many of which would have dated back to the medieval period. They 'are of mud and thatch, the lower division consisting of a kitchen and an apartment dignified with the name of parlour but called provincially the higher side, a cellar and a dairy room, but these latter frequently under a lean-to roof. The rooms very low, not ceiled, and two bed-chambers over, the floors of the chambers are of oak plank, the ground floor earth, lime-ash or flagstone; the farm offices built of the same materials, consisting of a barn, cow and ox-sheds and hogsties standing in confusion about the dwelling'. Nonetheless, Worgan also noted that some modern farmhouses were appearing by the beginning of the 1800s, built higher, with stone walls and slate roofs.

Most farmers kept a 'good best parlour', but this was a room used only on special occasions. The life of the farm revolved around the farm kitchen. While towards the end of the *Poldark* years the tick of a grandfather clock might add to the crackle of the fire at quiet times, in daylight hours these were drowned by the clatter and bustle of meal preparation and the echoes from the lean-to scullery where the washing and messier work was going on. To this was added the confusion of smells from the bags of herbs, or the salted bacon and pilchards hanging from the ceiling beams, the smell of the fire and any food being got ready. When darkness fell, to this mix was added the pungent odour of the pilchard oil burnt in the earthenware lamps which, together with candles, provided a glimmer of light.

Here would also be found the large kitchen table around which the family and farm servants would gather at mealtimes, often seated on benches rather than chairs. In addition, no farm kitchen would be complete without its high-backed settle. The back helped keep the draught out when the settle was drawn nearer to the fireplace on cold winter evenings. The massive open hearth, big enough for a wood corner and chimney-stool, would have its fire kept burning all year round. This was necessary because the cooking might all be done on an open hearth, although cloam ovens would have been more common in east Cornwall.

The wood corner would contain bundles of dried furze. Furze burnt too quickly to serve as the sole fuel and it was combined with wood or, in the tree-starved areas, turves. Cooking was done on this hearth. Bread, pasties and cakes were all baked on an iron sheet placed directly on the embers with a 'kettle' (a bowl with three legs) inverted over it. The fire would be built up over the kettle and removed when baking was done. Such an operation must have required a huge degree of skill and experience in estimating the time needed to bake the food. For boiling, a crock was used, either placed on a stand over the fire or hung from bars built into the chimney.

An account from the 1830s gives us a hint of what the farmer's household might expect when they arrived to eat at the kitchen table. Their fare:

> consists of salt pork, salted fish (near the coast),
> dumplings, broth, milk porridge and, above all, of
> potatoes, always boiled with the skins on. Turnips and
> some of the commoner garden vegetables are also in
> use. Twice or three times a week a favourite pie is
> made of sliced potatoes with bits of pork and some
> seasoning, having a crust four inches thick running
> around it, but open in the middle. Apples have of late
> years come much into use in the cookery.

For drink, there was usually just water or tea, save at harvest time when beer and cider (more common then than now in Cornwall) was drunk. Cheese was a rarity, reserved for harvest and special occasions, and strangely, there was no mention of pasties in this particular account.

'a great spirit of industry in Cornwall in the improvement of land'

Most of these farms were taken by the farmers on fixed rent leases of 14 years length. These were tending to replace any three-life leases still used for farms during the eighteenth century. From their farmhouses the farmers and their labourers were putting around a third of Cornwall's land area under the plough at this time. Cornish farmers were the same as their colleagues across the Tamar, believing there was 'nothing like corn in sacks, for making money'. In fact, the long wars with France from 1793 to 1815 had made importing more difficult, while the number of mouths that needed to be fed was steadily rising. This had resulted in high prices for grain. In Cornwall, the continuing growth of the mining population added to demand and 'excited a great spirit of industry ... in the improvement of land'. According to the *Times* in 1801 'large tracts of ground, hitherto wholly barren, have produced considerable crops'. Even the summit of Castle an

Dinas in mid-Cornwall, the paper reported, had been cultivated for the previous two years, providing a 'fine crop of potatoes and turnips'.

The high prices of wartime did not survive its end. By 1816 Cornish farmers, like those upcountry, had been plunged into a severe depression. The debts that had been taken on when prices were high and rising were now proving to be burdensome, along with higher taxes and poor rates. Admittedly, rents were falling, but they were not falling as fast as incomes. In 1816 a Board of Agriculture Enquiry asked farmers about their situation. The Penzance Agricultural Society claimed that in one parish two thirds were unable to pay their taxes. At Veryan on the Roseland rents had fallen by 30 per cent. Despite that, many remained unpaid, cattle had been sold off and farmers were quitting their farms as soon as their leases ended. If farmers were 'dispirited, gloomy and discontented', the plight of their labourers was that much worse. At Veryan the labouring poor were 'daily losing their employ' and their conditions were 'very distressing'. The Cornwall Agricultural Society thought that the depression was 'far beyond anything that had ever come within the knowledge of the Society'.

Before the surge of cultivation during the Napoleonic Wars, when land under the plough reached limits only previously attained before the Black Death of the mid-1300s, around a third of Cornwall had been open common land or 'waste' and another third crofts. On these last every 25 or 30 years the vegetation was rooted up and the land dressed with manure or sea-sand and seaweed, or pilchards that were bruised or otherwise unfit for sale. One or two cereal crops were then taken, before it was allowed to revert to furze. In fact, even so-called 'waste' often had value as summer pasture for animals. In 1812 the *West Briton* advertised summer pastureland to be let at Hawke's Tor and Butter Tor on Bodmin Moor, for the grazing of cattle and sheep. Moreover, in the west the waste land was an important source for the peat and furze used for fuel.

By 1820 the haphazard and primitive occasional cultivation of crofts was being replaced by more scientific crop rotations. In the fertile stretch of land between Newquay and Camelford Samuel Drew in 1824 reported the common rotation to be wheat, barley, grass and then rest for a year. The cultivation of potatoes and turnips had also become part of these crop rotations. Potatoes, of which two crops could be grown in the west, the first drawn in May, at which time the second was planted, helped to plug the gap between the capability of Cornwall's grain-producing land and the growing number of people who required feeding. Turnips, planted in June, were also used for fattening cattle and oxen, feeding sheep and boiled and mixed with potatoes for pigfeed.

'Cornish sheep .... [are] still as wild as cats'

Worgan reported 'very few bad pigs' in Cornwall. They were 'good grass eaters, orchard and lane grubbers'. The 'true Cornish breed' of pig was a 'large, white, long-sided, razor-backed pig'. By 1800 this was being crossed with shorter, but fatter, breeds from Devon, the East Midlands and East Anglia. We have already met the flocks of goats in the mining districts of the west, reared for their meat and free to roam, that sparked comment from several visitors. To these should be added perambulating pigs. While some pigs, especially in the backyards and gardens of the towns and on the smallholdings of the miners, would have been kept closely confined, they were often allowed to wander. Worgan suggested that 'the present unwarrantable liberty of this animal should be abridged.'

To pigs and goats might be added sheep. Francis Basset in the 1790s commented that the 'majority of Cornish sheep .... [are] still as wild as cats'. For Thomas Preston, visiting Cornwall in 1821, the local sheep were 'inferior' to those of his native Norfolk. The Cornish breed was already becoming rare by this time. Worgan stated that Dorset stock had been introduced in the 1760s and Leicestershire breeds by the 1790s. The original Cornish sheep had 'grey faces and legs, coarse short thick necks, stand lower before than behind, narrow backs, flattish sides, a fleece of coarse wool.'

In similar fashion, by 1800 the native Cornish cattle – 'very small, of a black colour, short-haired, coarse-boned, and large offal; very hardy', were being replaced by larger Devon breeds along with some Jersey and Guernsey cattle. Cornwall in Poldark's days was not the dairying country it later became. Milk was difficult to obtain beyond the farm, while the cheese was 'very trifling' and of an 'inferior kind'. However, the practice of letting out milk cows in the far west may have improved the supply of milk and butter there. Raising cattle for beef was of more consequence to farmers than dairying. Cattle helped meet the supply needs of the Royal Navy during the wars and those not sold and slaughtered locally met a ready market at Plymouth. Others were driven to Somerset for grazing before being sold on to markets further east.

The true peculiarity of Cornwall at this time was the preference for oxen. Housed from November to May, these were worked from the age of three to seven or eight years, when they were slaughtered for their meat. 'In no county does the ox stand in higher estimation for all kinds of work, than in

Cornwall .... everywhere to be met with, drawing the butt, the wain and the wagon, on the roads; in the fields, the plough and the harrow'. Oxen were joined by farm horses, 'rather small, but hardy and active'. Oxen and horses provided the pulling power for the carts and wagons that were a relatively recent innovation. In Poldark's days, it was only within the lifetime of the oldest local residents that the roads had been sufficiently improved to enable him to travel in a coach, as we shall see in the next chapter.

4
The Road

In the *Poldark* books we first meet Ross travelling in a coach from St Austell to Truro in 1783. This must have been a precociously early coach service. Coaches there were, but not many of them, with irregular and infrequent services. In fact, coaches of any description were late to appear in Cornwall. The first coach was spotted at Falmouth in the 1760s and at St Ives as late as 1778. Meanwhile, the establishment of a coachmaker's business at Truro in 1813 was novel enough to be reported in the newspaper. When Ross got back from overseas there was still no regular mail coach service, the first one being attempted a year after his return. Even that proved to be a temporary addition to travel options and did not last long. Although some of the gentry had obtained coaches earlier in the 1700s, these were more for show than practical use. When contemplating a ride out, preparations were sometimes made for a band of servants to be on hand 'armed with ropes, spades and spare horses, to haul it out of holes and ruts'. Moreover, what passed for roads would have often looked to us to be little more than bridleways or even footpaths.

'remaining just in the same rude situation in which the deluge left them'
Maybe it was the penny-pinching of the parishes who were responsible for the upkeep of the roads. Maybe it was a question of Cornwall's hilly topography. But contemporaries were agreed; Cornwall's roads were atrocious. In 1754 a writer in the *Gentleman's Magazine* memorably concluded that:

> Cornwall, I believe, at present has the worst roads in
> all England, a great part of which are intolerable,
> remaining just in the same rude situation in which the

deluge left them, and most of those which have been
improved are still so extremely narrow and uneven,
that they are almost inaccessible to all kinds of
wheeled vehicles.

Insiders tended not to dispute the point. Thomas Tonkin in the 1730s thought, with more than a hint of pride, that 'there are not any roads in the whole kingdom worst kept than ours.' A century later, by which time, as we shall see in this chapter, Cornish roads had improved considerably, they could still be described as 'very hilly, and abounding in steep, inclined places.' In fact, with nowhere in Cornwall that far from the sea, coastal shipping would have often provided a more convenient and equally quick mode of transport.

Bad as they already were, the roads of west Cornwall could not have been improved by the growing number of mule trains that trekked to and from the ports, carrying ore to the ships and bringing back coal and mines supplies. In 1832, even after alternatives by rail became available, it could still be noted that 'the primitive mode of conveyance on the backs of mules is still continued in some of the mines west of Redruth. These animals go in troops of 20 or more, under the guidance of one man: each carries two bags containing ore, hanging across his back'. Stockdale, visiting in 1824, encountered troops of 30 to 50 mules and commented that 'the cruelty which is often exercised towards these poor animals deserves the severest reprehension'.

Mule trains were an unavoidable sight on the highways of west Cornwall, especially on those routes near the mines and leading to the ports. Indeed, on his first day back Ross encountered one on his dejected ride home after hearing that Elizabeth was marrying his cousin Francis. After 1810 the practice was becoming more common in mid-Cornwall too. In 1813 a tender for a contract to carry ore from Crinnis mine east of St Austell to Charlestown, a distance of around a mile, calculated that the 'number of mules necessary to carry the said ores is supposed to be from 25 to 30'. In consequence there was a vigorous trade breeding and selling mules. In 1811, 20 'very capital young mules and horses, in good condition, with their saddles and sacks' were being offered for sale at the Oxford Inn, Redruth. Overall, it's been estimated that by the 1790s as many as a thousand mules a day were carrying copper ore to the ports. The damage done by the trampling of these mule trains was sometimes worsened by the narrow wheels of the carts in use at the turn of the century. In 1818 a notice was issued to the mining and smelting companies at Hayle not to employ carriers with cartwheels narrower than six inches as they were causing large ruts to appear in the local roads.

'suitable for light goods and the lower classes'

However, change was in the air. Coach services could be contemplated in Poldark's times, as turnpike trusts began to make some improvements, at least on the main routes. Traditionally, road repairs were the responsibility of the parish authorities. Each parish would appoint its unpaid highway surveyor who had the unenvied responsibility of keeping the roads in a passable condition. The surveyor could call on local farmers who were supposed to supply six days labour and/or carts or oxen and horses to help mend the roads. Not surprisingly, farmers were sometimes reluctant to do this and the surveyors were not always perfectly conscientious about their task. Maintaining the roads was often regarded by parish authorities more as a way of creating work for the poor than as an ongoing means of keeping the roads in good repair. This was particularly problematic when a main route passed through a parish but was not much used or needed by people in that parish. One way around the problem appeared with the introduction of turnpike trusts. These were privately financed and run ventures which undertook the maintenance of an existing road or sometimes built new roads, over a longer distance. They employed paid surveyors and were financed by tolls on road users. These privately run roads added a measure of predictability to the more variable quality of the parish-maintained roads.

The first turnpike trust appeared in 1754 and was responsible for roads from Truro to Falmouth and to Grampound, as well as taking over the road to Redruth through Chacewater. Others soon followed. By 1760 there was a turnpike all the way from Truro to Launceston via Camelford and in 1770 a turnpike road from Liskeard to Torpoint followed, improving the notoriously poor southern route into Cornwall. This was followed by a ferry across the Tamar (although not then steam powered), linking the new town of Torpoint to Devonport from 1791. This was in addition to the existing ferry services upriver at Saltash and the rather more dangerous crossing at Cremyll.

By 1820 there were over 300 miles of properly maintained turnpike roads in Cornwall, good enough for regular long-distance coach services to have been initiated in the 1790s. Indeed, in 1814 the mail coach roads could even be described as 'very good'. A mail coach service, replacing the post boys who had previously carried the mail on horseback, was first tried in 1784, but it was not until 1798 that a permanent mail coach service was in place.

This travelled daily from Falmouth, where it picked up the overseas mail from the packet boats, to London and vice versa. Earlier, in 1791, there had been a service of four coaches a week, leaving Falmouth at 6am. It took 16 hours to arrive at Exeter by 10pm, when there was an overnight stop. Leaving early the following morning, the coach would arrive in London in the afternoon. The service in 1798 left Falmouth at the extremely early time of 3.45am, getting to London within two days.

Travelling by mail coach was not cheap, to say the least. In 1815 an inside seat in the coach cost £5 and four shillings. That would be around £470 these days. It wasn't that comfortable either. When Ross Poldark travelled back to Truro in 1783, he shared his coach with three others. They would have been cramped, as the interior of mail coaches was only between three and a half to four feet in width. There was always the cheaper option of an outside seat, perched on top of the coach. That cost £2 and 18 shillings in 1815 (or a mere £260 in modern terms). That is if you were prepared to be frozen in winter, burnt in summer or, more usually, soaked through from the rain.

Mail coaches were the luxury travel of the early 1800s, averaging a stupendous seven to ten miles an hour. They were supplemented by a variety of local coaches, fly wagons (in 1814 these were advertised as suitable for light goods and the 'lower classes') and horse buses. The cheapest form of travel were stage wagons, slow, lumbering carts mainly carrying goods but willing to take passengers. These averaged around three miles an hour and could take two or three weeks to make their ponderous way to London. For those unable to afford the wagon there was always walking, not that much slower a mode of travel than wagons in fact. Local coaches from Truro to Falmouth began running in 1799, the fare a guinea (a guinea was one pound and a shilling, worth £120 in today's money). The price even makes our bus services look remarkably cheap. In 1814 a local coach leaving Redruth at eight in the morning would arrive at Marazion at two in the afternoon, a journey of six hours. There were four inside seats on offer for ten shillings each (or £40) and ten places outside, which sounds a mite perilous, for seven shillings (or £28), equivalent to almost five day's wages for an agricultural labourer, who would be most unlikely to be using this service in any case.

'the snow ... was as high as the horses' shoulders'
In Poldark's days those prepared to fork out a considerable amount of cash to travel by coach might face additional hazards. In 1812 the:

mail coach for London was passing over Polson Bridge
[over the Tamar east of Launceston], one of the wheels
came in contact with an angle in the wall, and the
coach overset. There were four outside passengers ...
three of whom were precipitated over the bridge, the
fourth hung by his hands on the top of the wall, until
he was delivered by the guard.'

One passenger suffered a badly fractured leg while another, a Portuguese,
suffered 'several wounds' and a coachman was 'seriously hurt'. Bridges
could be dangerous places even on foot. In 1792 at Truro William Tonkin,
a former chief bailiff of the Stannaries, 'fell through a hole on one of the
decayed bridges into the mud' and died from his injuries.

Snowstorms then, as in more recent times, could cause chaos on Cornish
roads. In January 1814 the weather was reported as the most severe for 20
years. The snow was piled so high that travel was 'dangerous'. The mail
coach going east at Mitchell Common lost the road entirely and overturned.
In other places 'the snow ... was as high as the horses' shoulders', while
travel across Goss Moor was suspended as it was impossible to discern the
road. The deep streamworks nearby made it too dangerous to proceed.

At the growing port of Hayle the shortest route to Lelant and St Ives,
before the building of the causeway in 1825, lay across the estuary. John
Wesley had almost come to grief here, not allowing for the rapidity of the
tide rising across the flat estuary sands. Later, in 1815, a cart was crossing
but got stuck in the centre as the tide was turning. Most of the passengers
managed to scramble away and wade to safety, apart from one pregnant
woman who was unable to escape the tide and drowned.

Finally, the road was not always the safest place for other reasons. Mail
coaches had guards and were rarely troubled, at least not in Cornwall. But
lone travellers on foot, especially women, were always potential prey for
the desperate or the criminal. This wasn't exactly the classic Dick Turpin
type of highway robbery but something altogether shabbier. In 1795 James
Frederick was 'capitally convicted' for assaulting Sara Lean 'on the high
road and robbing her of three pence'. In 1826 a case of highway robbery
was brought against Richard Groves, a chimney sweep. He had stolen a bag
of flour and three loaves from a woman on the road near Liskeard. In the
end he was found guilty not of highway robbery but of straightforward
felony and given three months in jail.

New modes of transport were beginning to make their appearance by
1820. Canals had proliferated upcountry in the later 1700s, moving heavy

goods and linking industrial regions. Cornwall already had its ready-made means of water-borne transport by sea and its hilly terrain hardly made it canal country in any case. Nonetheless, the Bude Canal Act was passed in 1819 to build a canal to bring lime inland to farmers in north Cornwall and north west Devon. A similar canal had been proposed as early as 1777 to serve farmers in the Liskeard district. Nothing happened and it was proposed again in 1795. It finally got underway in 1825.

Ross Poldark had moved no faster than the speed of a galloping horse. Canals wouldn't change that, but railways would. His children would experience the great jump in speed of travel that occurred in the Victorian years. While Cornwall was relatively slow to obtain its first canals, it was quick to get a railway, although not at first a railway powered by steam. That came after the time we're discussing in this book, in the shape of the Bodmin and Wadebridge Railway, which opened in 1834. In the meantime, the first railway in Cornwall was constructed as early as 1809, linking Poldice mine at Gwennap to the port of Portreath on the north coast. This railway, sometimes called a tramroad, continued to use horses to draw its wagons, despite being only a few miles from the birthplace of Richard Trevithick, inventor of the word's first steam locomotive. The development of the steam-powered railway was left to engineers and inventors elsewhere more focused on the task and with more abundant coal supplies near at hand.

'fetid and disagreeable odour of stinking pilchards'

Let's leave this hint of the coming modern world behind and return to the dusty, or more usually muddy and rutted lanes that passed for roads in Poldark's days. It's time to use those roads to visit Cornwall's main towns around the turn of the century. We are in fact lucky to have several accounts written by visitors between 1792 and 1824. Using these as our guide, what would the curious tourist of Poldark's times have seen as he or she trudged or rode around Cornwall, or if sufficiently well-heeled, took the coach?

If our traveller chose to cross the Tamar on the new-fangled ferry to Torpoint they would have landed on the Cornish side in the large village of Torpoint. This was a new town planned on land owned by the Carews of nearby Antony House, a speculative venture to house workers at the dockyards on the other side of the river. In 1787 it had the grand total of 44 houses. As no contemporary account actually mentions the place, we have to assume that their authors had arrived instead by the traditional ferry at Saltash. In the 1790s visitors described Saltash as 'but a poor town'. A decent guildhall, built around 1789, and a 'large assembly room' were insufficient to make up for 'narrow, crooked and ill-built' streets, 'chiefly inhabited by poor fishermen.' Nonetheless, in 1799 it was reported to have a good market, benefiting from the growth of Plymouth across the river.

Negotiating the hilly country between Saltash and Looe, the traveller would eventually overlook the Looe River, relieved at having survived a road 'so exceedingly narrow, that in several places it would be impossible for a horse and carriage going different ways to pass each other'. From a distance the two boroughs of East and West Looe might look delightful, but being 'chiefly supported by the fishing industry', they were places 'not very likely to recommend themselves to visitors' because of the 'fetid and disagreeable odour of stinking pilchards and train (pilchard) oil.' Despite between them returning four MPs to the House of Commons, the two Looes were 'small' and 'miserable'.

Making their way up the Looe River our traveller might meet with an altogether more superior sort of town – Liskeard. A visitor in 1795 described this as 'one of the largest market towns in Cornwall, with 'many good shops, a capital town-hall' and a 'large market-place', rebuilt in 1782. A leather trade was reported as flourishing here in 1799 with some spinning encouraged by the clothiers of Devon. However, 'the pavements are very bad'. The pavements of Cornish towns were a perennial source of complaint from visitors, because at this time they were 'generally paved with pebbles from the shore, the points of which being turned upwards form a footing neither safe nor pleasant'. Nonetheless, Liskeard in 1824 was described as extensive and populous (even though its population amounted to no more than 2,500) with houses that were 'in general substantial, and slate-roofed'.

At least Liskeard had 'two good inns', unlike the small town, or overgrown village, to its east – Callington – with just 400 people in 1800. A visitor in 1795 found the Bull's Head there a 'very poor inn'. It was clearly not exceptional. In 1786 the *Times* reported the death of the Reverend Samuel Nanjulian, aged just 22, at Plymouth, 'of a fever, caught by sleeping in a damp bed at an inn in Cornwall'. It wasn't just the inn at Callington that was uninspiring. In the 1790s dependent mainly on woolcombing, Callington was 'one short street of very poor houses', described by another visitor as 'a shabby place'. Nothing much had changed a generation later. In 1824 it was being described as 'one broad street; and being very irregularly built, and very much out of repair, has rather a poor appearance'.

'the mound studded with pigsties, and the lofty keep undermined by gardens'

Launceston was another matter entirely. Here the White Hart was in 1795 a 'good inn and they charge for beds one shilling a night'. The dining room also doubled up as an assembly room for the occasional theatrical performance. Another visitor around the same time found it 'a very populous and extensive place ... [with] ... altogether a very respectable appearance'. In 1799 it was described as 'pleasantly situated on the side of a hill ... surrounded with excellent meadow land and fine gardens. All kinds of provision are exceedingly cheap; but coals are dear'. Appearances could be deceptive, however. Its streets were, as usual, found to be 'badly paved' in 1824 and although its castle made for a grand view from a distance, on nearing it you would find it 'hazardous from neglect; the mound studded with pigsties, and the lofty keep undermined by gardens,' according to the *West Briton* in 1814. This was of course next to the squalid and disease-ridden jail from which Ross Poldark and Dwight Enys had rescued Jim Carter from his incarceration, only to see him die from fever and a badly infected arm.

While Richard Warner in 1809 found 'nothing in [Stratton] that can fix the attention', he was more impressed by the 'decent inn and several neat lodging houses' he encountered at a 'little creek called Bude'. Fifteen years later, Bude was being 'much frequented in the summer season for bathing'. Heading west from Cornwall's northernmost outposts, the visitor would pass through Camelford and Wadebridge, both 'inconsiderable places' in 1794. Warner was distinctly unimpressed by the 'affectation in dress ... of the inferior classes' at Camelford, a contrast with the 'wretched hovels' in which they lived. How dare the poor dress well!

'several carts loaded with barrels, containing a white, earthy substance'

In mid-Cornwall Bodmin was, along with Launceston, one of Cornwall's two assize towns and features in the *Poldark* saga as the place where Ross was put on trial and where Francis Poldark mused over thoughts of suicide. Cornwall's oldest town, the only one described as such in Domesday Book, it had seen better days. In 1794 William Maton thought it 'must have been formerly very flourishing' although it still had a 'wide street, inferior to none' in Cornwall. Yet, a few years later in 1799, George Lipscomb found it 'a mean, ill-built town' and in 1824 its houses were described as 'low, decayed and irregular', although there had been 'much improvement' since the 1790s. Two of the 'improvements' were the jail, first built in 1779 and later, the asylum, begun in 1817. The people in the rest of Cornwall may have looked on both of these 'improvements' in a more jaundiced way. They had set Bodmin on its path to become the place to avoid, the phrase 'you'll be sent to Bodmin' taking on a particular meaning for generations of folk elsewhere in Cornwall, where it was used as a way to scare the children.

Down the river Fowey, Lostwithiel, the old Duchy capital, was by 1799 'once flourishing, but now a decayed place'. By the 1820s its houses were 'generally neat' but its trade had disappeared as the river silted up and business departed downriver to Fowey. Just along the coast, St Austell was described as the 'Peru of England' in 1788, presumably because of the wealth of nearby Polgooth Mine. This would seem to have been a little over-enthusiastic, as in 1795 it was found to have 'a few good houses but the rest very old and indifferent', with the inevitable 'very bad pavements'. William Maton, also writing in the mid-1790s, found it nothing more than a 'a small place', with 'nothing to recommend it to attention'. In 1799 however, George Lipscomb eulogised over the White Hart at St Austell 'the best [inn] we had seen in Cornwall'. He strongly recommended to his readers 'the careful and spontaneous attentions of our host and hostess, the goodness of their accommodations in every respect, and the air of willing and cheerful alacrity with which they almost anticipated our wishes.' Lipscomb noticed that 'many large shops' had 'sprung up within these few years ... [the] increase in wealth and population ... chiefly owing to the vicinity of the mines.' By 1809 Richard Warner was meeting with 'several carts loaded with barrels, containing a white, earthy substance' being taken for export from the newly built port of Charlestown. This was china clay, the harbinger of St Austell's future, although the doubling of the town's population in the 15 years or so after 1810 was the result of new copper mines opening up nearby rather than china clay extraction.

Somewhat off the beaten track, St Columb was an older town than St Austell but in the 1790s 'not more likely to detain a traveller than Mitchell'. A decade later, it was still unable to give Richard Warner a 'more favourable impression of the Cornish towns than we had before entertained, being straggling, narrow and paved with execrable pebbles'. It's interesting to note also the places these travellers ignored entirely. While passing through Grampound – a 'decayed and mean' place – there was no mention of Newquay, at this time an insignificant and overlooked fishing village.

'The women ... are very fair and in general genteel'

Once west of St Columb and St Austell, travellers were anticipating the heady delights of Truro. In 1795 this was 'a considerable town, with wide and regular streets and a number of very capital houses.' 'The women ... are very fair and in general genteel' while 'the poorer part of the population are in general neat and industrious'. A few years later the *Universal British Directory* thought 'the people of this town live so elegantly, that the pride of Truro is one of the by-words of the county', although we might suspect that the phrase 'the pride of Truro', could have been intended as an insult, as people elsewhere sneered at the pretentious snobbery of the place. That aside, the Truro that Ross and Demelza regularly visited was undergoing considerable change at this time. The combined assembly rooms and theatre at High Cross, built in 1780, was the best such building in Cornwall. During the 1790s too, the row of houses in the middle of Boscawen Street was pulled down, to create the present broad street. From 1794 Lemon Street began to be built and by 1798 there was a new bridge at the bottom of Lemon Street and an entirely new entrance into Boscawen Street. Moreover, in 1794 it had been 'new paved, which makes it very pleasant to walk over'. For William Maton in 1797 Truro was 'unquestionably the handsomest town in Cornwall'. Not just handsome but busy. The blocks of tin brought to the town for the regular coinages and, too heavy to steal, left lying around the streets were unmissable evidence of its role as a coinage town while its quays were capable of receiving ships of up to 120 tons.

Even James Boswell, on his visit in 1792, felt compelled to mention Truro and its 'appearance of business and wealth', although he was usually more concerned to describe at great length the vast quantity and variety of alcoholic drinks he had guzzled at Cornwall's various country houses. For the Reverend Warner in 1809 Truro was 'in extent, regularity and beauty ... the metropolis of Cornwall', with 'genteel houses, elegant hospitality, fashionable apparel and courteous manners'. In 1824, it was 'well paved, watered and lighted with gas' and 'more comfortable than any other town'. There were the additional refinements of a library established in 1792 and the County Infirmary in 1799. No doubt the frequent presence of many of the local gentry, some with town houses there, others, like Ross and Demelza, making use of its banks, assembly rooms and the choice of inns and shops, made it the place to be seen. To cater for this genteel market, in 1811 Mr Roberts, a tailor at Truro, was offering 'spring fashions ... everything that is useful and ornamental in gentleman's dress and ladies' habits'. Although five years later 65 shopkeepers and millers at Truro were found guilty of using defective weights and measures.

'a parcel of low, dirty people collected there'

Redruth and, somewhat later, Camborne had grown into populous market towns by this time. Redruth in 1799 had 'by far the largest' market in Cornwall, 'owing to the vast number of tinners employed in the neighbourhood'. Meanwhile, Camborne was described as 'uniform and elegant', reflecting the straight streets being developed to house the growing number of mining families. But these towns did not have the social cachet of Truro and were passed over relatively quickly. As was the busy town of Hayle, although Warner in 1809 noted its 'considerable fleet of trading ships for Bristol and Wales, which bring in iron and coal for the mines, and limestone for flux, and load back with copper'.

St Ives got more mentions, but not always very complimentary. It was a 'populous seaport', according to William Maton in the 1790s but 'the stench arising from the (pilchard) stores, and from the putrid rejectamenta lying about the town, is to strangers almost intolerable'. The smell meant that its 'narrow streets which run in the most intricate and capricious directions' were free of visitors. On the other hand, the remark in 1824 that, as the streets were 'dirty, the town has but a poor appearance, yet when viewed from the environs, it has a very picturesque effect' was a hint of what was to come. Little did the residents of Poldark's days anticipate that 200 years later the smell of fish would be replaced by the redolence of sun cream and sweat from a heaving mass of visitors wandering through its streets.

Passing rapidly through St Just in Penwith, a 'sad, dismal place, situated in a most inhospitable and cheerless corner', our traveller in the 1790s would confront the sight of Mount's Bay. Along with Truro, Penzance received the most favourable notices of the time. The town (of over 3,000 inhabitants in 1801) was 'well-built and populous'. As early as 1794 Penzance was being lauded for 'the mildness of its air, the agreeableness of the situation, and the respectability of its inhabitants [which] render Penzance a particularly inviting residence'. By 1809 it was being stated that the town had been 'for many years past the retreat of that happier description of invalids on whom fortune has bestowed the power of seeking health in a more genial air than other parts ... afford'. It was no coincidence that the towns receiving the highest praise from visitors were places that were home to a larger middle-class element or which regularly received visitors from the landed classes, places such as Truro and Penzance, where the well-off

70

recuperating residents boosted its status in the eyes of middle-class contemporaries.

The inhabitants of Penzance could also gaze with satisfaction at the view of St Michael's Mount rearing majestically out of the sea a couple of miles to the east. Not that everyone was enamoured by the Mount. James Boswell pontificated after visiting it that 'it is a disgusting nuisance to have a parcel of low, dirty people collected there' (in the village at its foot), with 'a vile smell of spoiled fish and garbage lying about it'.

'the great variety it exhibits of human countenances'

Moving back east, Helston, like Penzance, was generally well regarded by its visitors. It was also described variously as 'populous' (its population was just over 2,000 in 1801), 'large and respectable', 'neat and regular' and 'decent'. Moreover, it had a good inn. Richard Thomas of the Angel advertised in the *Sherborne Mercury* in 1784 that 'the said inn has been lately improved by the addition of two very elegant dining rooms, three lodging rooms and a new and commodious 16 stall stable'. Reviews of Penryn were more mixed. Richard Warner in 1809 commended the place for the granite moorstones that were replacing those damned pebbles on its pavements and making walking around a less painful and dangerous business. On the other hand, Stockdale in 1824 found the market house and town hall 'not very pleasing'. It's unclear why.

Finally, we arrive at Falmouth. Although Boswell wasn't particularly taken by its 'narrow streets' in 1792, a few years later it was described as 'by much the richest and best trading town' in Cornwall. With 'many rich merchants' resident, Falmouth would clearly, like Truro and Penzance, be complimented by visitors. William Maton, writing in the same decade, felt it was 'unquestionably one of the noblest parts of the kingdom', let alone Cornwall. However, although a place of 'great population, wealth and respectability', the Reverend Richard Warner in 1809 thought it had 'no claim to attention' apart from 'the bustle of its quays and the great variety it exhibits of human countenances'. Its shipping links with all parts of the globe had made Falmouth one of what would now be called the most multicultural towns in Britain. The regular visits of trading ships, the Royal Navy vessels constantly putting in there during the long wars with France, the packet boats bringing news from North and South America, the West Indies, Spain and Portugal not only made for a busy and diverse place. They also provided a market for all sorts of goods and services. Some of these were less praised in visitors' accounts. In 1813 for example Catherine

Mitchell was found guilty of keeping a brothel in the town and given a £10 fine and two months in prison.

But Falmouth was Cornwall's window onto a wider world, the first place in Britain to get the news in pre-telegraph days and the terminus of the mail coach from London. Indeed, it's the perfect place to step away from the roads and the land and look at what role the sea played in Poldark's Cornwall.

5
The Sea

Nowhere in Cornwall is more than 20 miles from the sea. It comes as no surprise therefore that the sea played a large part in the life of its people in the past. Nowadays, for most of us, the sea is something to be gazed at or played in or on. This is presumably why the Poldark series spent so much time lingering longingly on clifftop shots of the sea, feeding a voracious and apparently inexhaustible appetite for Cornish seascapes. However, in the real world, the sea was not just a backdrop for galloping gentlemen or wistful women. It was Cornwall's main highway, a communications and trade route with the wider world. It was a place of conflict, of privateering and violent wartime clashes. Finally, it was an invaluable source of food. Let's look at each of these in turn.

'spectacular rackets'

The taciturn and brooding Captain Andrew Blamey, who married Ross's cousin Verity, was the commander of a packet boat employed on the Falmouth to Lisbon run. Packets were speedy ships, relatively small and lightly armed. In the days before the telegraph, they were used to carry mail, high value goods and also some passengers overseas – as many as 3,000 a year by the 1800s - and were the responsibility of the Post Office. The ships were not owned directly by the Post Office but would be hired by it as long as they met the Post Office specifications. Packet commanders like Blamey had to equip their ships and find the crew, who then became part of the packet service and were protected from being pressed into the Royal Navy.

By the 1790s Blamey would have been one of many such packet boat commanders. Falmouth had first become a packet station in 1688, the terminus of a route from Britain to Spain and Portugal. The original packet boats, plying the seas to the Iberian coast, were later supplemented by others on transatlantic routes, by the 1800s to North America, the West Indies and South America, as well as to the eastern Mediterranean. By 1808 there were as many as 39 packet boats based at Falmouth with crews numbering a total of around 1,200 men. Its role as a packet station made Falmouth (and Cornwall) the best-informed place in the kingdom, the first to get the news from the wider world. The presence of the packets also ensured Falmouth's prosperity. The crews stationed at the port, the victuals the boats required, and the generally well-off passengers who travelled by packet boat and passed through the town, served to boost its economy.

All of which made the temporary removal of the packet service from Falmouth to Plymouth in 1810 such a major blow for the town. How did this disaster come about? The packet crews on the Lisbon service had long been used to selling small amounts of goods on commission overseas for Bristol merchants. This was technically illegal but relatively small scale when compared with the 'spectacular rackets' that were uncovered by a Post Office investigation in 1784. This found that commanders had been claiming for full crews but sailing with fewer, making bogus claims for illness and condoning widespread avoidance of customs duties, all of which resulted in the suicide of the Post Office agent at Falmouth in 1785. Despite that scandal, afterwards the small 'private ventures' of the crews were still winked at and had come to be regarded as a customary supplement to their wages.

'serious spirit of insubordination'

On October 24, 1810, customs officers boarded the two Falmouth packets *Prince Adolphus* and *Duke of Marlborough*, which were about to leave port for the Mediterranean and Lisbon. They broke open the chests of the seamen, confiscating any 'private ventures' that they discovered. Enraged, the two crews refused to put to sea. Thus began what became known as the Falmouth Mutiny. However, there was more to it than a suppression of illegal trading, even though the Post Office and Government claimed to have acted because, at a time of war, the presence of goods on board the packets made them more tempting targets for enemy ships and privateers. In contrast, the packet crews felt that this was merely an excuse for a heavy-handed crackdown by the authorities in response to growing restlessness over their rates of pay.

Earlier, in the summer of 1810, packet crews had assembled at the Post Office Agent's office in Falmouth and presented a demand for higher pay to be forwarded to the Post Office headquarters in London. Their pay had been agreed a decade earlier, but wartime inflation had eaten into its value. In actual fact, after peaking at nine per cent in 1809, the inflation rate fell to just over two per cent in 1810 and in 1811 prices were to fall. But the seamen could hardly predict this. After some delay, a commission was set up to look into their rate of pay. The Post Office concluded that the packet seaman's pay of 28 to 31 shillings a month was higher than that in the Royal Navy and passed the buck back to the packet commanders who were directly responsible for paying their crews out of the general sum they were paid by the Post Office.

Up to this point the men's demands had been couched in a respectful and moderate tone and everything had been peaceable. The action of the customs officers in curtailing the men's supplementary income abruptly changed this. For, not content with merely confiscating their ventures, 13 men from each of the two packet boats that had refused to set sail were forcibly pressed into the Navy, ignoring their traditional exemption. Not too pleased by this, to say the least, seamen from all the packets met the following day. They demanded the release of the pressed men and reaffirmed their call for more pay, pledging not to put to sea until these demands were met. Alarmed, the Mayor was induced by the Post Office agent to read the Riot Act, even though there appears to have been no actual riot. The men dispersed, calling a meeting at the Seven Stars Inn, across the river at Flushing, to formulate their demands and elect delegates to represent them.

On hearing of this meeting, the Royal Navy dispatched a crew in secrecy to Mylor in order to cross the neck of land to Flushing and arrest the ringleaders. By the time they arrived however, the birds had flown and the Seven Stars was innocently empty of any plotting packet seamen. Either the packet crews' intelligence had been spot on or, as the Post Office agent and Navy suspected, they'd been tipped off by sympathisers among Falmouth's elite. Lurid and inaccurate reports soon began circulating in the London newspapers. The *Times* reported a 'civil disturbance' so 'alarming that it was found necessary to call in the civil power, and subsequently the military. The Cornish miners came down in great numbers' while several had been wounded during the 'tumult'. Three months later, the same paper admitted that rumours of involvement of the miners and reports of riots by the townsfolk were 'wholly unfounded' but failed to remind its readers of its own part in spreading the fake news.

In the meantime, the packet crews had elected two delegates – John Parker and Richard Pascoe – to go to London and present the Post Office directly with their demands. At the same time rumours began to surface that the Government was thinking of moving the packet station from Falmouth. Panicked by this, a meeting of the town's leading lights was hastily convened. It was decided to encourage the Post Office agent to promise any man returning to the packets that they would have the traditional protection from impressment. This he did, apart from six named 'ringleaders'. Assured by this, the packet crews began to drift back to their boats.

However, it was too late. While tension was building at Falmouth, the authorities in London had seen their plans to deal with the two expected delegates frustrated. Far from listening to their demands, it had been determined to arrest the pair on their arrival. This the Lord Mayor of London did, but then discovered that he didn't actually have the legal authority to do it. After a few days in jail, Parker and Pascoe were both released. It was claimed that Parker was an 'American', which may have meant he was from the States or that he had 'American' views of democracy, while Pascoe had the local nickname of 'Sir Francis Burdett', a prominent radical politician who called for parliamentary reform.

Stung by this failure, the Government then leant on the Post Office to remove the packet station from Falmouth, even though by now the men were back at work. This it did on November 6, two weeks after the 'mutiny' began. It gave as its reason the 'serious spirit of insubordination' at Falmouth and the 'encouragement and support from the inhabitants' for the packet crews. A lesson had to be learnt and the town punished, so the packets were moved to Plymouth. As it turned out, poorer and less suitable berthing facilities there combined with heartfelt pleas and assurances of loyalty from Falmouth made the stay at Plymouth fairly short-lived. By June of the following year the packets were safely back at Falmouth. By then too, falling prices were defusing the men's demands for more pay.

'a heavy swell and sudden gust of wind swept them all off'

The demand for speedy packet ships played its part in helping to fuel a growing shipbuilding industry in Cornwall by the early 1800s. This was centred on the Fal but Mevagissey, Mount's Bay and other coastal sites also had their shipbuilding concerns. Most of these were small yards, employing no more than a dozen men and turning out sailing ships of up to 100 or 150 tons. The majority were destined for the coastal trade, bringing into Cornish ports the salt needed to cure fish and preserve food and the coal and timber used in the mines as well as an increasing amount of grain and consumer goods. The main export was the mineral produce of Cornwall – its copper and tin. In 1805 more than 800 individual voyages were being made up-channel from west Cornwall to Bristol and South Wales. It's been estimated that by 1824 over 100 vessels were engaged in the trade to Swansea alone, taking copper there and returning with coal. Over three quarters of the ships involved in this growing trade were owned in Cornwall, mostly by relatively small investors, family shipowners, widows, tradespeople and the captains of the vessels themselves. St Ives had many such owners, their ships using the harbours at Hayle and Portreath.

This was a great period for pier and harbour improvements. On the south coast Charles Rashleigh financed the development of the port of Charlestown from 1791. Business boomed in the 1810s when new mines opened east of St Austell. Later, Charlestown prospered from the export of china clay. However, when superseded by the bigger port of Par, it became a quiet backwater. This made it perfect for extensive use when filming the *Poldark* series and other films using Cornwall as their location. Also on the south coast, Point Quay was constructed in 1800 in the Fal estuary. On the opposite coast Trevaunance harbour was rebuilt in 1794. It had been destroyed by storms in 1736 and was to be destroyed again in the 1800s.

Improvements to Hayle harbour in the 1780s were longer lasting, while at Portreath Sir Francis Basset had bought all the harbour shares and rebuilt the pier, on which he spent £12,000 (almost £2 million now) in 1788-91. More basins were cut at Portreath by 1805 and the number of ships negotiating the narrow entrance to the harbour grew quickly in the early 1800s. However, Portreath was never an easy harbour to enter. Even pilot boats could get into difficulty. For example, in December 1810 the sea 'rose suddenly' and a pilot boat was having trouble getting back into the harbour. Four men 'got on the pier head to watch what course the boat would take ... a heavy swell and sudden gust of wind swept them all off'. Three were drowned, while the pilot boat and crew abandoned their efforts to return and made it safely down the coast to St Ives.

Bouts of such stormy weather buffeting Cornwall's exposed coastline plus the reliance of sailing ships on the strength and direction of winds and currents made such 'melancholy' incidents a regular occurrence. Every year saw, on average, ten vessels wrecked on Cornish coasts. Such spectacular wrecks kept Cornwall in the news although the number of wrecks on its coasts was actually lower than that in south-east England where, although the weather was kinder, the quantity of shipping was far greater. Nonetheless, sometimes hundreds would perish in such shipwrecks. In January 1814 the transport ship *Queen*, bound from Spain to Portsmouth, put into Carrick Roads at Falmouth to anchor and wait out the storm. But its cable parted in the gale and the ship was blown onto nearby Trefusis Point. Over 200 men, women and children lost their lives.

In those days navigation in a raging gale wasn't made easier by the fact that some lighthouses were using coal fires to produce their light. For example, those at the Lizard Point, Britain's most southerly lighthouse, were only replaced by oil lights in 1812. Sometimes there were no lights at all. In 1811 in just one month three vessels ran onto the shore and 11 lives were lost at Harlyn Bay near Padstow. The ships had mistaken a headland for the entrance to Padstow, a situation blamed on the lack of a lighthouse on Trevose Head. Similar shipwrecks were still being reported three years later and still being put down to the lack of a lighthouse.

Probably the biggest disaster of this time was the loss of a troop ship in 1796, wrecked at Loe Bar near Porthleven. Not one person survived and an estimated 600 crew, plus soldiers and passengers perished. In the same place, 20 years later, in 1807, the HMS *Anson*, a Royal Navy frigate, was trapped with 'huge seas breaking over the entire ship, the weight of which were slowly tearing her to pieces.' Hundreds of spectators just yards away on the beach could do nothing to help. Appalled at the sight of the scores of corpses lying washed up on the sand, Henry Trengrouse, a carpenter and cabinet maker at nearby Helston, developed a rocket apparatus that could shoot a line to a ship in distress to help more people escape, an early type of breeches buoy. The rocket was successfully tested at Porthleven harbour in 1816 and the first lives were saved using it in 1821.

'quantities of bacon, beef and pork, butter and lard'

Where there were wrecks, there were also wreckers, those who spirited away the goods being carried on the ships. In the fictional world of *Poldark*, when the Warleggans' ship *Queen Charlotte* was wrecked at Hendrawna Beach, hundreds of people descended to take away the goods washed ashore. On the ebb tide they climbed onto the wrecked ship, smashed the hatches and took away the goods. The next tide brought to grief on the same beach the *Pride of Madras*, with a 'cargo of silks, tea and spices'. Some of its crew got ashore but were stripped of their clothes and robbed of everything they had by miners who had by now arrived in large numbers looking for loot.

What Winston Graham was describing here in fiction was a somewhat exaggerated version of two different aspects of wrecking. These are comprehensively described in Cathryn Pearce's superb book *Cornish*

Wrecking, which also punctures the many myths surrounding the subject. In the parallel real universe of Poldark's days there were basically two kinds of wrecking. The first were beach harvests, taking goods that had been washed up on the shore. This was generally regarded by the community as a customary right and a justifiable bounty for the lucky finder. However, it was not viewed that way by the law, which gave the right of wrecks to various landowners and the crown, or the Duchy in Cornwall's case. Those finding goods from a wreck were supposed to deliver them to the lord of the manor and then wait for a year. If the owner had not claimed them by then, they would receive a salvage reward.

The second, more ambiguously regarded kind of wrecking was plunder, actually attacking a wrecked vessel and removing goods from it. The *Fly* was plundered in Mount's Bay in 1794 and in 1795 there was a reported plundering attempt on the *John* at Poldhu Cove, Mullion, when two miners were killed by soldiers brought in to protect the wreck. Significantly, reports of plunder peaked in the unsettled decade of the 1790s, when the authorities tended to see subversion and revolution lurking under every stone and infecting every crowd of boisterous wreckers. Overall, however, such violent incidents and direct looting of wrecks were quite rare.

Wreckers had become folk devils. The relatively infrequent instances of plundering were inflated in the media of the time. Completely fabricated stories of lights being deliberately set on clifftops to lure passing ships to their doom only served to add to the paranoia. Wreckers became 'barbarians' in the columns of the *West Briton* in 1815 and a 'ferocious multitude' in the *Times* in 1817. Yet, exaggerated initial accounts of violent wrecking often had to be toned down or retracted. In 1792 claims that the country people tore the clothes from survivors as they struggled ashore from the Dutch ship *Brielle* on the Lizard turned out to be 'totally destitute of the truth'. The *Sherborne Mercury* reported that it was 'happy to contradict a paragraph that lately appeared in the *Whitehall Evening Post* and which stated that great barbarities had been made in Cornwall towards the Dutchmen lost near Falmouth, as it is manifest that they not only saved the Dutchmen from being totally lost, but launched into great dangers to preserve the ship and stores'.

While the 'barbarians' were to a large extent figments of an over-excited imagination, beach harvesting, taking away washed-up cargo, was commonplace. In 1815 the *West Briton* carried an account of the wreck of the Russian ship *Flora* at Praa Sands, when the presence of the militia failed to stop local people carrying a 'great part of her and her cargo ... into the country'. After 1800 militia or other military were often present at wrecks but it seems more to deter any plunder or violence among the crowds, rather than to stop the removal of goods from the shore. That went on seemingly under their very noses. In 1818, just north of the Camel estuary, three vessels were wrecked in the same storm. Despite a military presence, 'numbers of the peasantry' took away 'quantities of bacon, beef and pork, butter and lard', although two men drowned when wading out too far to collect the bounty.

This example did not occur in a mining district and shows that wrecking was not confined to the mining population. It involved most levels of society. Furthermore, if wrecking in the sense of beach harvesting and without resorting to violence was generally regarded as a customary right, so was the obligation to try to rescue those being wrecked. Cathryn Pearce reports that in the Penzance customs district from 1738 to 1860 almost 100 lives were saved. Lifesaving activity occurred in three quarters of the shipwrecks reported. Wrecking and lifesaving were not necessarily opposed but could be mutually compatible.

'with 900 ankers ... of spirits on board'

It is interesting to compare the reputation of Cornish wreckers as 'barbarians' with the often-romanticised activities of those engaged in illegal trade by sea – smugglers. During the eighteenth century the Government in London slapped increasingly high customs duties on certain goods, realising that their growing consumption could be a lucrative source of income and a convenient means of keeping the land tax, paid by the gentry and themselves, low. Among these were duties on tobacco, spirits and tea, although that on tea was lowered in 1784. As duties rose it didn't take a genius to grasp that a tidy profit could be made bringing in goods, avoiding the customs duty and selling them on the black market. By the end of the century reports like the following from January 1793 were an everyday occurrence – 'at 6pm was seized the sloop *Maria* of Looe ... having on board 210 casks of foreign spirits, a quantity of tea, coffee, tobacco, cards, cotton and lace'. This was accomplished by one customs officer 'in defiance of four very able and desperate smugglers'.

Smuggling in the eighteenth century was big business, estimated to have generated three times the income of all the pilchard exports of that century. It was a business directly and indirectly employing hundreds, not just seamen but those involved in the distribution networks, as well as shipbuilders and suppliers. The business peaked precisely in the *Poldark* period when war disrupted normal trading patterns with the continent and when the authorities were preoccupied with other matters. In addition to the war with the French there was what amounted to another, smaller war daily waged between smugglers and the revenue and customs officers whose job it was to ensure that duty was paid and to confiscate smuggled goods.

Although smuggling was clearly a major activity in Cornwall, it should be noted that its particular association with Cornwall is another myth. This owes more to the prevalence of romantic fiction of the likes of Daphne Du Maurier's *Jamaica Inn* than it does to the actual frequency of smuggling. In fact, smuggling was an even bigger business in the south east of England - in Kent and Sussex - closer to the French coast and with the huge London market close at hand. Nevertheless, bringing goods in without paying duty was commonplace in Poldark's Cornwall. It was also surprisingly open. Newspapers carried reports of the building of new smuggling cutters, '*Goddess of Voyages* ... a new smuggling cutter lately built at Mevagissey' was wrecked off north Devon in a gale in 1790 on her first journey from Guernsey in the Channel Isles, with 900 ankers (casks containing around ten gallons) of spirits on board. The crew were nowhere to be seen. Most of the boats engaged in smuggling were around 50 to 100 tons, carried a crew of ten or a dozen and were armed with a dozen light guns. James Dunn of Mevagissey kept records of his orders from the smugglers and the boats he built between 1802 and 1807 averaged around 80 tons. However, the size of some smuggling craft could be as large as 150 or 160 tons, with 16 to 20 guns.

'riotously and feloniously assembled with firearms'

Once landed at the many coves and beaches along the south coast of Cornwall, the smuggled goods would be spirited away inland via a complex distribution network. Sometimes, customs officers focused their efforts on tackling this inland network as:

> near the seashore, smuggling was carried on to such an
> extent, and with so great a force, that the officers ... not
> thinking it safe for them to attempt making any
> seizures there, or preventing the landing of goods, were
> obliged to wait and stop them as they were carried into
> the country for home consumption.

In 1799 two excisemen at Braddock in east Cornwall, well inland, came across five men 'driving horses ... laden with small casks called ankers, exactly of the same kind with those in which smuggled liquors are always carried on shore, and being fastened with slings and cords in the same way as they are on smuggling vessels'. The casks were also marked with a B or a G which the customs officers assumed stood for brandy and gin. If all that wasn't enough, they were stamped with the initials of persons in Guernsey 'remarkable for selling smuggled liquors'. Moreover, on their demand to examine the casks, one of the smugglers 'struck the customs officer and his horse with a pole', and the officers retreated. Reinforced by the arrival of a third officer, they then again approached the five, 'who defended themselves with sticks'. After some difficulty, they were arrested and brought to the Old Bailey in London for trial. They were found guilty of obstructing the revenue officers, their rather feeble defence claiming the casks just contained water.

On another occasion, a smuggler with two ankers of brandy was spotted by excisemen near King Harry Ferry on the Fal. Pursued down the steep hill to the river, he 'plunged his horse into the water, and attempted to gain the opposite shore'. The horse was on the point of sinking halfway across, clearly exhausted from the chase. The rider slid off, swam alongside and then cut the slings of the ankers. Although the poor horse drowned, the man 'with difficulty reached the shore' and escaped on foot. The brandy was recovered.

Confrontation and conflict did not just occur inland. Accounts of violent clashes between smugglers and the authorities in these years were not unusual. In 1785 two smuggling vessels, the *Happy-Go-Lucky* and the *Stag*, were landing cargoes near Rame Head in south east Cornwall when they were challenged by a small boat sent from a revenue cutter. The midshipman on the boat boarded the *Stag* but was seen by a man in the rigging. He gave the alarm and 'immediately a man came upon deck with a blunderbuss in his hand, and was advancing towards the midshipman, upon which he (the midshipman) fired a musket at him ... and he dropped'. The smugglers then returned fire into the revenue boat, killing one and wounding two others before moving off westward to unload the rest of their cargo. Several months later in 1786 the *Happy-Go-Lucky* was taken 'after a desperate struggle' with another revenue cutter off the Lizard Point. John Martin was charged with wilful murder and held at Pendennis Castle, Falmouth. He managed to escape from there but was eventually recaptured after a reward of £100 was offered.

Another clash in south east Cornwall in September 1798 resulted in the death of Humphrey Glynn, a revenue officer. Following the shooting, the smugglers' vessel, the sloop *Lottery*, delivered its cargo at Polperro and then made off for the safety of Guernsey. In May 1799 however, a man called Roger Toms was taken from the *Lottery* by customs officers. Toms implicated Thomas Potter and two others in the murder but was then unwisely set free by the authorities, pending the trial. He then promptly disappeared. 'It was supposed that he was kept as a prisoner in a cave by smugglers ... for the purpose of preventing him from appearing as a witness.' This ploy worked and the trial had to be postponed. Toms was finally found more than a year later and the trial took place. Four or five witnesses appeared on behalf of the three men accused: 'they all swore [Toms] was a thief, a liar and a man of the most infamous character'.

Support from the community was widespread, whether from fear and intimidation as the Government contended, or from appreciation for the supply of luxury goods at considerably reduced prices. This context enabled gangs of smugglers to operate openly and brazenly. It also meant that cases against smugglers were often brought to London to be tried before the King's Bench at the Old Bailey in order, the Government claimed, to guarantee a fair trial and an unbiased jury. This occurred in 1800 when William Strick was indicted 'with other malefactors and disturbers of the peace' for having at St Keverne in 1799 'riotously and feloniously assembled with firearms and aided and assisted other persons in recovering and taking away from certain revenue officers, 50 gallons of brandy and 40 gallons of geneva [a cross between gin and whisky], after the seizure of the same by the officers'. The liquor had been discovered buried in a field. While the revenue men waited for horses to arrive to carry off the casks of spirits, eight armed men had appeared and retaken the goods. They 'told the officers in a threatening manner to stand, said the goods were theirs; that they had hazarded their lives for them, and would lose their lives in protecting them'. They were found guilty although the jury recommended mercy as no violence had actually occurred.

The revenue officers could not be confident of retaining confiscated goods in these circumstances. In 1815 a reward of £200 was being offered to apprehend a band who had assaulted customs men at St Ives and rescued 200 to 300 casks of smuggled spirits. In 1820 a large smuggling cutter of 16 guns landed 500 tubs of spirits near Padstow. This was discovered by a customs boat from Boscastle which took possession of the spirits. No sooner had that happened than the smugglers rescued the spirits and made off with the customs boat for good measure.

'such wayward consciences with regard to smuggling'

Throughout the *Poldark* years the simmering conflict between smuggling gangs and customs officers provided a constant background noise. Sometimes it erupted into violence, with the authorities struggling and failing to control it. If we dig beneath the veneer of romanticism that surrounds Cornish smuggling, the smugglers rowing into secluded moonlit coves, the mules padding away into the countryside with the smuggled goods, we might note the similarities with the Prohibition era in the States in the 1920s or the current 'war on drugs'. Folk heroes such as John Carter, the 'King of Prussia' and his brothers Francis and Harry were quite ready to resort to violence when necessary to protect their considerable financial investment in the illegal trade. This was despite their Methodist affiliations. Harry had to go on the run to America via the Mediterranean in 1788 but the family business at Porth Leah, later renamed Prussia Cove, was backed up by a shore battery which they were fully prepared to use. In the early 1790s this fired on a revenue cutter to prevent it intercepting contraband and in 1794 the Captain of the Penzance Volunteers reported helping the revenue to secure and destroy a 'large quantity of contraband' at Prussia Cove 'in the face of armed opposition'.

As with later illegal trades in drink or drugs the Government had unwittingly created a lucrative source of profit. A black market then emerged to meet the demand from a considerable number of consumers, who provided tacit or active support for the smugglers. The money they had invested or borrowed to buy the goods meant that the smuggling gangs were very willing to resort to force and intimidation when necessary. However, while modern-day Mexican drug cartels may rely more on the violent end of the spectrum, in Cornwall in the 1790s and 1800s smugglers appear to have been able to call on considerable genuine community support for their activities.

Even local elites could be found among the consumers of the luxury goods that were smuggled into Cornwall. In 1824 for example, £300 worth of brandy was seized from the house of the Mayor of Fowey. Moreover, examples of support for smugglers can be found in places miles away from the coast. In 1801 a number of men were brought to London for trial and convicted of resisting revenue officers. One of them, a Jacob Crabb from Liskeard, received an 'excellent character' from the magistrates of that town despite having recently completed a jail term for a similar offence. Somewhat surprised at this, the judges asked the attorney-general to make enquiries. This done, he concluded that 'the only way he could account for giving this man such a character was, that they in that quarter ... had such wayward consciences with regard to smuggling as to conceive it to be no crime whatever'. Also inland, in 1819 two men from Bodmin, one of them aged 78, who had given evidence against smugglers in another trial in London, were assaulted on their return to the town. Mud was thrown at them by a crowd estimated to number 200, who called them 'old rogues, old informers'.

Smugglers relied on a network of contacts who could supply them with goods from France and further afield. This was done mainly by merchants in Guernsey who acted as intermediaries between the producers and the smugglers. Smugglers usually obtained the cash to pay for goods on credit and repaid the loan once the goods were sold. In the *Poldark* saga we meet smuggler Trencrom, the merchant who acts as the godfather of the local smuggling fraternity. His real-life equivalent was Zephaniah Job of Polperro. Job became known as 'the smugglers' banker', supplying the credit they required for their activities and acting as a link to the Guernsey merchants. Zephaniah had actually been born (in 1750) and brought up in Poldark country at St Agnes but fled east to Polperro as a young man after an obscure violent incident. He began acting as agent for a group of Guernsey merchants in 1778. Part ownership of a privateer and the money from six French prizes enabled him to start advancing cash to the smugglers while also trading all sorts of goods legally. By the 1790s he was the acknowledged go-between, linking smugglers in Cornwall with merchants in Guernsey. He vouched for the 'honesty' of his Cornish clients and acted as the merchants' trusted banker by receiving payments to them from the smugglers to whom he had advanced credit. It's been estimated that Zephaniah made £6,000 a year (equal to around £700,000 now) for 20 years from Polperro smugglers alone.

staggering home a little too well lubricated

Cornwall's close relationship with the sea didn't end with illegal trade. At times of war illegality shaded into legality when privateering, getting commissions that allowed ships to take prizes from the enemy, became an accepted activity. There was certainly plenty of opportunity in these years. Britain had been at war with France from 1778 to 1783, after the French pitched in on the American side. In 1793 war again broke out, following the

French Revolution of 1789, when the central European powers of Prussia and Austria tried to stifle the revolution. That shaded into the Napoleonic Wars after 1799 when Napoleon took power. War then continued with only a couple of breaks until 1815. During these wars, armed smuggling boats could equally well serve as privateers and prey on defenceless merchant shipping. In the American War from which Ross returned in 1783, 83 Cornish ships, half of them based at Falmouth or Penzance but with most other ports also represented, were recognised as privateers. Between them they took 67 prizes during that war, a welcome boost to the local economy.

In the *Poldark* books we meet Scottish army officers but surprisingly few men from the Royal Navy. The army led by Bevill Grenville was remembered as the martial Cornish heroes of the 1600s. But by the 1700s that accolade had shifted onto the shoulders of the men of the Navy. The many merchant seamen, fishermen and smugglers around the coast ran a permanent risk in wartime of being pressed into service with the Royal Navy. Cornwall, with its stock of experienced mariners, was a ready-made, although not altogether willing, reservoir of the sea-going skills that might be commandeered by the Navy. Press gangs had been active in Cornwall in earlier wars. In the wars with France that followed 1793 they again stalked the narrow streets of Cornwall's ports on the look-out for any unwary seaman staggering home a little too well lubricated by the numerous pubs and beerhouses of these places. Five permanent press gangs were active in 1795, at Looe, Fowey and Penzance, with two at Falmouth. As a result, Cornwall supplied far more than its fair share of naval manpower. At the Battle of Trafalgar three per cent of the fleet had been born in Cornwall, although the Cornish population only amounted to about one per cent of the British total.

Among these, some men gained lasting reputations for bravery and heroism. Earlier in the eighteenth century, there was Edward Boscawen of Tregothnan, rear-admiral by the age of 36, dead of typhus before 50, who became known for his exploits in the recurring French wars of the eighteenth century and was nicknamed 'Old Dreadnought'. The Boscawen influence also reached into the Poldark period, and sponsored the career of Edward Pellew. Pellew was the Cornish maritime hero of the French wars of the 1790s. One of Poldark's generation, he was born in 1757 of a Cornish family although not in Cornwall, in fact at Dover, his mother bringing him back to Penzance when his father died in 1768.

At the age of 13 Pellew ran away to sea from Truro Grammar School and with the help of Boscawen patronage obtained a post as captain's servant.

He served in the Mediterranean before having to trek back to Britain from Marseilles where he had been deposited after a disagreement with the captain. By 1777 Pellew was in North America and was involved in helping the British army whose campaign was halted at Saratoga. There he had played a key role commanding a party of seamen and on returning home was promoted to lieutenant in 1778 and in 1782 to captain. The war ended in 1783 and Pellew turned to civilian life, marrying Susan Froud of Wiltshire and living at Truro and then Flushing when his brother Samuel became customs collector at Falmouth. After a period of service commanding a frigate in the 1780s, Pellew turned his hand to farming, with a notable lack of success.

War with revolutionary France in 1793 was Edwards Pellew's salvation. Once again with Boscawen help, he was given the command of the frigate *Nymphe*. Short of crew, Pellew recruited some Cornish miners to help man his ship when he started to accompany convoys in the Channel. Six months later in June 1793 he captured the French frigate *Cleopâtre*, the first British success of the war, for which he was knighted. Pellew was then part of a Falmouth-based squadron of frigates that cruised the Western Approaches hunting down French ships. In 1794 another French frigate *Pomore*, the largest such ship in service, was taken after a brisk half hour engagement. By 1796, by now commanding the frigate *Indefatigable* and the entire squadron, Pellew captured two French frigates after a 15-hour chase. In 1797 he engaged the 74-gun French ship of the line *Droits de l'homme* south west of Ushant. In the teeth of a severe gale and rough seas the *Droits de l'homme* was driven onto a sandbank, dismasted and all aboard lost. In 1799 Pellew was promoted to command a ship of the line, the 74-gun *Impetueux*, captured from the French in 1794. This was something he wasn't too keen on as it ended his days leading the western squadron and meant no more income from the lucrative prizes they took. However, he went on to become rear-admiral in charge of the East Indies command, where the capture of a Spanish treasure ship by one of his captains doubled his wealth overnight. From 1811 to 1814 he commanded Britain's Mediterranean fleet of 70 to 80 warships and became Baron Exmouth in 1814 before retiring in 1821.

Pellew's biographer describes him as one of the foremost frigate captains of his age. His glory years were indubitably when he was commander of the western squadron operating out of Falmouth in the 1790s. He had a reputation for fearlessness and was not slow to lead by example. In 1796 he personally took a rope onto a stranded troop transport driven onto rocks at Plymouth and led the rescue of the 500 people on board. On the other hand, he could also be short-tempered and brooked little disagreement. For example, he faced down a mutiny on board the *Impetueux* at Bantry Bay in Ireland in 1799 and made sure that three of the ringleaders were hanged. He also achieved posthumous fame by being portrayed in fiction many years later as Hornblower's captain in C.S.Forester's *Midshipman Hornblower*.

'the refulgent appearance of the scaly tribe'

The sea was Cornwall's means of communication with the wider world, while its presence threw Cornwall into the front line at times of war. But more directly, thousands depended on its bounty. Every year, the annual pilchard fishery was anticipated with hope and sometimes foreboding. As we saw in chapter 3 the diet of the average family revolved around the three staples of grain, potatoes and pilchards. If either of the first two failed, as happened later in the 1840s when west Cornwall, like Ireland, suffered from the potato blight, the success of the pilchard fishery became critical. In the 1840s it helped save Cornwall from hunger and famine on an Irish scale. But conversely, if the pilchards did not arrive in great numbers, the poor suffered difficult times and the authorities anticipated trouble in the form of food riots.

It was because of this that the success or otherwise of the pilchard season was regularly reported in the columns of the press. In 1793 for example, the *Times* reported that 'the pilchard fishery in Cornwall promises to be both plentiful and advantageous'. But in 1810, the *West Briton* was reporting a poor season. If there was no improvement 'the distress among the poor will be very serious'. The quantity of pilchards taken could vary immensely, as is shown in the number of pilchards exported to the Mediterranean. In 1817 an astonishing number of pilchards, amounting to over 70 million, were exported from Cornwall, but four years later just two million left Cornish ports.

Pilchards would appear off the coast in August and September. Some of them would be caught at sea by drift fishermen but the bulk were traditionally taken close to the shore by what were called seines. A seine comprised three boats, two carrying the nets with six or eight men on board, while a smaller one hosted the master seiner. These, directed by a wildly gesticulating 'huer' on a nearby cliff, would enclose a body of pilchards within a large seine net drawn in a wide semi-circle and hanging down to the sea-bottom. The gap between the ends of the seine net was closed by a smaller stop net to stop the fish escaping. The whole mass of trapped fish would then be pulled closer to shore before the fish were 'tucked', using a small tuck-net, drawn to the surface and pulled on board. The *West Briton* reported the scene during tucking at night:

> The operation is always performed at low water ... the
> number of boats sailing or rowing in all directions
> around the seine; the quantity of persons employed in
> taking up the fish with baskets; the refulgent
> appearance of the scaly tribe, struggling, springing and
> gleaming to the moon in every direction, the busy and
> contented hum of the fishermen, together with the
> plashing of the frequently-plying oar.

This picturesque scene caught the attention of visitors and inspired the talented wordsmiths of the local press although they rarely noted the wider context of this fishery.

The seine companies at Poldark's nearby village of Sawle must have been formed relatively recently as in the 1700s the main seine fishery was on the south coast, not the north. Mevagissey was the principal port. By the end of the century Mevagissey was fading as the pilchards became more prone to turn north, allowing the rise of seining at St Ives, which became the main centre of the fishery. By 1800 there were around 300 seine companies based in the ports and coves of Cornwall with about 200 being effective, the others temporarily or permanently laid up. At bigger places like Mevagissey or St Ives up to 40 or more different seine companies operated, having previously agreed to divide the coastal waters into separate zones in order to avoid a situation of chaos with all the boats competing for the same stretch of sea. A seine boat plus nets cost £1,000 (around £80-90,000 now) and for most of the year it would lie idle. For a couple of months at most, fishermen would be employed, each seine needing 16 or more men. These were part-time, having to find other work for the rest of the year. In addition to the cost of the seines and nets and payment for the men there were the cellars and other buildings on land, where the fish was stored, and the wages of the women who bulked (packed) and salted the fish. According to an estimate in the 1820s this almost doubled the cost of the seine itself. Clearly, all this required considerable capital and indeed seine companies were owned by merchants and groups of adventurers and had been since at least the 1400s. Picturesque it may have been, but seine fishing had been a profit-seeking, heavily capitalised venture for centuries.

In bad seine fishing seasons the poor would buy what fish they could from the drift boats that fished the waters further off the coast. After 1820 these began following the fish - mainly herring - to Irish waters and further afield. But in Poldark's days they would have usually stayed closer to home. In contrast to seine fishing, drift fishing was much less costly. A boat and nets cost around £250 in 1800 (or just over £20,000 in modern terms). This was within the reach of the better-off fishermen, who owned the boats, dividing the proceeds of the catch among the men, while retaining some of the income for the upkeep of nets and boat. In the 1830s, the difference between seine and drift fishing was neatly summarised: 'the gains of the seine owner are large but uncertain; the drift fishery affords smaller, but more certain profit. The seines are principally owned by persons of property; the drift boats and nets by poorer individuals: it may be called the poor man's fishery'.

During the pilchard season most of the fish caught by the seines were pressed to remove the oil and then packed in salt before being sold to the local market or exported overseas, mainly to the Mediterranean. Women were central to the curing and sale of fish, many being employed temporarily during the pilchard season. In other months the fish landed from the drift boats would be sold fresh. 'Jousters' were women who trudged inland carrying on their backs a large basket of fish, with a supply of salt in their side pockets. The women employed to cure fish could prove to be feisty and independent and fully prepared to defend their rights. Some years before Ross Poldark returned to Cornwall, Thomas Carlyon of Truro, who owned fish cellars at Mousehole, had to face down a strike by the women there after he attempted to abolish a custom whereby they could take the fish left over from a barrel. Five months later, as the women were still insisting on the custom and stating their refusal to work for him, he was beginning to consider bringing in women from other places for the coming season.

'every person drowned'

Meanwhile, their menfolk were out at sea. Mackerel were joining herrings and pilchards as the mainstay of the drift fishermen by the 1790s. In 1793 'the mackerel fishery on the coast of Cornwall has been abundant, near 30 boats loaded with mackerel on Monday sailed from Penzance to Southampton, to be there conveyed to town [London]'. The boats taking the fish to distant markets might not have been Cornish. In 1817 a Parliamentary enquiry found that Brixham smacks would travel to Mount's Bay in the early spring to buy mackerel for London as they were faster than the Cornish luggers. Nonetheless, in 1820 it was reported that some St Ives luggers were sailing mackerel to Bristol for onwards distribution. The mackerel fishery, usually from April to October, was followed by a local herring fishery, according to Samuel Drew in 1824.

Any fishing out at sea brought its own perils. In 1792 the *Sherborne Mercury* reported that herring were plentiful at St Ives. Sadly however, in this instance they were too plentiful. 'Two poor fellows were drowned out of a small boat employed in this fishery; the boat being over-laden with herrings'. It had capsized in a strong north-easterly gale just 400 yards from the shore. These were not the first and they would by no means be the last fatalities in a notoriously dangerous occupation. In 1817, a very unseasonable gale in June, 'the severest ... ever remembered at this time of year' caught boats fishing for mackerel off Mount's Bay by surprise. They promptly headed for harbour but two sank and 14 fishermen were lost overboard, leaving 37 dependent children, according to the *Times*.

Surveying the uses which Poldark's contemporaries made of the sea uncovers some similarities with our own times. It's still a means of trade, both legal and illegal, although international communications now depend on satellites rather than packet boats. Wars are still fought on the sea and the sea remains a resource for food, although an increasingly fragile one as humans continue, as in Poldark's days, to use it as a convenient dustbin. No doubt people in those times sometimes gazed at the sea, as we do nowadays, but they must surely have spent less time doing that than the characters in the *Poldark* TV series. The use of the sea as a place of leisure, relaxation and hedonism was much less prevalent in Poldark's times. There were coming signs of this though. In the summer of 1788, '33 men and boys and four women went out in a new fishing boat on a party of pleasure. By some means the boat was overset and every person drowned'. This 'melancholy accident' occurred off Porthleven.

No doubt the funerals were well-attended and the church packed. But in their religion too, for the Cornish this was a time of great change.

6

The Chapel

C hapels are a disappearing element in the Cornish landscape of the twenty-first century. Converted into housing, used as warehouses or for retail purposes or just slowly crumbling into decay, chapels, like engine houses, are a relic of old Cornwall. In Poldark's time it was quite the opposite. Chapels were fast becoming an iconic landscape element, along with the mine, its engine houses and the labourers' cottages, redolent of a new, industrialising Cornwall.

'we have lost the people'

Chapels began to sprout across the land from the 1760s. After mid-century, the new Methodist Societies which had emerged in the 1740s began to build their own meeting houses to supplement those of the established Church of England. By 1791, 64 Methodist chapels had been built in Cornwall, many of them small and primitive and most of them later rebuilt and extended by the Victorians, sometimes several times over. The number of chapels then multiplied more than three-fold from 1791 to 1820. Indeed, it was this period that saw the most explosive growth of Methodist membership. In 1785 fewer than a third of Cornish parishes had a Methodist Society. By 1820 only one in seven was without one. As early as 1800 it was being said that 'the Methodists have Redruth to themselves; theirs may be called the established religion'. More prosaically, an historian of Cornish Methodism has described Cornwall as 'a region where Methodism had a profound and perhaps unmatched effect in the early nineteenth century'. By the 1830s a vicar was lamenting that 'we have lost the people. The religion of the mass is become Wesleyan Methodism'.

In 1783, when Ross returned from America, that outcome was still uncertain. John Wesley, an Oxford-educated Church of England clergyman, had been converted to evangelical religion in 1738. He felt that God had urged him to preach to the people, to tell them that by faith and the love of God they could attain grace and holiness. Wesley then set about travelling relentlessly up and down the British Isles, leaving in his wake organised societies of Methodists. Nonetheless, he was careful to assure his listeners that he and his followers remained a part of the established church. His aim was merely to give it more 'method'.

It was only after Wesley's death in 1791 that Wesleyan Methodists moved beyond the orbit of the Anglican Church, and began their journey towards dissenting religion proper, a journey completed by the 1840s. By that time Methodists were viewed as a branch of dissent, along with Baptists, Congregationalists, Quakers and others who could trace their roots back to the religious schisms of the mid-1600s, when they had broken away from the Church of England. Wesley might have continued to deny that Methodists were dissenters and urge his supporters to attend and take communion at their parish church. But the expansion of chapel-building from the 1760s and the establishment of a parallel Methodist organisational structure, separate from traditional parochial authorities, suggested otherwise.

'a strange sight, the sun shining in Cornwall'

Cornwall regularly appeared on John Wesley's itinerary. However, it was not at the top of his list for its scenery. Or its weather. In 1743 Wesley noted in his *Journal* that 'I saw a strange sight, the sun shining in Cornwall'. John Wesley and his brother Charles, who actually made the first visit, came to Cornwall 32 times between 1743 and John's death in 1791. They first came because of reports of a small evangelical group that had already been formed at St Ives. The Wesleys brought a relatively simple message. Stripped of its theological justifications, it was a straightforward choice. There was heaven and there was hell, good and evil. People just had to make their decision. Anyone could have their past sins redeemed and be saved as long as they had faith. This message was transmitted to small groups and to large outdoor meetings, as well as in churches. In a real sense Wesley took religion to the people, in their towns and their villages. From an early point it meshed with their everyday life.

Moreover, this message was backed up by an extremely efficient and flexible organisation. Members were grouped in bands (if there were only a half a dozen or so of them in a locality), classes (of up to a dozen people) and societies. When societies grew, they were sub-divided. Societies were also grouped into circuits and as Methodist membership rose, circuits were themselves divided and then divided again. This organisational structure proved to be beautifully adaptable to the shifting geography of Cornwall, as mines rose and fell, people moved readily from one parish to another in search of work, and new hamlets and villages sprang up in places remote from the existing towns.

Later, Methodists claimed that their success was largely due to a corrupt and uncaring Church of England, a church that had lost its way and failed to meet the spiritual needs of the people as it turned a blind eye to the moral depravities of society. It's certainly true that the Anglican Church in the 1700s in Cornwall was in serious decline. Attendances were falling. In the copper mining parish of Gwennap around 100 people were taking the sacrament in the parish church in 1744. By 1779 this had fallen to 40 despite a large jump in the population. A similar story was told at nearby Redruth, where attendance was reported as plummeting from 250 to 50 over the same period. In the west at St Just in Penwith numbers attending the church halved. Falls were less serious in towns such as St Austell or Liskeard and in the rural farming parishes, but even there most places recorded declines in church attendance between 1744 and 1779.

'his necessary attendance on his affairs in Berkshire'

Low attendance at church was traditionally linked to the twin problems of non-resident clergy (where the clergyman who held the living - and got the income - did not live in the parish) and pluralism (where a clergyman had the living of more than one parish.) In 1765 for example the Vicar of St Cleer was also the Rector of Mary Tavy, just across the border in Devon, but had actually been living for the previous 34 years at Looe. The Vicar of Tintagel was living and working as a schoolmaster at Penryn, many miles to the west. The Rector of Creed (who was also Vicar of St Austell) had been living in Bath for five years, while the Rector of Marhamchurch was absent 'by reason of his necessary attendance on his affairs in Berkshire'. In 1779 around 40 per cent of Cornish parishes had no resident clergyman. Instead, poorly paid curates like the harassed Reverend Mr Odgers, the curate of Sawle, undertook their pastoral duties for them, often for a relatively small salary.

The situation did not improve during Poldark's time. In fact, if anything, it got worse. In 1821 it was reported from Gwennap, by then a parish containing over 6,000 souls, that the attendance at the parish church was 'not many'. Non-residence and pluralism continued to be commonplace. At

Gwinear, the clergyman with the living was actually to be found teaching at a grammar school in Kent. At Kenwyn and Kea the livings were held by a vicar who lived in London. The Vicar of Perranzabuloe also lived in London, as did the Vicars of Sancreed and Sithney. Indeed, the Church of England reached its lowest point around 1820, before it began to revive.

Nonetheless, despite these abuses, the success of Methodism in Cornwall cannot be ascribed entirely to the shortcomings of the established Church of England. For one thing, there was no actual link between non-residence and low attendances. Some of the better attended churches were precisely those that had no resident clergyman. Moreover, even the worldly eighteenth century church had its share of clergy who, like Wesley, had been caught up in the 'Great Awakening', the revivalist, evangelical wave that had gripped Protestant communities in parts of north-west Europe and North America during the 1700s. Wesley avoided Truro on his visits between 1746 and 1760 because of the presence there of the evangelical clergyman Samuel Walker (who was himself the non-resident Vicar of Talland, near Looe). In north Cornwall a small group of evangelical Anglican clergymen in the mid-1700s meant that this was another area Wesley avoided in consequence, although the lack of large numbers of labourers there would also have made it less attractive territory.

It might be expected that Cornwall would attract more than its fair share of pluralists in the 1700s as livings were relatively poor and the church was often situated well away from urban conveniences and 'polite society'. Rather than pluralism as such, the problems that the Church of England was facing in the eighteenth century lay more in the social and geographical distance between its clergy and the mass of the people. Non-residence only exacerbated this social gulf. By the 1700s the clergy were dominated by the sons of gentry, who tended to be allocated the most lucrative livings. They had little direct experience of the life of the poor. At the same time, their social status more generally in Cornwall was in decline. Mining and trade had created new families with new money and had shaken up the existing social hierarchy. When those at the bottom could remember the time when those at the top had also been at the bottom, it became harder to keep up any innate respect or deference for the landed class. This was especially so given the poor quality of some of the more notoriously worldly hunting and feasting clerical gentry or the insipid or incomprehensible sermonising of some of the others. It comes as little surprise that the clergy were finding it ever more difficult to prevent their flocks grazing in the more sustaining fields of Methodism.

'much excitement among the public'

The loss of social status was not helped by other changes wrought by industrialisation. Copper mining had injected a volatility into the settlement pattern. Cottages or even whole villages sprang up in places well away from the parish church. A new settlement pattern was superimposed on a medieval geography that was in any case problematic for the Church. Cornwall's dispersed settlements combined with large parishes (often with no resident gentry) had always made social control difficult to exercise. Sometimes, as at Redruth, the churchtown was a mile or so away from the actual town. Other large mining parishes such as nearby Gwennap or Wendron had churchtowns that were located well away from new mining communities. Methodism's flexible organisation gave it a head start over the lumbering parochial institutions of the Church. It could speak to the people in the places where they lived. Moreover, by the use of local preachers, it could do this in their own accents and using familiar and meaningful metaphors.

The flexibility of Methodist organisation can be illustrated by the example of Francis Brenton, born in 1793 at St Wenn in mid-Cornwall 'of industrious parents', his father being a shoemaker. After an early spell with the Methodists, Francis became a 'backslider', giving up his membership. But he re-joined in 1817. As there was no chapel in his hamlet, 'he and three other young men of Tregonetha commenced an informal prayer meeting in an out-house in the village'. Francis and his friends took the initiative and formed a society and obtained a barn for their prayer meetings. 'The numbers attending ... rapidly increased and in a little time the barn was crowded; many became concerned for their eternal well-being, the number of converts ... increased and a class meeting was established'. In 1818 the Bible Christians, a recently formed Methodist sect, introduced preaching into the vicinity. Their female preachers, by now frowned upon by Wesleyan Methodism, 'caused much excitement among the public'. Francis and his fledgling society at Tregonetha invited the Bible Christians to establish regular preaching there, which they did. 'For a while they occupied an old, dilapidated barn, with the window place stopped with straw,' eventually enlarging and rebuilding it as a chapel in 1836. In this haphazard way, in fits and starts, rough hewn chapels blossomed and Methodism more generally advanced.

These over-crowded meeting houses, together with the enthusiasm of the people attending, were not always the safest of places. The *Sherborne Mercury* in 1784 reported that at St Mawes a dissenting congregation was meeting in a room above a cooper's shop. 'It was supposed there were near 400 persons in it; and just as the preacher was beginning his discourse, the beams gave way, and about one-third of the congregation fell into the shop below'. Fortunately, no lives were lost although several suffered fractures and bruising.

'always hairy and with eyes that glowed fiery red'

The Methodist message was first taken on board in the western mining parishes. There, the religious vacuum that industrialisation was helping to produce created the perfect opportunity for Methodists to fill the gaps. Within those communities however, miners themselves were not necessarily the first to be drawn to this new creed. Instead it was their wives and daughters. Women made up the majority of early Methodist membership lists. Moreover, at first, women preachers were tolerated by Wesleyan Methodism. When, in 1771, Ann Gilbert of Gwinear attended a service the preacher didn't show up. She gave out the hymn and then began to 'entreat [the congregation] and beseech them to repent and turn to the Lord. The people were melted with tears, and many were convinced of sin'. Ann was totally blind but found a new respect and status through her preaching.

This was also the case for working men like Drake Carne in *Poldark*, who could enhance their community standing by becoming local preachers in their Methodist circuit, conducting services and acting as class leaders. The Methodist magazines of the time are full of their obituaries, usually recounting a standard rite of passage from sin via conviction of that sin and then conversion to a holy life. One example among multitudes was that of Thomas Trethewey, born at St Dennis in mid-Cornwall in 1786. He was from a large family and had received little schooling; 'obliged at an early age to work out of doors' to help the family finances. Although learning to read at evening school and a 'constant' attender at the parish church, he 'grew in sin ... taking great delight in wrestling, dancing, music and all other sinful amusements'. In 1808, aged 22, he began to reassess his life. Marriage increased his seriousness; he attended one of William O'Bryan's sermons and became convinced of his sinful ways. After a little while he was 'set at liberty whilst down a mine' near Luxulyan. By 1820 he was a local preacher and a class leader, tasks which he conscientiously undertook up to his death in 1841. That occurred after a mine accident, when he slipped from a broken ladder, fell over 40 feet down a shaft and shattered several bones. His funeral was 'attended by upwards of a thousand persons'.

It's been proposed that the Methodist emphasis on the humble cottage, the class meetings in people's houses, the open-air gatherings in their hamlets, all helped to reaffirm the status of the cottage at times of uncertainty. Far away events in global mining markets could suddenly threaten their lives, but Methodism helped to provide certainty, or in modern terms, resilience. It gave people a sense of domestic security, simultaneously reminding them that they were part of a shared community. During the time the *Poldark* saga was unfolding, more and more men and women like Drake Carne were getting involved in Methodism. Local Methodism tended to reflect the communities it served. For instance, in the mining village of Blackwater in 1815 the trustees of the Wesleyan chapel were 14 miners, a carpenter and a labourer. However, in the towns, Methodism was more diverse and more middle class. John Probert, historian of Cornish Methodism, has shown that in Redruth in 1815 trustees of the Wesleyan chapel included six shopkeepers, a brewer and three farmers, with just five miners and a shoemaker.

Although there was more diversity in town Methodism than in the countryside, nonetheless the rough equality of Methodism contrasted with the stuffy, hidebound social hierarchy of the Anglican Church. Methodism resonated with the broad equality found in the poor but independent mining communities that were emerging in the 1700s. Its message also seemed to be more suited to people's day to day concerns. The first historians of Methodism also tended to stress how this new creed, with its emphasis on self-discipline, orderly behaviour and hard work fitted into the needs of a new industrial society. However, things were not quite so straightforward.

As well as being a harbinger of changing manners, Methodism in addition seemed to be perfectly compatible with widespread pre-existing superstitions. In the 1790s a Helston lawyer noted the 'giants, fairies, piskies, mermaids and demons' that populated the imaginations of ordinary folk. Cunning women and white witches were widely endowed with the ability to heal sick people and animals. Some of their skills no doubt flowed from a close knowledge of herbal remedies and traditional treatments. At other times, they were ascribed to witchcraft.

Meanwhile, in the mines, most miners accepted the existence of knockers or knackers. These were underground spirits, little people who could at times be heard hammering away in the depths of a mine. They had to be left pieces of pasty as they could lead miners to riches or, if they took a dislike to them, to disaster. The presence or absence of knockers explained the chance occurrence of prosperity or poverty. For a Methodist tributer,

God took over. It was God that had to be kept content, rewarding men with riches or casting them into penury. The hand of God was everywhere, as a contemporary put it, 'from bee stings to earthquakes'. According to Samuel Drew, there was, conversely, a belief in a physical devil, constantly ready to terrorise the unwary traveller. 'In form the devil, or his agent, was usually bestial, resembling a large, shaggy dog, or even a bear, but always hairy and with eyes that glowed fiery red'. Methodism did not so much replace superstition but merge with it. It was a two-way relationship. Methodism was made to fit existing folk religion, but that folk religion was being remoulded and reinterpreted by Methodism.

'produced a perspiration which fell from their face to the ground'

Cornish Methodism was also at this point starting to see periods of intense excitement, waves of religious revivals. In this way it differed from elsewhere, where patient evangelising and the conversion of small groups of people was the preferred method of building up membership. In contrast, in Cornwall in the 1780s mass revivals were fast becoming the main way of attracting members. They could be spectacular. In the five years from 1793 to 1798 Methodist membership in Cornwall grew by 63 per cent. Then, in the space of the one year of 1799 it shot up by 72 per cent. Similarly, in the five years to 1813 membership expanded by 52 per cent. But in 1814 it grew by 49 per cent in one year. Ross Poldark's life span encompassed both of the dramatic revivals of 1799 and 1814. These outbursts of mass religious frenzy sealed Methodism's position as the most popular religious denomination in Cornwall. They marked the beginning of its dominance over the Cornish people's spiritual world, a sway that persisted until the 1960s.

Revivals were periods of mass conversion, when thousands underwent the experience now known as being 'born again'. More generally, conversion was the expected route to becoming a good Methodist by the late 1700s. This first involved a process of becoming 'serious', aware and concerned about the sinful life currently being led. That inevitably progressed to a period of conviction, a time of anguish when the individual became convinced that he or she was doomed to the everlasting fires of hell. Yet there was light at the end of the tunnel. For, given the right support and encouragement, the person became assured that their sins had been forgiven and they could start life afresh. Revivals were merely periods of mass conversion, when hundreds went through this process simultaneously, sometimes in a startlingly public manner.

The first major revivals took place at St Just in Penwith in 1782 and St Austell in 1785, indicating that Methodism in those places had already reached the numbers necessary to support the phenomenon. The two 'great' revivals of 1799 and 1814 burned across the land in mid and west Cornwall as village after village succumbed to the excitement of revivalism. Thomas Langley, a Yorkshireman who was a Wesleyan Minister at Redruth, described the 1799 revival there:

> Meetings continued long and very late, sometimes till
> midnight, or one, two, or three o'clock next morning
> before they broke up, sometimes great noises and
> much confusion, so that at times there appeared no
> serious devotion at all, some singing, some praying,
> some talking to, and exhorting, in different parts of the
> chapel, and at the same time, so that no regularity, or
> order were attended to.

Langley was distinctly unimpressed, as were the Wesleyan authorities. The Cornish took a different view. In 1814 the revival soon spread to Redruth. There, it was observed that:

> the chapel doors were not shut till ... seven nights after
> ... at their first conviction the people dropped down as
> dead and became quite stiff, and after some time
> revived again, and the first words were 'Christ have
> mercy upon us, Lord have mercy upon us', and this
> repeated (in some cases) not only for hours, but for
> days, till the Lord on whom they called sent salvation
> in an answer of peace to their souls.

This account continued:

> men crying with loud and bitter cries, till the anguish
> of their souls had opened every pore of the body, and
> produced a perspiration which fell from their face to
> the ground ... Almost all business was at a stand, and
> the shops mostly shut up. When market day came there
> was scarce any buying or selling. The cries for mercy
> were not confined to the chapel, but extended to the
> streets, and men and women were seen ... supported on

each side from the chapel to their houses, for they
could neither stand nor walk.

That report from an anonymous Methodist is corroborated by William
Jenkin, who was a Quaker and consequently could remain more detached.
Describing the 1814 revival, Jenkin reported that 'for a few weeks there was
'a great noise', then:

> the great current seemed to run westwards. It was not
> so very noisy or rapid about Truro and its vicinity, as it
> was in the parish of Gwennap. At Illogan and
> Camborne it was more violent, but at Hayle
> Copperhouse and the surrounding villages ... the
> torrent bore down everything that stood in its way.
> Were I to attempt to describe it, I could not find words
> sufficient to draw it in colours strong enough.

Jenkin noted that 'some were merely imitators [and] others were worked up
by the force of their heated imaginations', implying a form of mass hysteria.

Sceptics noted the role of preachers in whipping up this hysteria,
threatening the 'convinced' with hellfire and perdition. For them revivals
resembled a form of moral terrorism, playing on the fears of an emotional
and suggestible people. For others, doubts were submerged by the examples
of real behavioural change that followed revivals. William Jenkin claimed
that public drunkenness had disappeared while attendances at all churches
soared in the months following the 1814 revival. Yet such changes proved
to be temporary for at least some of those converted. The broader effects
inevitably faded over time and, following a revival, complaints inevitably
surfaced about 'backsliding'. Although the 1799 revival had led to a 72 per
cent increase in Methodist membership, over the following five years a third
of those on the bloated membership lists dropped out. The same thing
happened, although not to the same degree, in the five years after 1814,
which saw an 18 per cent drop in membership.

'convinced that they were sinful perishing, helpless creatures'
How can these mass revivals be explained? Various ingenious attempts have
been made to link them to external events such as war, economic depression,
or outbreaks of infectious disease. It may indeed be possible that some
external concern acted as a trigger to detonate a revival. Both the revivals
of 1799 and 1814 occurred in wartime for example. Yet the real engine of

revivals may be more prosaic. Significantly, contemporaries noted that, of those converted in 1814, the 'greatest number are young persons of both sexes, from about 14 to 28 years of age'. They were 'convinced that they were sinful perishing, helpless creatures ... driven to the throne of mercy by terror'. Others noted that when 'young people' were prominent, 'the torrent broke down everything that stood in its path'. In addition, we should note that most of those converted were already leading what might seem to us to be exemplary lives, attending chapel, of good character and the like. It was not unknown, but reports of inveterate and older drinkers, gamblers and hedonists being suddenly converted were very rare.

If we add the youth of those converted in revivals to the growing role of the Methodist chapel in Cornish life, we come closer to the mechanism through which revivals occurred. They are best seen as rites of passage, times when a new generation of young people was inducted into membership of the Methodist connexion. This would happen more easily once there was a large circle of regular chapel-goers who were non-members. These provided a convenient pool that was ripe for conversion to full membership. It was also a group that, through regular attendance at chapel, was susceptible to the urgings of the preachers and aware of the language of revivalism. Moreover, once established, the idea of a periodic renewal of Methodist societies through revivals became an anticipated event. Preachers would begin actively to work up a revival if it had been a few years since the last one. Methodists would be on the lookout for any sign or portent that might herald the glorious event. That sign may have been an external event, the declaration of war or the arrival of an epidemic disease. Or it may have been something much simpler. At St Ives it was claimed that a group of small children who, in imitation of their elders, 'began singing a hymn and uttering the expressions which they had heard at chapel' was enough to start a revival.

Revivals seemed to suit the Cornish temperament of the time. Robert Lowery, a visiting Chartist, later described the Cornish as 'full of warm religious feeling' with a 'daily language ... replete with rapturous exclamations'. Some of this comes through in the later, nineteenth-century biographies of charismatic local preachers. This might sometimes be difficult to imagine nowadays. Years exposed to chronic economic hardship and the more socially conservative late nineteenth-century Methodism made the Cornish much more likely to be dour, self-contained and unemotional than rapturous or excitable. But so it was in Poldark's times and for a generation or two afterwards.

'very willing to govern the preachers'

Such characteristics predisposed the population to mass revivals. However, this enthusiasm was not shared by the Methodist authorities which viewed revivals and the subsequent backsliding with suspicion. They preferred an altogether safer and steadier route to building their organisation. This inevitably led to tensions and conflicts between Cornish Methodists and the Methodist hierarchy. These strains began to appear almost as soon as John Wesley died in 1791.

The gap in perception was exacerbated by another tendency, a restlessness among local Methodists, who were quick to find fault with the leadership and reluctant to accept the authority of the itinerant ministers, often from outside Cornwall, who were allocated to the local circuits. Towards the end of his life the autocratic John Wesley became irritated by the lack of obedience he received in Cornwall. 'It has been observed for many years', he wrote, 'that some at Redruth were apt to despise and very willing to govern the preachers.' After his death these simmering tensions became more visible. In 1791, 51 leading Methodists met at Redruth to discuss the administration of Methodism. The remarkable document they produced would have, as John Probert has observed, 'revolutionised Methodism'. Those attending, principally mine captains and tradesmen, the products of Cornwall's industrialisation, were demanding nothing less than a democratic revolution. They called for the right of members to elect their class leaders and society stewards and for circuits to have a right of veto over the itinerant ministers appointed by the centre. More strikingly, the language of the document strongly echoed that of the American Constitution of 1787.

Methodism's leaders had other ideas. In 1795 their Plan of Pacification ensured that the central Wesleyan Conference would retain its authority while demands such as those issued at Redruth were brusquely ignored. That set the tone for an ongoing mistrust between local circuits in Cornwall and the Wesleyan Conference. This was made worse in 1807 when the Conference rejected the outdoor 'camp meetings' popular in Cornwall and implicitly spurned revivalism. To some local Methodists this looked like a direct attack on the spiritual energy that had underpinned Cornish Methodism and fuelled its growth.

Change was in the air by the 1810s. New urban chapels were appearing, as at Falmouth in 1815, catering for the more respectable middle classes of the town. Wesleyan Methodism in the towns began to diverge from the simpler, more socially homogenous chapels of the countryside. In doing so differences came to the fore. In 1802 there was a dispute at Redruth when the trustees introduced pew rents against the wishes of many members. In 1814 two women at Truro were expelled after the revival of that year, for 'jumping, shouting and recounting visions.' They went on to help create, for a time, a small sect of revivalists in the town. These gathering clouds betokened the gale of schisms that were to blow apart the main body of Wesleyan Methodism in the first half of the nineteenth century. Usually in Cornwall these revolved around issues of evangelism and revivalism, with Conference being viewed as unduly restrictive, or they arose from disputes over administrative priorities or challenges to local autonomy.

'ravings and shrieks of the preacher'

In Poldark's time most of these splits lay in the future. The exception was the Bible Christian denomination. Its followers were often dubbed Bryanites, after the name of their founder William O'Bryan, although he was actually christened William Bryant, who had founded his chapel at Gunwen in Luxulyan. The Bible Christians chafed at the refusal of the Wesleyan leadership to evangelise those, mainly agricultural, districts of Cornwall where Methodism was less strong. The leadership preferred to consolidate their existing organisation before expanding. This allowed the Bible Christians to establish a presence in farming country in north Cornwall and on the Lizard. The Bryanites deliberately encouraged a spiritual and revivalist style. At St Columb in 1827 the *West Briton* reported a local disturbance caused by the 'ravings and shrieks of the preacher and their disciples within and the shouts and laughter of the crowds outside'.

Nevertheless, the more explicitly revivalist Bible Christians were unable to trigger revivals in the rural areas. The population there was not sufficiently concentrated and Methodism not the preponderant religious practice. In consequence, and paradoxically, revivals remained largely a Wesleyan phenomenon, despite the disapproval of the Wesleyan authorities. The result was a stark contrast. By 1820 a more revivalist Methodism was located in the west, particularly outside the towns. In the east Methodism was more orderly and administratively stable. This was the result of differences in the timing of Methodist growth. In industrial west Cornwall mass revivals predated the establishment of the formal machinery of Methodism, leaving a popular, indigenous Methodism intact. In the east, in contrast, administrative structures were already in place before the number of Methodists had reached a critical point, stifling the revivalist impulse.

This leaves us with the final paradox of Methodism in Poldark's Cornwall. In 1808 the visiting Reverend Richard Warner observed that:

> the customs which some years ago brutalised the
> miners of Cornwall and kept them in a state little better
> than that of savages are now in a great manner
> exploded. The desperate wrestling matches for prizes
> ... the inhuman cock-fights ... the pitched battles which
> were fought between the working men of different
> mines ... the riotous revellings ... are now of a very rare
> occurrence.

He ascribed this change to Wesleyan Methodism. Local Methodists were quick to bask in the credit for this moral revolution. Yet they overplayed things.

There had been change, but many of the old customs were still alive in 1820, well after the rise of Methodism. In fact, they endured longest in precisely those districts where Methodism was strongest. Rather than being an agent of external, foreign influence disrupting local traditions, Methodism, in the 1790s and early 1800s, had buttressed the defences against change. It acted to shore up those aspects of life that provided continuity with former times - the folk beliefs, the smallholdings, the centrality of the cottage, even the wrestling matches, which peaked not in the 1790s but the 1850s. These traditional features of Cornish life were of course themselves undergoing change and coming under pressure from outside forces. But the chapel had not displaced them. Instead, it had taken its place at the heart of Cornishness by the end of the Poldark era, joining older pursuits, both reputable and disreputable, pursuits we shall meet in the next chapter.

7
The Plain an Gwarry

(The *plain an gwarry*, in English 'the play place', was a circular ampitheatre used to present religious dramas in Cornish-speaking communities before the Reformation of the 1500s.)

In Poldark's times what did people do for fun? The miner Mark Daniel at one point complains that the only break he had from work was on feast days. That was probably an over-statement. Annual feast days were supplemented by a number of other holidays into the early years of the nineteenth century. These included the obvious religious holidays, such as Christmas, Easter and, particularly associated with sports and games, Whitsun. There was also midsummer day and a large number of local fairs plus special occasions held to celebrate local or wider events. One such took place in 1792 when laying the foundations of a new quay at Trevaunance Cove, near St Agnes, in the heart of Poldark country. This was accompanied by 'the innocent sports of the country, such as wrestling, hurling, football ... practiced with infinite hilarity and good humour'.

'a game fit only for barbarians'
In the 1700s Cornwall's two national sports were hurling and wrestling. It is intriguing that hurling and football were mentioned separately in the above account from 1792. In fact, what was known as hurling in Cornwall was a regional version of the rough and ready football that had been played in towns and villages across the length and breadth of the British Isles since medieval times. Unlimited numbers could take part, the aim being to kick, carry, throw or by any other means possible convey a ball to the goals. These were sometimes a considerable distance apart and the game could range chaotically over a wide expanse of ground. With few rules, this type of hurling was often more like a battle. Moreover, at times, such hurling matches in Cornwall could involve contests between men of nearby parishes. In the Camborne burial register, there is an entry from 1705 recording the death of William Trevarthen, killed during a hurling

match with Redruth men 'at the high downs'. It's hardly surprising that twenty years later Daniel Defoe memorably summed up Cornish hurling as 'a game fit only for barbarians'.

However, more than a century before that, Richard Carew had written a detailed description of two separate types of what he called hurling. The first was the unregulated mass brawl of traditional football. But the second was a game played in a confined space, with approximately equal numbers of players on each side and with defined rules. This second form, more akin to modern rugby, may have been implied in the distinction made in 1792 between 'hurling' and 'football'. Paradoxically however, the 'football' of 1792 may have been the confused pandemonium of the violent rough and tumble version Defoe observed, whereas by 'hurling' the observer may have meant the more ordered, rule-bound version Carew had described. But we have no way of knowing, as no contemporary in Poldark's time bothered to describe hurling of either type in detail, or distinguish between them, as Carew had done. The hurling that survived, as at St Columb, where town still confronts country, is the traditional mass version. The other, if it had survived, was later swept up by the Victorians into the codified sports of association and rugby football. But whatever the precise meaning of the term, it is clear that by the 1790s hurling was in decline. Richard Polwhele wrote in 1797 that it was almost extinct, although it was recorded as late as 1822 from the parish of Germoe, to the west of Helston. Gentry patronage had been withdrawn, presumably because of the collateral damage to person and property that was associated with it.

'the lower classes are addicted to athletic and pugilistic exercises'

Hurling and traditional football were on the way out. But wrestling survived. While there is only passing reference to it in the *Poldark* saga, it was noted that Demelza's father, Tom Carne, had been an 'expert wrestler'. It did more than survive, becoming Cornwall's major spectator sport in the first half of the nineteenth century. Cornish wrestling pitched two men against each other, both wearing a loose jacket. This was gripped by the opponent, who then attempted to induce a fall, or a 'back', when three of the four points of shoulders and hips touched the ground. It was somewhat similar to judo but with no grappling on the floor. Wrestling could take place in three contexts: informal contests, organised tournaments, or challenge matches, when one wrestler might respond to a public challenge issued by another. The main form that Poldark witnessed would have been tournaments, usually held on or immediately after the parish feast days or at Whitsun or other summer holidays.

Tournaments were often organised by publicans, keen to drum up some extra trade. A piece of ground sufficiently large was needed for a ring in which the wrestling would take place, plus room for the spectators and some booths selling beer and other consumables. Tournaments were also held on traditional sites, such as downland, greens or even the local plain an gwarry. A committee was formed and local gentry were approached to provide subscriptions for prizes. Most of them seemed quite prepared to respond at this time. The Trevanions at Caerhays even held a wrestling match in their grounds in 1823. Prizes were usually in the form of gold or silver laced hats or silver cups. Sometimes money prizes were on offer and this form of reward was on the increase by the end of the 1700s. At Bodmin in 1786 for example, the winner received five guineas, the second placed man three guineas and the third two guineas. These would be worth around £800/£500/£300 respectively nowadays and would have been a considerable supplement to a miner's wage. Before 1820 however, only around half the tournaments offered money prizes, either on their own or in conjunction with material goods, while the other half held out prospects of items of clothing or gold and silverware only.

The committee would also appoint the sticklers, those who would referee the contests and adjudicate when 'backs' had been achieved and the winners when they were not. Sticklers were often ex-wrestlers and sometimes mine captains, reflecting the latter's standing in the community. The presence of mine captains as sticklers also suggests that many of the wrestlers competing were themselves miners. This was the case later in the 1800s and no doubt applied to earlier times as well. Tournaments had two phases. In the first, 'standards' were awarded to those wrestlers who had beaten two opponents or just one but had shown 'good play'. In the second, sometimes taking place on a second day, wrestlers would be matched up in knock-out rounds before an eventual winner emerged. As the individual contests had no set length of time, matches could stretch out late into the evening. At Bodmin in 1811 the wrestling 'continued by moonlight until near midnight'.

Wrestling tournaments were popular attractions. In 1817 it was observed that in Cornwall 'the lower classes are addicted to athletic and pugilistic exercises', while earlier the Reverend John Whitaker at Ruanlanihorne wrote that the (wrestling) 'ring-close was a busy scene of life' at the parish feast. Spectators on horseback, presumably farmers and the minor gentry, watched the wrestling separated by ropes from those on foot in front of them. At Bodmin in 1815 'a great concourse' from the neighbouring parishes 'flocked to the wrestling', while it was estimated in 1818 that 6,000 attended the annual Probus wrestling. This seems a high number, but similar figures were quoted for tournaments later in the nineteenth century. No doubt some of the crowd would have been enticed by the plentiful opportunities for gambling that the drawn-out tournaments allowed. Others may have been more tempted by the supplementary activities on offer. Cudgelling contests were popular, as at Liskeard in 1791, while at Millbrook, next to the Tamar estuary, in 1784 there was also 'running for pigs, racing by asses, running for smocks, and jumping in bags.'

Challenge matches between wrestlers from Cornwall and Devon began to be reported after the turn of the century. In 1811 a Devon wrestler named Jordan met a Cornishman called Parkyn at Saltash. 'Parkyn won with fantastic ease', despite Jordan being permitted to wear the heavy boots employed in Devonian wrestling to batter the shins of their opponents. He was described in Cornwall as a 'real savage Devon kicker'. Cornish wrestlers in contrast fought bare footed or in soft footwear and kicking was expressly forbidden, a much more civilised version.

'the barbarous practice has afforded mirth to the savage spectators'

'Civilised' might be a word applicable to Cornish wrestling, which had a long history. It was less applicable to some other 'amusements' that failed to survive the nineteenth century. A set of these involved cruelty to animals, either setting them to fight each other and betting on the outcome or baiting animals with dogs. At Mabe, near Penryn, in 1785 a silver collar was awarded to the best dog in a bull baiting contest. In this 'sport' a bull was chained to a suitable post and dogs set onto it. Sometimes pepper was blown into the bull's nose to make it more aggressive. In 1814 the *West Briton* carried an account of a bull baiting at Penzance, where the bull was fastened to a stake and dogs set on it for four or five hours. Ten years later, in 1824, Samuel Drew was claiming that Penzance had been the last place 'in which the barbarous practice has afforded mirth to the savage spectators' and that bull baiting was by then 'almost unknown'. The last bull baiting at Liskeard took place as early as the 1770s, although a bull baiting a few miles outside town on the edge of Bodmin Moor a decade or so later had resulted in a fight. During the ensuing mayhem, the bull had 'broke loose ... and ran into the town, terrifying the inhabitants.' Bull baiting at Liskeard was however survived by badger baiting, which carried on until at least the 1820s.

Drew reported that even cock-fighting was 'scarcely known' in 1824. It took longer to eradicate this 'sport' as it attracted considerable support from the gentry. Clearing the room after dining for a cock-fight was apparently not restricted to the fictional world of Charles Poldark and George Warleggan in the 1780s. The steel or silver spurs that were fastened to the legs of George's prize fighting cock 'Red Gauntlet' were not unusual. Cock-pits in towns like Truro in the late 1700s attest to the popularity of the sport as do reports of major tournaments in east Cornwall. In 1792 one took place at Launceston between 'the gentlemen of Cornwall and gentlemen of Devon', with 14 cocks on each side, 100 guineas (about £15,000 these days) for the winner and ten guineas for each individual battle. This was clearly a regular occasion as two years later the *Sherborne Mercury* carried a similar advert for a cock-fight at Ivybridge in Devon between 'gentlemen of Devonshire and the gentlemen of Cornwall', with 31 battles over two days and a similar level of prize money.

Condemnation from evangelical churchmen and changing sensibilities were tending to push cock-fighting underground by the 1820s although it had little effect on another sport targeting animals – fox hunting. This had become popular upcountry in the second half of the eighteenth century, an opportunity to show off the landowners' horses and symbolically assert their control over the countryside. In 1780 a hunt club was formed at Truro. The annual subscription of £25 (over £3,500 now) ensured the right class of person was a member. This led later to the Four Burrow Hunt and more organised fox-hunting in Cornwall. That was followed in 1820 by the Western Hunt, formed at Penzance and led by the irascible Sir Rose Price of Trengwainton, a man who had made his money from Jamaican sugar plantations and the exploitation of black slaves.

'idle, absurd practices'

In 1794 William Temple, the Vicar of St Gluvias, preached a sermon attacking inhumanity to animals after a bull baiting at Penryn. Temple and other evangelical churchmen were joined by a growing chorus of condemnation of 'idle sports' from Methodists. By this time, the Methodist clamour was reaching its crescendo. This went a lot further than merely condemning cruel sports and was extended to all the traditional pursuits. A Methodist in 1814 listed the three 'most prominent vices' of the Cornish as wrestling, hurling and an 'excessive love of ardent spirits.' Some were claiming that this Methodist and evangelical offensive had already produced change. As we have already seen, in 1809 Richard Warner wrote that 'the desperate wrestling matches ... the inhuman cock-fights ... the pitched battles which were fought between the workmen of different mines or different parishes ... the riotous revellings held on particular days ... are now of very rare occurrence.' This, he argued, was the result of the reformation of manners wrought by Methodism, which had transformed a former 'state little better than that of savages' into calm decorum. A few years later, in 1817, a historian of Cornwall, C.S. Gilbert, plagiarising Warner, re-emphasised the point: 'desperate wrestling matches, inhuman cock-fights, pitched battles and riotous revellings, are happily now of much rarer occurrence than heretofore; the spirit of sport has evaporated, and that of industry has supplied its place'.

Condemnation of the 'idle' pursuits of former times extended to the traditional festivals. Although many survived even into modern times, others fell foul of the reformation of manners. Mayday celebrations were abandoned and midsummer bonfires extinguished at Liskeard soon after the end of the eighteenth century, along with other 'idle, absurd practices', although ridings continued in east Cornwall at Bodmin, Liskeard and Lostwithiel. These were processions around the parish, probably originally connected to beating the bounds. Even midsummer celebrations continued until later in the west, the *West Briton* reporting the midsummer eve bonfires at Penzance in 1816. There were also fireworks and sea trips, 'accompanied by fiddlers', offered by local fishermen on the payment of a penny or two.

Furthermore, the censure of the more relaxed older customs was applied to the annual feast days. These, according to Samuel Drew in 1824, had 'degenerated into public revels ... the character they sustain is too conspicuous to warrant any comment'. Occasionally, it is true, feast days included drunken brawls. One such occurred in 1816 at Lanivet, near Bodmin. A wrestling tournament held at a local pub led to a fight between 'the lads of Roche and Luxulyan' and the 'youths of Bodmin'. The 'combatants armed themselves with bludgeons from a large wood-rick ... heads were laid open, teeth knocked out, and the field of battle was quickly strewn with the maimed'. The fight reputedly went on for two hours before the arrival of reinforcements in the shape of miners from Roche and Luxulyan forced the Bodmin boys to 'fly in disorder'. Such an incident was rare but fuelled the quasi-hysterical campaign against the older customs.

'promises of full work, better wages and a liberal allowance of beer'

Even events such as the Obby Oss at Padstow were not immune. Samuel Drew primly observed that Padstow's May Day 'generally ends in riot and dissipation', which 'the more enlightened grow ashamed of.' However, the Obby Oss was, as we say these days, 'too big to fail' and survived attacks on it from the reformers. As did another iconic event on the Cornish festival calendar – Furry Day at Helston. This, with its cross-community involvement embracing the local gentry as well as the common people, studiously ignored the growing clamour against 'idleness'. Nonetheless, its more boisterous element, the *hal an tow* procession and mummers' play, came under fire for its associated demands for cash and its noise and drinking. Like other similar events it was being increasingly 'consigned over to the conduct and management of the illiterate and vulgar'. The main

Furry Day dances survived but the original *hal an tow* eventually succumbed, as did the various mock mayor ceremonies held up and down Cornwall.

Mock mayors were parodies of the real thing. For a day someone was chosen to be a mock mayor, inverting the normal order of things. A later description from Polperro explains what happened:

> some half-witted or drunken fellow, tricked out in
> tinsel finery, elected his staff of constables, and these
> armed with staves, accompanied his chariot (some
> fish-jowster's cart, dressed with green boughs)
> through the town, stopping at each inn, where he
> made a speech full of promises of full work, better
> wages and a liberal allowance of beer during his term
> of office.

At Penryn the wittiest journeyman tailor was chosen as mock mayor. At Budock it was the one who 'could drink the most beer and tell the tallest yarn'. At St Austell he was 'selected for his wit, drollery and love of drink'.

In Poldark's days, mock mayors in the main were still surviving the growing hue and cry from the 'respectable' classes. So were the more innocent entertainments that accompanied the multitude of fairs. At Bodmin fair in 1820 there were three days of 'horsemanship, wild beasts, waxworks, puppet shows, glass-blowing, tightrope dancing, giants, dwarves and jugglers' to delight the curious. Meanwhile, the visit of a fire-eater was a great draw at Penzance in 1819. Wider events often triggered more organised celebrations. In 1813 Wellington's victories in Spain were celebrated at Penzance and Newlyn by setting fire to three tar-barrels. A year later, the first defeat of Napoleon was greeted with 'great rejoicing' at Crinnis mine near St Austell, when the workers were treated to a roasted ox, 1,000 loaves of bread, ten hogsheads of beer and a 'grand display' of fireworks. At United Mines at Gwennap, 1,200 sat down to dinner, consuming 600 gallons of strong beer in the process, four pints each!

The annual guise dancing at Christmas was also a feature of the times. Those participating would cross-dress, black up their faces or in other ways disguise themselves. They would then traverse the town or village singing, dancing, playing music or performing a traditional play. A time of some licence, the changing sensibilities of the middling classes were beginning to look askance at some behaviour which in former times would have been casually tolerated. By Samuel Drew's days, in the 1820s, Christmas plays and guise dancing too were coming under growing scrutiny as the custom became increasingly likely to be left to a younger and poorer section of the population. Indeed, Drew dismissed the Christmas plays as 'almost wholly confined to children ... they learn to repeat a barbarous jargon in the form of a drama, which has been handed down from distant generations'.

'no one thought ... intoxication unbecoming, but rather the mark of a gentleman'

Christmas was celebrated with a drink or two. But when the consumption of alcoholic drink exceeded the normal limits, it reinforced the growing doubts in the minds of the 'respectable' classes about the festivities associated with it. Drink and the public house were accepted as central to popular culture in the eighteenth century. The involvement of publicans in the national sport of wrestling has already been noted. Many pubs would also have a skittles or kayle alley built on to attract extra custom. Moreover, pubs were unlicensed at this time and could open whenever they liked. They would range from the up-market inns with stables and facilities for the gentlemanly traveller to the two-roomed cottage, locally termed a kiddlywink, selling beer, as did widow Tregothnan's kiddly at Sawle.

In proportion to the population there would also have been a lot more pubs than now, although of course they did not suffer competition from supermarkets and other outlets. Celebrations involving drinking were not limited to special occasions, feast days and holidays. On first pay days or promotion there were various 'treating' customs and paying for a drink for workmates was expected, if not demanded. Funerals were also occasions for heavy drinking. Richard Polwhele in 1822 criticised Cornish funerals as resembling the Irish, with 'such excess of drinking' and 'such howling at the graves of the deceased'. Concerns about levels of alcohol consumption had reached the point where in 1805 the first temperance organisation in Cornwall - the Society for the Suppression of Drunkenness - was formed, significantly at Redruth in the heart of the mining country.

The growing concerns being raised about the demon drink had not only to overcome the customs of the poor but contend with the culture of the rich. Of the 1790s it was written that 'no one thought ... intoxication unbecoming, but rather the mark of a gentleman, as indicator of high breeding: the higher classes, clergy, as well as laity, seemed more frequently inebriated than the lower, their means of indulgence being more ample'. There was a strong element of hypocrisy when condemnations of the drinking habits of the poor emanated from magistrates and clergy with well-stocked wine cellars.

James Boswell's account of his journey to Cornwall in 1792 reads more like a drinking tour of the great houses of the gentry. At dinner with Sir

Francis Basset and his family at Tehidy, there was burgundy, champagne, Bordeaux wine, two kinds of madeira fortified wine, sherry, port, claret and liqueurs. While at Tregothnan Boswell sank three bottles with George Boscawen, the third Viscount Falmouth. They both got very drunk and next morning Boswell 'rose considerably disturbed'. At Port Eliot Boswell sampled more madeira, hock (a German white wine), a 27-year old sherry, port, claret and champagne, with 'excellent cider and admirable beer'. Nonetheless, he was still 'displeased that neither my lord nor his son ... encouraged a brisk circulation of the bottle, which in many houses is recognised as a test of hospitable reception'. In fact, he felt it was a 'strange mode of Cornwall, where I could say I had never been asked to drink a little more'. Not that he seems to have needed much encouragement.

six silver laced hats
While the upper classes were drinking themselves under the table and, when they could, the poor guzzling themselves into the gutter and the newly respectable or religious railing against such follies, there remained many other forms of amusement that escaped moral censure. These were safely well away from the front lines of the culture wars between traditional and 'rational' recreation. As such they received less attention from the press or moralists.

First, there were competitions and contests of all kinds, some organised, some less so. Horse racing was common, that at Bodmin in 1784 taking place over three days. However, those races were reported as having been discontinued by 1799. Ploughing matches, under the auspices of the newly formed Cornwall Agricultural Society, were being held at Liskeard in 1794 and no doubt at many other locations. In the new century bell ringing competitions became the fashion. A ringing match at St Austell in 1815 offered a prize of eight guineas for the winning team, comparable to that of wrestling tournaments, although this would be shared. The team from Camborne that won a ringing match at Gwennap church in 1817 received six silver laced hats. Near the coast or estuaries, competitiveness could extend onto the water. By 1820 an annual sailing match was being held at Truro while at Torpoint there were reports in 1782 of a rowing match, with a silver oar as first prize.

The team sport of cricket had long antecedents and had become popular in south-east England by the late 1700s. However, it was slower to catch on in Cornwall. The earliest record of cricketing appeared in 1781, as an adjunct to a cattle show at St Teath, although this was a single wicket competition (for a silver laced hat) rather than a team match. By 1813 there were cricket clubs at Truro and Bodmin and by 1819 Penzance. However, it may be significant that all the matches reported on in the press before 1820 took place in the more rural districts east of Bodmin, with the exception of Truro. In the west wrestling retained its position as the most popular spectator sport while cricket clubs provided more of an excuse for 'gentrified sociability' than a regularly played sport. The number of rainy days in Cornwall may also have dampened enthusiasm for cricket, not to mention the difficulty of finding level pitches.

In addition to organised contests there were unorganised events which served as spectacles for those with time on their hands. For example, in the 1820s walking challenges were increasingly reported. It's likely that these had also taken place in earlier decades. In 1825 a man tried to walk five times the distance from Helston to Penzance over six days. He collapsed, but another man, a 50-year old miner at Wheal Vor, in the same year succeeded in walking from Falmouth to Truro five days in a row. These events may have been associated with gambling. Some indoor games certainly were. Ross Poldark's cousin Francis won and lost heavily at the faro table. Faro was a French gambling game of the late seventeenth century that became popular in Britain in the 1700s and in the nineteenth century in the States. It involved betting against the bank on the next cards dealt. Whist, the most popular card game of the time, was also often played for money, sometimes quite high stakes.

'the house was very mean, being two rooms at a low inn'
Other indoor amusements were those associated with the arts of drama, music and painting. The travelling players that arrived at the fictional Nampara bore more than a passing resemblance to the theatre parties that toured up and down the peninsula at this time. A typical evening's entertainment might include a comedy or farce followed by a tragedy or more serious play, with songs in the interludes. There would sometimes be specifically Cornish plays, for example one had the title 'Great Hewas Mine', referring to a mine near St Austell. Travelling parties of actors came under some suspicion from those desiring to clean up popular culture. Strangers to the locality, men and women travelling together, dressing up, attracting crowds of people, crowds that could be boisterous and unpredictable. This all seemed a bit dubious to some.

Local theatrical companies were a bit more acceptable. Truro had its purpose-built theatre in 1787 and Falmouth in 1802, while there were also theatres at Penzance and later at Bodmin and Redruth. Local theatrical companies could be semi-professional, the Falmouth company going on tours to other places. Success did not automatically follow. Experiments with a summer season of performances from May to June proved a financial disaster for the Truro theatre in 1807 and thereafter it stuck to its traditional winter seasons. Before purpose-built theatres, the venue was more likely to be a local pub. James Boswell was present at one in Falmouth in 1792; 'the house was very mean, being two rooms at a low inn'. He saw three plays, accompanied by music which was 'only two fiddlers, played one by a white and one by a negro, who sat in a little recess close by one side of the stage'. This was clearly not the well-known figure of Joseph Emidy, the talented black violinist who only arrived in Falmouth in 1799.

'his colour would be so much against him, that there would be a great risk of failure'

Although Emidy was not the first black violinist at Falmouth he was possibly one of the most talented classical music composers with a connection to Cornwall before Michael Tippett in the twentieth century. Joseph Antonio Emidy was no native of Cornwall. Instead, he had been born in Guinea in west Africa at some time between 1770 and 1775. As a child he was sold to Portuguese slavers who, after baptising and converting their captives to Christianity, sold them on to a slave master in Brazil. By the later 1780s Emidy had been moved to Lisbon in Portugal. There, his master recognised his precocious musical talents and paid for a violin and music lessons. In the more racially relaxed atmosphere of Portugal Emidy flourished and by his 20s he had gained an established place as a violinist with the prestigious Lisbon Opera.

A promising musical career in Lisbon was cut short by the British navy. Sir Edward Pellew had put in at Lisbon and attended a concert at the opera. Lacking a fiddler to play the jigs and reels to which his sailors would dance in their time off, Pellew pressed, that is effectively kidnapped, the young musician. Emidy then spent five years as a fiddler on Pellew's ship. In that time, he would have witnessed ferocious sea battles and endured howling gales. His views of his situation are perhaps hinted at by the fact Pellew did not allow him ashore, no doubt fearing he would run away. Emidy had exchanged a theoretical but comfortable slavery in Lisbon for a practical slavery as a 'free man' in the Royal Navy. Eventually, Pellew moved on to another command and in 1799 Emidy was discharged at Falmouth, where he took up residence.

In Cornwall he made his living from teaching the violin and guitar, while playing in the concerts of the local amateur harmonic societies. His prowess as a very skilled musician rapidly became apparent. Not only did he play but also compose, the first of his compositions being noted in 1802. Unfortunately however, none of his works has survived. In the same year of 1802 Joseph married local girl Jenefer Hutchins. The next decade was spent teaching and performing to support his young family. Six children were born, of whom five survived into adulthood. At some point around 1812 the family moved from Falmouth, where the harmonic society was fading fast, to Truro, where he became leader of the Truro Philharmonic Society.

While at Falmouth, Emidy's patron, James Silk Buckingham, had taken examples of his compositions to London. There they were 'highly approved' by a meeting of professional musicians. However, the consensus was that 'his colour would be so much against him, that there would be a great risk of failure'. The narrow attitudes towards racial difference that prevailed in London scuppered Joseph Emidy's chance to achieve fame on a wider stage. Nonetheless, his background had not hindered his acceptance or the 'high reputation' he enjoyed in Cornwall.

'a blaze of beauty and fashion'

Music was central to entertainment in the Poldark era, even though choral societies and brass bands had to await the 1820s and 30s. Much music-making was spontaneous and self-made. In 1792 Boswell noted that at St Gluvias, next to Penryn, 'several young people sung sacred music in the churchyard at night, which it seems is a usage here'. At the opposite end of Cornwall, at Liskeard, it was reported in 1795 that 'it is the custom ... of a fine evening after supper about ten o'clock for the young men to sing songs in different parts of the town. They stand in rings to the number of near a dozen'. This tradition presumably shaded into the growing popularity of hymn-singing in public places beyond the chapel, using the considerable repertoire supplied by the Wesleys. Carol-singing at Christmas clearly retained its role as part of the local culture, Davies Gilbert producing the first collection of Cornish carols in 1822 at the end of our period,

At concerts songs were interspersed with orchestral music. Vocalists were usually local with the occasional visits of 'stars' from London or Bath. One of these was the tenor Charles Incledon, who visited in 1808. Incledon was actually a native of St Keverne but rarely sang in Cornwall. Tours of prodigies such as Miss Randles, a seven-year old pianist who visited Truro and Falmouth in 1807, piqued interest but the market in Cornwall was insufficient for a professional musician to survive solely from performing. As Emidy had found, it was necessary also to teach music. Another compatible occupation was church organist. Charles Hempel was a Londoner who came to Cornwall and worked as a bank clerk at Truro. A proficient organist, he landed a post at St Mary's Church and became a full-time organist and composer in 1809.

Presumably, Hempel would have been one of those, along with Emidy, who provided some of the music for the Truro Philharmonic Society's annual concerts, of which half a dozen would take place every winter between November and April. In 1806 the Society had been more ambitious, organising a grand music festival at Truro, with visiting professionals from London supplementing the local amateurs. This was deemed a great success. However, a second such festival in 1809 did not receive such glowing reviews; its vocalists were not so good and the attendance fell away. The third and final such festival in 1813 was reduced to three evening concerts, although the *West Briton* claimed that it 'will be attended by almost all the gentry in the county'.

While orchestras supplied a fashionable diet of Handel and the baroque, with Haydn and Mozart's compositions sometimes added, bands were restricted to churches and the military. Few churches at this time possessed organs, which had been removed in the seventeenth century after the Reformation. Nonetheless, some of the larger churches were re-installing them by the late 1700s. St Mary's organ at Truro had been acquired second hand in 1750 and there was a new one at Bodmin Church in 1775. But more usually, church music was supplied by a small band of two to six instruments. These included a bass viol, flutes, violins and sometimes a serpent, a 'now obsolete brass wind instrument'. The first church choirs were beginning to appear by the end of the 1810s although it was usually left to someone in the congregation to pitch the tune and lead the singing. As attendances at Anglican churches at this time were pitifully sparse the singing may well have been drowned out by the church band.

The other type of band was military bands. Regimental bands date from the mid-1700s and there was militia band at Bodmin by 1777. The expansion of the militia and the formation of volunteer forces in 1794 led to further small volunteer and militia bands of clarinets, horns and trumpets with the occasional serpent, which played music based on marches. The Royal Cornwall Militia was giving concerts in Falmouth and Penryn by 1801. Regimental bands were presumably not the main providers of music at the balls of the time. As Demelza discovered, with some trepidation, these were places of a 'blaze of beauty and fashion' as the *West Briton* put it. They were occasions where anyone who was anyone had to be seen. Balls took place in most Cornish towns but the most prestigious were at Truro's assembly rooms, where the local professional classes would go to admire themselves and rub shoulders with the landed gentry. The dancing at such balls would be minuets and cotillions, a gentrified country dance. By the 1810s the fashion had turned to the quadrille, a genteel square dance not dissimilar to a cotillion.

'like Caravaggio, but finer'

A less energetic pursuit was gazing at fine art. Ross Poldark's rival George Warleggan had had his portrait painted by 'Opie'. Opie was no fictional creation but a real portrait painter who, ghost-like, flits through the background of the *Poldark* tales. In fact, by the time Ross is supposed to have returned from America in 1783 John Opie was living in London. Infrequent visits he paid back home to Cornwall notwithstanding, he remained in London until his death in 1807. But Opie had been born in 1761 at Mithian, a small hamlet near St Agnes, not far from the fictional Nampara. The son of a mine carpenter, he was destined for a life as a sawyer until his natural drawing skills were recognised by Dr John Wolcot of Truro. Wolcot, who wrote satires and poetry under the name Peter Pindar, took Opie off to the bright lights of Truro to cultivate his artistic talent.

Opie became an accomplished portrait painter, painting the local gentry of west Cornwall and being commissioned by John St Aubyn of Clowance near Helston to paint more ordinary folk – beggars, children and Dolly Pentreath, the supposed last Cornish speaker. In 1781 Opie and Wolcot finally made it to London, where Opie soon attracted considerable numbers of the well-off, keen to have their likenesses painted. Sir Joshua Reynolds, regarded at the time as the grand old man of British art, described Opie as 'like Caravaggio, but finer'. From 1786 a member of the Royal Academy and later its professor of painting, Opie took his place among the other Cornish exiles of his generation, such as Davy and Trevithick, at the leading edge of their professions. Like them he corresponded with that inveterate behind the scenes string puller Davies Gilbert. Opie moved on to historical and Shakespearian paintings, which although largely dismissed now as overly melodramatic, were at the time among the wonders of the art world.

Moving in the 1790s in circles that included the feminist Mary Wollstonecraft and the anarchist thinker William Godwin, Opie was described in 1789 by the poet Robert Southey as 'without anything of politeness. His manners are pleasing, though their freedom is out of the common; and his conversation, though in a half-uttered, half Cornish, half croak, is interesting. There is a strange contrast between his genius, which is not confined to painting, and the vulgarity of his appearance'. It is difficult to know how much of this 'vulgarity' was merely a direct Cornish bluntness alien to the mannered ways of London society and how much was a deliberate creation of Wolcot, Opie's mentor and business partner until Opie's marriage in 1782. Wolcot had done a superb public relations job when Opie first arrived in London, presenting him as the 'Cornish wonder', an untutored savant from the sticks, natural talent untainted by any formal training. Although Opie had in fact received much training from Wolcot himself while they were at Truro and later Helston, this image was clearly designed to appeal to metropolitan stereotypes of the 'noble savage' from the uttermost margins of civilised society.

This was an image that Opie seems to have relished playing up to. Even his biographer in the Oxford Dictionary of National Biography, while noting his 'remarkable reputation', also mentions his 'idiosyncratic character' and his sarcasm, probably honed by the even more sarcastic Wolcot. This was an 'idiosyncracy' carefully nurtured at first by Wolcot to stimulate interest and then cultivated by Opie himself, who played up to the image and fed other people's expectations while quietly having a laugh to himself at their expense, a not uncommon Cornish trait.

'There's scarce a witch in all the land, the world has grown so learn'd and grand'

Even less energetic than painting or visiting a country house to view the paintings (art galleries were yet to appear) was reading. Reading secular literature became more fashionable during the 1700s, a demand later met by novelists such as Jane Austen. There was a Ladies' Book Club in Penzance as early as 1770. As well as novels such as Goldsmith's The Vicar of Wakefield, its acquisitions included guide books, travelogues and collected letters. Books were circulated for a year, after which they were sold to the members. Of course, reading had to be learnt and many people – between a third and a half of adults - would not have been able to read in Poldark's Cornwall. Mark Daniel for example had to sign his name with a mark when he married the actress Keren Smith. She, on the other hand, could write her name. The ability to write, something rarely required by labourers in those days, was less common than a rudimentary ability to read, taught by the charity schools and dame schools of the day and the Sunday schools that were beginning to appear by the early 1800s.

Reading shaded into the 'rational recreation' that was beginning to make its appearance. This was signposted by the formation of the Cornwall Library in 1792, the Geological Society of Cornwall at Penzance in 1814 and the Cornwall (later Royal Cornwall) Institution at Truro in 1818. All these were gentry-led institutions that also encompassed the urban professional and middle classes. The world of museums, literary institutions, self-improvement and frighteningly long lectures on worthy subjects that became typical of the Victorian years was just around the corner.

Meanwhile, the world of the itinerant droll-teller was on the wane. The last purported droll teller, making a living by touring the hamlets and villages of Cornwall, bringing the news and selling and reciting poems and ballads, was Henry Quick of Zennor, who was born in 1792 and died in 1857. Quick was an anachronism, plying his wares in competition with the newspapers that were being published in Cornwall from 1800. Although the price of newspapers restricted their circulation largely to the gentry and middle class until the onset of a cheap newspaper press in the 1850s, every time Ross Poldark opened his copy of the *Sherborne Mercury* another nail was driven into the coffin of the droll-tellers. As Quick lamented:

The Cornish drolls are dead, each one;
The fairies from their haunts are gone:
There's scarce a witch in all the land,
The world has grown so learn'd and grand.'

'fortune telling and gabbling Cornish'
Among Henry Quick's departed ways was the plain an gwarry itself. Not its physical form, which endured intact in places such as St Just in Penwith or Rose, near Perranporth, but its purpose. The plain an gwarry had long lost its original function as a setting for mystery plays and saints' life stories performed in the Cornish language. During the 1500s the echoes of these had faded as the Reformation emphasised the message of the Word over any lessons taught by drama and spectacle. Literacy in order to read the Bible now became more necessary. As the Bible did not get published in Cornish, literacy in that language became unnecessary. Around 1680 the Cornish language revivalist Nicholas Boson was bemoaning the fact that '*ugge an teez goth tho merwal akar, ny a wele an teez younk tho e clappia le ha le, ha lacka ha lacka, ha andelna eve a vedden leha durt termen tho termen*' (after the old people die off, we see the young speaking it (Cornish) less and less, and worse and worse, and therefore it will lessen over time).

By Ross Poldark's time, a century later, although a plethora of dialect words had come from the old tongue, the Cornish language was on its last legs. In the 1780s it was confined to a handful of old people in out of the way locations. In 1777 or 1778 William Bodinar, a fisherman at Mousehole on Mount's Bay, wrote a letter (in Cornish and English) to the antiquarian Daines Barrington in London. In it he reported that '*nag es moye vel pager po pemp en dreav nye ell clapia Cornoack leben, poble coath pager egence blouth. Cornoack ewe oll neceaves gen poble younk*' (there are no more than four or five in our town that can speak Cornish now, old folk aged 80. Cornish is entirely forgotten by the young people'.) Bodinar was responding to Barrington's account of a visit to Cornwall in 1775 when he had met Dolly Pentreath of Mousehole, who maintained herself 'partly by fortune telling and gabbling Cornish'. Dolly had died in 1777 but was clearly not the 'last speaker' of Cornish as posterity remembers her.

As the Cornish copper mines struggled to recover from the depression of the 1780s, as Methodism strengthened its hold over the emotional life of the people, as the smuggling gangs ratcheted up their slow-burning war with the excise men, the Cornish language was quietly dying. Its last speakers were uttering their last breaths in small fishing coves scattered along the coasts of West Penwith or the Lizard or in some poverty-stricken and remote hovel or smallholding high up on the moors of West Penwith, their farm animals possibly the last living creatures to hear the old language.

The Cornish language and with it the old, traditional Cornwall was fading quietly away, unnoticed, largely unmourned at the time, making way for a new vibrant Cornwall of mines, money-making and Methodism. As we have seen Methodism was making great strides and rapidly becoming the religion of the mass of the people after the 'great' revivals of 1799 and 1814. When that stage was reached, a Methodist recreational culture began to spread beyond the bounds of the class meeting and the chapel. It penetrated the everyday life of the people and became unavoidable. It offered an alternative to the boisterous wrestling tournaments, the fairs and the feast days that ran parallel to it. Probably more importantly, it slowly altered those amusements by influencing their participants. Here was a more populist alternative to the genteel seeds of rational recreation in the towns. Tea treats, with their saffron buns and mugs of tea, were emerging right at the end of our period. The less organised and more spontaneous hymn-singing had already escaped the confines of the chapel and was periodically heard in streets and workplaces up and down the land by the 1800s. Then there were the love feasts, popular by the 1800s. These were not quite as exciting as they sound, involving a shared simple meal of cake (again probably a saffron bun) and a cup (of tea), along with prayer, preaching, hymn-singing and personal testimony.

In stark contrast to the older pastimes of wrestling and hurling, Methodist culture gave relatively equal space as participants to women, a key reason for its growing attraction. Like the earlier pursuits however, it also brought communities and villages together in groups and crowds. Furthermore, crowds might sometimes gather in ways that those who had more to lose could find altogether more menacing. Angry crowds of people could rally to protest, to demand bread, to threaten the social order of a very unequal society, as we shall discover in the next chapter.

8
The Crowd

Attending a copper sale one day, Ross Poldark overheard someone describe a riot at Bodmin. A smashed coach, attacks on corn merchants, looting and a pitched battle with the military all featured in the colourful account. It was certainly the case that the Cornish by Ross's days, and particularly the miners, had a fearsome reputation for food rioting. But wait. Is 'riot' the best word to describe these events? They did not usually resemble the outraged spasms of unorganised and angry violence aimed at the nearest bystander that the word 'riot' might conjure up. On the contrary, by the 1790s there was a predictability to their timing and their location and a ritual to both the proceedings of the crowd and the response of the authorities to them.

'superfluities ... scarcely enough to supply the deficiencies of other parts'
Food riots occurred when the grain needed to make bread was in short supply. As we saw in chapter 3, barley bread was one of the three staples of the Cornish diet. In the 1600s Cornwall had been self-sufficient in barley and wheat but the population growth of the 1700s in the west meant that by the 1780s usually around a third of the grain consumed had to be imported. Even in a good year, as a history of 1814 put it, the 'superfluities' of the grain growing districts of Cornwall were 'scarcely enough to supply the deficiencies of other parts'. Poor harvests meant less grain came to market while the grain that was there sold for a higher price. This situation was made worse as competition for what grain was available became more intense at the very time supplies were low and prices high. This was because, at the times when grain was in short supply in Cornwall, it was also very likely to be scarce elsewhere too.

By the late 1700s a network of merchants was actively seeking out supplies for the vast London market. Nearer home, the growing towns of Plymouth and Devonport added another large demand for grain. Merchants might offer to buy the farmers' harvests in bulk, which saved the farmers the considerable time and labour of taking their grain to the various local markets that served the scattered towns and villages of Cornwall. However, labouring families required grain sold in small quantities at local markets, from where they took it to the miller who would grind it into flour. At times of shortage this supply faltered. At that point, farmers had the luxury of choosing to sell to the merchants more energetically combing the countryside for supplies. Paradoxically therefore, it was at the point when grain was needed locally that there was most temptation to sell it to distant markets. The suspicion that grain was being exported at the same time as emergency supplies were imported was one trigger for food riots. When suspicion seeded rumour and rumours flowered, miners and others would descend on the ports to stop such corn exports.

'if they attempted to fire they would kill every man of them and level the whole town'

Trouble was brewing in the winter of 1792/93. A worried clergyman wrote to the Home Office in early January. The 'tinners' were becoming impatient as the price of corn and bread remained high. The previous month Sir William Molesworth was telling the government that Francis Basset had been buying corn at Wadebridge and shipping it to Portreath down the coast. Basset was trying to counter the rumours circulating in the mining districts that corn was being exported upcountry from Wadebridge and Padstow. However, there may have been more to the growing unrest than concerns over grain scarcity. Another report to the Home Office spoke of 'seditious proceedings' in Cornwall 'on account of wages' in these months. It should be noted that this was only a few years after the French Revolution had left Britain's ruling elite distinctly nervous of popular disorder.

Basset's initiative did not succeed. The fears of the authorities were proved right later in January 1793 when bands of miners descended on 'several towns' in search of concealed corn. The *Times* continued: 'At Wadebridge they found about 24,000 bushels in store, which they obliged the owners to sell at reduced prices. At Looe upwards of 6,000 bushels of grain were stopped by them from being shipped'. Francis Gregor, a magistrate, reported that there were no serious consequences at Wadebridge, while the *Sherborne Mercury* described events at Looe as merely involving 'a few [tin] streamers' who carried away a small number of bushels. In the meantime, 1,200 miners arrived at Padstow, where they discovered wheat and barley.

John Clift happened to be staying at the Molesworths' country house at Pencarrow, near Wadebridge, at the time and was in Padstow during the riot. He wrote to his brother back in London:

> They got about 40 soldiers there thinking they could bid defiance to the Cornish heroes, but it only served to raise their undaunted spirits. When they first met the commanding officer with his drawn sword, who bid them stand, one of them with his little shelley club gave the sword a blow and told him to come on if he was for that fun, but if they attempted to fire they would kill every man of them and level the whole town; so the soldiers and tinners were as friendly as men could be in a short time.

The miners took some grain, at a reduced price, the wheat from 20 shillings to 16 shillings a bushel and barley from 12 to eight.

At some point during these events the miners sent a messenger across the peninsula to Polgooth mine near St Austell to persuade the men there to come and join them. However, the messenger was arrested. On hearing of this, a body of miners from St Stephen in Brannel marched to Lostwithiel and rescued him from the Duchy jail. The rescue of the messenger and the relatively modest reduction of prices imposed at Padstow, when the miners could easily, given their numbers, have taken all the grain by force and paid nothing, indicate a considerable level of self-discipline and organisation. This was far from a haphazard and chaotic 'riot'. The same level of discipline was seen four months later in 1793 when 200 to 300 miners arrived in Falmouth and came to an agreement with the town's corporation on a reduced price of 16 shillings a bushel for grain.

A year later, in 1794, the people of Padstow had to put up with another visit. According to the *Times*:

> a party of tinners, from the neighbourhood of St Austell and Roche, consisting of about 300, assembled at Padstow ... and forcibly took possession of five sloops with barley on board, bound for Bristol and Wales and on [the next day] there came from the same

neighbourhood a great many women and boys, with
horses and sacks; they then began to fill their sacks and
were carrying off the cargo.

Then the militia arrived, the Riot Act was read and they dispersed. This
nicely illustrates the involvement of the whole community in such events.

'upwards of 450 men ... assembled with clubs in their hands'

The usual season for food rioting was the spring, in March and April, when
shortages were at their height and before the potato harvest or the arrival of
the pilchards. Another poor harvest in 1794 threatened continuing shortages
the following year. By April 1795 Francis Basset was claiming that there
was no more than 14 days stock of corn left in Cornwall. In such a situation
the miners were again determined to stop any exports. Predictably, a month
earlier in March 1795 they had taken matters into their own hands and once
again headed for the ports.

This time, the first confrontation occurred at Penzance. Two hundred
miners arrived there on March 10th. Searching the ships at harbour, they
found a quantity of corn on one of them. The captain agreed to release it for
sale locally instead of taking it for export and the miners left, apparently
content with this promise. There had been little trouble and in other
circumstances this visit might easily have left no record at all. However, as
the first group of miners was leaving, another arrived from St Just in the
west. This second crowd was bigger, estimated at 600 and behaving 'in a
more tumultuous manner'. They were met by the local Volunteer force (of
which more later) with fixed bayonets. After a tense stand-off, the crowd
dispersed, although as they did so they threatened to return the next day. On
that day, the ominous news duly came that 200 miners had begun to gather
north of Penzance with the intention of heading for the town. The
magistrates, backed by the Volunteers, decided to take the initiative. Secure
in their possession of two small cannons, they sallied forth to meet the
miners. When they heard of the approaching armed force the miners
prudently decided to retire.

By this time the townsfolk of Padstow must have been gearing up to
expect their annual visit of miners bent on stopping the export of corn, as
had occurred in 1793 and 1794. They were not disappointed. Later in March
1795 a group of miners from the St Agnes and Redruth districts estimated
to number 'upwards of 450 men ... assembled with clubs in their hands' in
Padstow according to the *Sherborne Mercury*. The paper reported that they

dispersed around midday 'after destroying and carrying away with them a quantity of grain out of the warehouses and shipping'. This was corroborated by a letter to the Home Office from an army general then in Cornwall. The miners had taken corn from four vessels. He also noted that as they passed through St Columb, they had received refreshments from the residents.

The distance from Redruth to Padstow is not inconsiderable - around 30 miles - and shows the determination of the miners to walk far and wide in search of grain. The original plan had been to go to Penryn, closer at hand. A Penryn resident speculated that they had decided against that because yellow fever was raging in the town after being introduced on a prize taken from the French in the West Indies. Another Penryn resident claimed the 500 or so miners who had earlier assembled with the intention of descending on Penryn had decided not to do so, 'due to the adverse weather'. It seems unlikely that a band prepared to trek 30 miles would be put off by a spot of rain. It's more likely that Penryn was avoided because the miners were aware that a strong force of Volunteers from Penryn and Falmouth was fully prepared for their visit.

In April and May of 1795 there was also news of trouble at other places. Delabole quarrymen took barley from a merchant at Boscastle, paying a reduced price for it. Tin miners at Polgooth travelled to Ruanlanihorne on the Roseland to visit farmers in that vicinity. This was no social visit. One report stated that a 'little damage' was done, another that they had 'broke open a granary and seized corn which was the property of a merchant who had previously sold them bad grain'. Visiting farms in the countryside in search of stored grain was in fact the second main tactic adopted by food 'rioters' in the 1790s. The parish of Ruanlanihorne seems to feature regularly in such expeditions, more than its size warrants. It was either used to mean the Roseland (a grain growing area) in general or suggests a ritual element to proceedings - 'off to Ruanlanihorne' perhaps more broadly indicating a call on local farmers.

In east Cornwall there were also reports of threats in the spring by 'tinners and others' to 'regulate' the market at Callington. The Callington Volunteers were mobilised and nothing came of this although 'some depredations' occurred at nearby Liskeard. Later in 1795, concerns were still being raised. Shortages would continue even after the harvest and things did not bode well. There were fevered accounts in the press in October of 'several insurrections' in the west. Forced sales at reduced prices were reported from Camborne market, although Sir Francis Basset later claimed these were not forced and that farmers had willingly reduced their prices. At Helford ships were seized and grain retrieved for the people. At the other end of Cornwall, mine captains at Gunnislake on the border with Devon were reported as having great difficulty restraining their men who were intending to demand the local magistrates reduce the price of corn. As one wrote, 'their children were crying out for bread and if nothing was done they would plunder the farmers'.

At Bodmin in July only three bushels of wheat and 'a little' barley had been brought to market and the people were 'in great distress'. Appealing to the Privy Council, Bodmin's leaders were brusquely told that buyers at Bodmin 'should purchase some of the wheat at Plymouth'. Even some local Justices of the Peace could be distinctly unsympathetic to the plight of the poor. The Mayor of Helston, where there had been some unspecified trouble earlier in the year, told the government that while a subscription was being raised to buy corn, it would not be 'at a reduced rate as we conceive that to be yielding too much to threats of the Mob'. Later in 1795, the Helston magistrates were among the loudest in calling for more troops to be sent to Cornwall.

'it is unsafe for any civil power to venture alone without the military'

For the third year in a row, in 1796 there was yet another bout of food rioting. This time the focus was inland rather than at the ports. Moreover, while unrest was relatively short-lived, confined to the early part of April, the temper was a lot more fraught. At Sithney, to the west of Helston, miners were urged to assemble this time armed so as not to be 'awed by the Volunteers' as they were the previous year. They then proceeded to visit local farms looking for any grain stored there. This involved the traditional device of a 'rope and contract'. The farmers would be asked to sign a contract promising to sell their grain to local people at a certain price. If they refused the rope would come into play and they would be hanged. This was a bit of theatre and rarely carried out. In fact, there was no instance of any farmer actually being lynched during any disturbance. However, in 1796 miners in the neighbouring Breage parish came close, with reports of two farmers, who had stubbornly refused their demands, being strung up. They were quickly cut down.

In fiction, Demelza, Verity and Andrew Blamey managed to get trapped in a riot of miners at Truro, heading for some corn warehouses. This event had its counterpart in reality in 1796 when a large crowd of miners, variously estimated as between 1,000 and 3,000, entered Truro. It's not clear exactly what their objective was although one rioter was reported as saying he 'would as soon be killed as starved'. They were confronted by the Worcestershire Militia, then stationed in Cornwall. There had been bad blood between this militia and the miners, with a corporal of militia having been badly beaten by some miners three miles outside Truro on the road to Redruth. As the *Times* reported, once the Riot Act was read:

> a field-piece was elevated, and fired over their (the rioters') heads with canister shot. This at first had a good effect, and the tinners retreated; but rallied again; when Major St John addressed them with great humanity, and told them, if they did not disperse, he must be compelled to point the field-piece, and fire amongst them. The tinners not regarding his humane advice, became more riotous, when the Worcestershire Militia advanced, with great vivacity, and notwithstanding showers of brickbats and stones hurled upon them, they made a brisk charge with fixed bayonets, and put the motley group to the rout.

During this riot, ten people were arrested. Seven of them were miners, four from the nearby parishes of Kenwyn and Kea, two from Redruth and one from Crowan. There was also a shoemaker and a farmer from Redruth, whose surnames suggest they may have been brothers. The ten also included one woman – Elizabeth Bray. Although her residence was not identified, her presence among those arrested suggest the crowd was a little more diverse than the term 'tinners' might suggest and would have included some women as well as men who were not miners.

General support for the food rioters from the community is also indicated by a letter from the commanding officer of the Worcestershire Militia to the Home Office a month or so later. He had been asked to accompany local magistrates to arrest some 'ringleaders'. He responded that 'it seems that every individual in the mining area is involved in the riots and it is unsafe for any civil power to venture alone without the military. Rioters can only be taken at dead of night, as during the day they hide in the mines'. Although the riots of 1796 were not prolonged, the authorities were sufficiently alarmed to call for regular troops to be sent to Helston, Truro and Redruth.

'poor people won't find all this bustle fills their children's bellies'

Better harvests then removed any further threat of riots for a few years. But not for long. In the spring of 1801 two consecutive bad harvests re-awoke the spirit of rebellion. Moreover, the events of 1801 were relatively unusual in that trouble began in Devon and then spread into Cornwall from east to west rather than being focused first on the mining districts. In March 200 women at Launceston market seized some corn from a farmer trying to sell it to a middleman and sold it themselves at a reduced price of ten shillings a bushel. Unrest then spread quickly through east Cornwall. A reward of £50 was offered for information leading to the conviction of those waylaying and plundering farmers bringing grain to Devonport. This was particularly prevalent near Torpoint. Meanwhile, the dockyard workers at Devonport were themselves increasingly restive. Their influence was even claimed to spread as far as Fowey, where their agents were linked to the harassment of farmers and butchers.

Whether or not that was really the case, unrest soon spread to the west. Women at Falmouth were again at the forefront in April when they insisted on a lower price for potatoes. When they were refused, they took the potatoes anyway. It was some considerable time before order was restored. A letter to the Home Office from the town reported that 'riot and tumult' had only subsided when some of the ringleaders were clapped into jail. Inevitably, the mining districts then began to get in on the act. At St Austell, Polgooth miners were again in the vanguard, adopting the familiar rope and contract tactic: 'large bodies of tinners ...visited the farmers ... carrying a written paper in one hand, a rope in the other. If the farmers hesitated to sign this paper ...the rope was fastened around their necks and they were terrified and tortured into compliance'.

William Jenkin at Redruth watched the unrest 'drawing very near to us. Gwennap mines pour forth their hundreds of desperate labourers who can with great caution and difficulty be prevailed on to be quiet.' Later he added a postscript: 'Since I wrote this I have had the disgusting sight of a riotous assemblage of tinners from Gwennap who broke into the market and are now compelling the people to sell potatoes, fish, butter and salt pork etc. at the prices they choose to fix'. At the following week's market, a magistrate attended with soldiers and a 'large number of new-made constables', although Jenkin added that 'the poor people won't find all this bustle fills their children's bellies'. At markets in the west – at Helston, Penzance and St Ives – prices were also driven down before the disturbances petered out during May.

'paraded the streets with a drum, and soon collected a large concourse of people'

Things were relatively quiet for a decade until early in 1812. Reports then surfaced of an 'alarming scarcity of grain'. To make matters worse the potato harvest of 1811 had also been deficient. When grain got short, miners began to leave work and gather in the traditional way to hunt down what grain supplies were available. In March, the tin streamers of the Bodmin district made a traditional foray to Padstow. They found the warehouses empty, were reported to be 'orderly and peaceable' and returned home. Miners in the much more populous district between Truro and Redruth then began to stir themselves. A letter to the *Times* from Truro reported the 'ascent of several thousand miners from the subterranean abode', although again there had been 'no disorder'. 'Workmen at several of the mines resolved to stop work till they were supplied ... [they] assembled in groups of considerable numbers, in the quarter between Redruth and Truro, and then dispersed over the country with their empty sacks, to purchase corn among the farmers'. At Redruth some miners took possession of the brewery and began taking away the stocks of malting barley before being dispersed by some militia hastily dispatched from Falmouth. After a week or two of some 'symptoms of commotion' things calmed down, helped by the arrival of 1,000 sacks of flour from Plymouth.

No further major food rioting occurred in our period, although substantial rioting again broke out in 1830 and, for the final time, in 1847. None that is except for an isolated incident in 1817. A long drought had led to a scarcity of potatoes in west Cornwall in that year and a near doubling of the price. Nonetheless, potatoes were still being exported from West Penwith. This 'excited great dissatisfaction among the poor at Penzance where ... a number of women assembled, paraded the streets with a drum, and soon collected a large concourse of people, who proceeded to the pier to prevent any further shipments'. The Mayor, scurrying to the scene, threatened to read the Riot Act. 'The menace had the desired effect' and 'the crowd dispersed' while 'the shipment of potatoes is resumed without molestation'.

'bayonets were drawn on each side; many were severely wounded'

The Cornish crowd regularly resorted to the food riot because it usually worked. It triggered an increase in the supply of grain and other foodstuffs.

To explain its success, we must look at the reaction of the authorities. This involved a three-fold combination: words of advice, repression and charity. The first, lecturing the rioters on the laws of supply and demand and the futility of challenging these had little effect. Neither did calls for 'patience' in the face of hunger and starvation. Meanwhile, the pledge of lawyers at Truro to discontinue the 'use of pies, custards, puddings etc. in their families' during the grain shortage of 1812 probably did little to impress the average mining family.

Repression involved bringing sufficient force to bear to stop forced sales of grain. Local magistrates would call for troops to be sent when trouble erupted. But in pre-railway days this took a considerable time. In 1793 a message was sent from Bodmin to Plymouth requesting military aid. Seventy men 'marched immediately for Bodmin and St Austell to quell the riots.' But they would have taken several hours to arrive, hours that provided the crowd with a window of opportunity.

By 1800, the regular army was backed up by two kinds of local force. First, there were the 'county' militias. These were part-time soldiers, brought together for several weeks each year. When the militia were on active service, they were usually sent to other places. This strategy was deemed prudent in order to reduce the risk that they would sympathise with the local population. Thus in 1795 the crowd at Truro confronted militia from Worcestershire. In 1812 it was the turn of the Monmouth and Brecon Militia to face down the food rioters. Militia were not always the most disciplined of forces however. The Cornwall Militia certainly was not. In September 1793 they were involved in a 'very serious riot' at Exeter:

> The Cornwall regiment of militia ... broke from their
> parade in a very riotous manner, and assembled
> themselves before the Guildhall, swearing they would
> liberate a comrade of theirs who had just been
> committed to prison for violently assaulting a chaise-
> driver and knocking out one of his eyes. After a
> considerable time in which many of them were
> wounded by their officers; swords, bayonets etc.
> broken, they were again brought to the ranks, where
> they were severely reprimanded by their officers and a
> few of the principal ringleaders taken into custody, but
> ... they swear vengeance to all who shall oppose them'.

The Cornwall Militia was again involved in a 'desperate affray' in 1809. This involved 'a party of Cornish Miners' (Militia), on permanent duty at Plymouth:

> and a detachment of the Third, or Old Buffs. A dispute
> having taken place between one of the former and one
> of the Buffs, the Cornishmen, in a body, marched from
> the barracks, to the amount of about 200, and fell
> furiously on the Buffs, whose numbers did not exceed
> 20: bayonets were drawn on each side; many were
> severely wounded ... when the fortunate arrival of the
> officers belonging to each corps put an end to the
> unequal contest.

From 1794 the militia was augmented by Volunteer companies. These were armed units organised and financed by local landowners. After some hesitation, when facing the possibility of a French invasion the Government encouraged their formation. One of the first to be formed, before being officially sanctioned, was at Penzance. Others very soon followed at Penryn, Illogan and other places in Cornwall. It was clear from the start that the impetus for this force was not just for defence against the French. In 1794 an advert in the *Times* called on 'gentlemen of Cornwall now in London' to consider subscribing to the plans for Volunteers, 'by having an independent and constitutional body of yeomanry armed, the minds of good citizens will be quieted, and the lurking seeds of Jacobinism destroyed'. The enemy was the potential revolutionary within as much as the actual revolutionary across the Channel.

John Whitaker, the Rector of Ruanlanihorne, a parish often visited by miners with their 'rope and contract', was one of those keen on forming an armed association that would be 'prepared to give a warm reception to the tinners, who have been lately visiting us'. Whitaker was also a regular contributor to the Anti-Jacobin Review, which demonised those calling for measures of reform, equating them with the French Jacobins. Whitaker clearly viewed the crowds of food rioters in much the same light as the French revolutionaries. Volunteer companies, keen to protect their property, were indeed usually fully prepared to confront the miners. The Penzance Volunteers in 1795 was said to be mainly shopkeepers, butchers and blacksmiths, led by the local gentry. But even the Volunteers might not always be reliable. In 1801 the Tregony Volunteers became 'mutinous and disorderly' and demanded a reduced price for corn on the same basis as the miners.

'derisory benefaction'

Despite the supplementary force of the Volunteers, the authorities could not rely on force alone to quell unrest. William Jenkin at Redruth wrote in 1801 that the rioters found 'no-one to stop them for we have neither magistrate or military here'. This gave the crowd in the mining districts an opportunity. Moreover, the charity the riots invariably triggered guaranteed that the strategy would continue through the Poldark years. A society that largely condoned smuggling and where many people lived in villages and hamlets remote from the influence of gentry or clergymen was not one to give up the tradition of food rioting lightly. And, of course, it was not just miners who resorted to 'riots'. The involvement of women was often a critical element in initiating direct action to reduce prices at markets while the presence of other occupational groups among those arrested point to a wider context than just 'tinners'. In 1801 for example the riots at Penzance were led by two brothers who were fishermen, John and William Richards, described as 'notorious for their turbulent dispositions'.

In 1812 it was stated that magistrates 'were doing all in their power to relieve them [the poor] and to punish the ringleaders in any further disorder'. In fact, threats of punishment always went hand in hand with frantic attempts to alleviate the situation by buying and distributing grain, free or at a reduced price. In 1795 the minister and inhabitants of St Merryn, for example, decided to supply every poor family in the parish with corn at a reduced price until the next harvest. At the end of 1792 a subscription was started, supported by the large landowners and MPs such as William Lemon, Francis Basset, the Earl of Mount Edgcumbe and merchants like the Foxes of Falmouth. This was intended to supply barley to miners and others and was started a week or two before crowds began descending on the ports.

Food riots, or even the threat of food riots, could therefore trigger charity from the better-off and an improved supply of grain at a reduced price. It was a message sent to the wealthy that the point had been reached where forbearance could not be continued. They had to intervene or face widespread commotion and danger to property. There was usually a ready response, although it was not always appreciated. In 1800 a notice was fixed to the church door at Duloe threatening the vicar and rejecting his 'derisory benefaction' to the poor of rice and salted pilchards.

'they were busy at each forging pikes and making cutlasses'

Unlike the fictional account painted in *Poldark*, when the prison at Bodmin became crammed with arrested rioters, the actual number arrested during these events was surprisingly low. Moreover, those involved knew that in normal times the penalties for taking part in a riot were quite light. In 1801, despite widespread rioting the total number of sentences handed out were three months prison for three of those found guilty, one month for one, two fines of £5 and nine of one shilling. In 1796 after the riot at Truro, six of the ten arrested were discharged and the rest bound over to keep the peace. All that is apart from one. Identified as a 'ringleader', John Hoskin, aged 55, conveniently nicknamed 'Wild Cat', was executed, the only one in the Poldark period to suffer this sentence for rioting. Even then, the magistrates at the assizes had been prepared to remit the sentence and be lenient, but Francis Basset had ridden back to Cornwall from London and insisted an example had to be made. He forced his reluctant fellow magistrates to go through with the death sentence. Several years later Basset claimed that the hanging was 'necessary for the benefit of society ... the manners of the people were suddenly changed from rudeness and disrespect to proper obedience.' If that were so it did not last long as four years later they were out on the streets and lanes again demanding bread.

Basset saw revolution lurking behind the crowds of food rioters. It is certainly true that the food riots between 1794 and 1796 were particularly tense, following as they did events in France that cast a shadow over them, or set an example, depending on one's viewpoint. The fall of the Bastille and the toppling of the French monarchy in 1789 was met with enthusiasm by those in Britain calling for the reform of a corrupt and unrepresentative system of government. Supporters of reform established the London Corresponding Society (LCS) to encourage contacts between reformers, who were avidly reading Tom Paine's *Rights of Man*, published in two parts in 1791 and 1792. This was a defence of the French Revolution and a call for democratic reform and an end to hereditary wealth more generally. A government of property owners was unlikely to be overjoyed about this. It responded with growing repression, prosecuting those calling for reform. It was helped when the Jacobins seized power in France in 1793 and launched the Terror, backed up by Madame Guillotine. As aristocratic heads rolled in France, government supporters in Britain condemned all reformers as 'Jacobins'. Even though the French Jacobins lost power in late 1794 the label stuck and was used in Britain as a general term of abuse for anyone supporting radical change.

There is evidence of some sympathy for reform in Cornwall in the mid-1790s. The LCS received a letter from west Cornwall in 1796 claiming that 'in this neighbourhood citizens abound', a reference to the citizens of France as opposed to the oppressed subjects of the British crown. Timothy Martin at Stithians corresponded regularly with the LCS and there were societies of reformers at Helston and Truro. A handful of reports of reforming sympathies surfaced in the generally loyalist and unsympathetic columns of the fledgling regional newspapers. An apprentice at St Columb was reported as having uttered 'some seditious expressions in a public house' in early 1794. The *Sherborne Mercury* continued: the 'effigy of the young man was afterwards burnt, amidst the applause of a large number of spectators'. In Redruth a miner was heard drinking health to Tom Paine and 'perdition to all kings.' A year later, in 1795, William Jenkin repeated a rumour he had heard that 'in St Just they went so far (during some food riots), in imitation of our Gallic neighbours, to plant the "tree of liberty" – and am sorry to hear several cant words among the tinners, much in use among the French'.

Alarm was certainly mounting among the propertied classes. It was reported in 1795 by the clerk of Kenwyn parish that, when his horse shed a shoe at St Agnes, he could not find a blacksmith to reshoe the horse, as 'they were busy at each forging pikes and making cutlasses'. This is an unlikely tale, as the miners seemed remarkably reluctant to use their newly forged weapons. The only weapons reported from the riots of 1795 and 1796 on the crowd's side were clubs and stones. The one example of a shot being fired in relation to a Cornish food riot came in 1795 when the High Constable of Pydar Hundred in mid-Cornwall took refuge in a house after trying to detain four miners who had removed corn. A shot was fired into the house. The sole incident with obvious political connotations occurred in 1800, but just over the border in Devon at Lifton. A tithe gatherer at an inn was met by a group with a 'bloody flag' (a red flag) who were crying 'liberty, equality and no tithes'. Their leader fired a shot through a window of the inn, although no-one was injured.

In Cornwall smuggling gangs readily resorted to firearms when needed, so there was no shortage of serious weaponry available. Incidents involving guns could also occur in other contexts. In 1801 there was an attack on the property of a Dr Flamank at Boscarne, Bodmin. According to the *Times*, this involved 'a banditti, supposed to consist of about 300 ... armed with guns, axes, saws and weapons of every description. They surrounded the dwelling house, guarded every avenue to the estate, and stopped travellers on the high road', before demolishing some salmon weirs and attacking mills. This was apparently the second such incident, with other attacks reported from mid-Cornwall. However, the cause of these look to be disputes over water rights and fishing rather than political reform.

'now is the time ... to take vengeance on your oppressors'
In 1795/96 in particular the authorities were paranoid, prone to see shadowy Jacobin influence behind every disturbance. A letter to the Home Office in 1796 from the St Aubyn estate steward at Helston claimed that miners in that neighbourhood were 'strongly tinged with Jacobinical principles', while the Mayor of Helston was also writing at the same time to the government reporting an 'incendiary paper' sent to the gentlemen of Camborne. This proposed a list of reduced prices for butter and salt pork 'or we will burn the town and you in the midst of it'. In actual fact, such letters and handbills were commonplace both before and during periods of riot. Despite limited literacy they were regularly employed either to call on people to assemble or to utter threats. In 1800 a paper was posted on the door of a smithy at Beer Ferris, just across the Tamar, threatening farmers with death for their treatment of the poor. In a similar vein, a handbill at Stratton in 1801 called on all 'labouring men and tradesmen in the hundred of Stratton that are willing to save their wives and children from the dreadful condition of being starved to death by the unfeeling and griping farmer ... now is the time ... to take vengeance on your oppressors'. At the opposite end of Cornwall, the miners of St Just sent circulars to other parishes in West Penwith in 1795 calling on them to assemble to prevent grain exports.

In the mid 1790s these letters and notices took on a new and more sinister connotation. Some were convinced mysterious agitators lay behind them. In 1793 a report on the 'very mutinous state' of miners in Cornwall in the *Times* declared, on no very apparent evidence, that 'some of our Jacobin emissaries have been sent among these deluded men, to preach up equality and the rights of man, which is now again recommended in little handbills around the streets.' At St Ives in 1799 two 'suspicious' Irishmen were seized and imprisoned in an inn, guarded by six constables. The local customs officer complained to the Home Office about the expense of keeping them under guard but Castlereagh for the Government agreed with the local magistrates that 'one object of the United Irishmen (at that time launching an abortive insurrection) has been to corrupt the miners of Cornwall'.

Handbills continued to agitate the mayor and corporation of Helston who seem to have been waging a private war on local reformers well after the peak of anti-Jacobin hysteria in 1795/96. In 1799 the mayor felt impelled to inform the government that 170 or more inhabitants had pledged themself against the LCS (which by this time had wound itself up) 'and any other association inimical to the constitution of the kingdom'. In 1801 the town council was reporting to the Home Office that seditious handbills had been found, calling on citizens to rise up. 'Cry Chains or Victory! Liberty or Death!' was the call, signed by 'Buonaparte of England'. The sheets also contained ballads including 'The complaints of the poor of Cornwall' and 'The weeping mother'. Helston corporation connected such subversive material with the fact that for several nights 'many of the larger houses ... have had their windows broken by disorderly persons'.

The loyalists of Helston were not alone. Later, in 1819, a pedlar was indicted by Penryn magistrates for uttering seditious libel. He had been selling copies of 'Sherwin's signs of the people coming to its senses', in which the clergy was attacked as debauched, protected in plundering the public by their friends in the aristocracy. Although pleading that he could not read and was thus unaware of the content of the pamphlets he was selling, the unfortunate pedlar was found guilty and given six months in prison. The publications were destroyed.

'a party chiefly composed of the lower orders'

Food riots were not new, having appeared at the end of the 1600s. They were to erupt again in Cornwall in 1830 and 1847 before petering out during the nineteenth century. In parallel with such rioting, but as we have seen largely unconnected, there was some political protest and demands for changes in the constitution and in particular parliamentary reform. This received a new lease of life in the 1780s with growing criticism of 'old corruption' and fears that King George III was attempting to increase the monarch's role. The demand for 'liberty and equality' (at least for white men) that echoed back across the Atlantic and then from France strengthened demands for reform and wider representation, one that had been ignited by the loss of the American colonies.

Historians have tended to regard Cornwall as a backwater in these campaigns for political change, its protests confined to 'primitive', although actually quite effective, food rioting. This underplays support for reform, especially after 1800, and owes a lot to Cornwall's current status as a place of holidaying, somewhere to escape from reality, where nothing much of consequence happens. Yet, when protests against the repressive policies of the government re-emerged in the 1810s, loud complaints also surfaced in Cornwall, just as they did elsewhere. This could be seen right at the end of the Poldark years, during the Queen Caroline affair in 1820. When George IV came to the throne in 1820, he was embarrassed by the unwanted arrival of his estranged wife Caroline of Brunswick, who turned up claiming the right to be Queen. The King pushed the House of Lords to annul the royal marriage to stop Caroline. She then became the unlikely beneficiary of a wave of protest against an overbearing government and an unpopular king. Despite the details of her torrid extra-marital sexual dalliances that were revealed in the course of the annulment debate, she became cast as a victim. This was made easier by the generally well-known and no less colourful sex life of the King. A series of defections of Tory MPs in the Commons gradually reduced the Government's majority and in November the divorce bill was abandoned amidst much public rejoicing.

This was a jubilation shared in Cornwall. Addresses in support of Caroline had included one from Truro in October 1820. This may have been from 'the female inhabitants of the borough of Truro', who Caroline replied to with thanks a week or so later. News of her victory gave rise to several demonstrations of support. At Newlyn and Penzance tar barrels were burnt and flags flown while 'parties, preceded by music, parade the streets, and rend the air by their acclamations of 'Long Live Queen Caroline''. At Bodmin, Launceston and St Austell the church bells were rung and fireworks let off. St Ives was 'pregnant with public rejoicings ... The principal gentlemen and tradesmen of the town walked in procession, with music playing', while free meat was distributed to the poor. At Truro there were 'the liveliest demonstrations of joy', although public opinion there was also described in another account as 'much divided'.

The Caroline affair soon subsided and Caroline herself was dead within a year. But the uproar encouraged those calling for less wasteful government spending and parliamentary reform. Nowhere more so than in Cornwall where a series of 'county' meetings were held in the 1820s demanding political change and parliamentary reform. These were led by the smaller landowners, exactly the same sort of men as Ross Poldark. Even though, on the surface, Cornwall benefited from it, they were calling for a reform of the system where Cornwall returned almost as many MPs to the House of Commons as did Scotland. Predictably, Francis Basset, by now with the pretentious title of Lord de Dunstanville, did not think too much of the mounting calls for reform. He later wrote that it was 'a disgrace to have a member forced upon the County by a party chiefly composed of the lower orders.'

Basset may have been getting a little worried. But he and his fellow landowners still remained firmly in control. Moreover, most of the gentry had gained disproportionally from the increased circulation of trade and money. This included relatively minor gentry such as the Poldarks, although on a rather more muted scale than the greater gentry. But who were those greater gentry neighbours and what did they do with themselves? It's time to knock on the door of the great house and ask for admittance.

9
The Great House

The houses of the greater gentry were a world away from the angry, seething crowds demanding bread or gathering to watch the feast day wrestling or flocking through the lanes to the nearest chapel. They stood in their own serene oases, patches of peace, surrounded by sylvan greenery and, increasingly, carefully manicured parkland vistas. They were seemingly untouched by the turmoil around them. Change lapped at the edges of their estates but the gentry kept it safely at bay. Or did they? The tendency is to see these two worlds, that of the crowd and that of the gentry, as entirely separate. Yet in reality there was no such stark boundary. As a reading of *Poldark* would suggest, the residents of the great house had their fingers in many pies and were fully engaged in the economic and social change going on around them. They were also active participants in politics as they fiercely clung on to their power and privileges.

As we have seen throughout this book, the *Poldark* saga was a mixture of the real and the fictional. While the main characters – Ross and Demelza and their children, Francis and Elizabeth, the Warleggans, Dwight Enys and Caroline Penvenen – are fictional, some of the secondary figures that flit through the pages were real. Three of Cornwall's major landowners made their entry in the pages of Winston Graham's books. These were Sir Francis Basset, made a baronet in 1770 and becoming Lord de Dunstanville in 1796, George Boscawen, the third Viscount Falmouth and first Earl Falmouth, and Sir Christopher Hawkins.

'high Tory talk'
Francis Basset was born in 1757. He was a relatively early participant in the gentry's growing preference for a public-school education for their male offspring, attending both Harrow and Eton for good measure. In the 1770s,

when Basset was there, public schools were still somewhat chaotic places, brutal, ill-disciplined and prone to riot. But they were beginning to be seen as valuable meeting places where useful life-long acquaintances could be struck. These gave the sons of the aristocracy and the wealthier gentry advantages in later life and helped to foster their sense of being a class separate from their 'inferiors'. After public school, Basset spent a year at Cambridge University. Like many of his peers at the time, he did not bother to graduate, instead embarking on the equally fashionable 'grand tour' of France and Italy.

Basset succeeded to the family estate, based at Tehidy between the growing towns of Camborne and Redruth, on the death of his father in 1769. He liked to stress the family's long roots, traced back to the Norman Conquest. However, their exalted position owed more to luck than to pedigree. They were fortunate in that their land and properties, relatively unproductive as farmland, happened to include the mining rights to what became some of Cornwall's major mines. Dolcoath at Camborne was the principal of these. Its exploitation in the eighteenth century considerably augmented the family fortunes, which had sunk to a low ebb a century earlier when financial difficulties following their support for the losing Royalist side in the civil wars led to the sale of St Michael's Mount in 1659 to the St Aubyns. Nonetheless, their status more than recovered during the 1700s as the mineral royalties flowed in. Neither Basset nor his father were reluctant to get their hands dirty, at least metaphorically, encouraging mining ventures, providing finance for harbours and other infrastructure, taking an active interest in the work of inventors such as Trevithick and getting centrally involved in Cornwall's infant banking system. This paradoxical mix of pride in lineage but aggressive business activity was echoed in Francis Basset's early political career.

Becoming MP for Penryn in 1780, Francis Basset was a member of the Commons until being raised to the peerage in 1796 and departing for the Lords. At first a supporter of Lord North and the war with the American colonists, he soon changed his stance and allied in 1783 with the opposition Whig group around Charles James Fox. This was not because of any great question of principle but occurred after they had promised him a peerage when and if they got into power. They didn't and the alliance was always a fragile one, as the central principle Francis Basset firmly held to throughout his adult life was a consistent opposition to parliamentary reform and an intense dislike of democracy. James Boswell, visiting Tehidy in 1792, observed that his 'high Tory talk' seemed incongruous given his theoretical attachment to the Whigs and Fox, who were supporting a moderate measure of reform. In fact, that attachment was soon broken, as Basset deserted the opposition to support the war against France in early 1793. He then became a constant follower of Pitt and a vigorous supporter of repression to deal with 'sedition', within which he included any calls for parliamentary reform.

In Cornwall he took, as we saw in the last chapter, a very hard line on food rioters, insisting on the death penalty for one of them. He even wrote a pamphlet in 1798 with the title *The Crimes of Democracy*. The Basset of the *Poldark* books is presented as a vaguely liberal, humane landlord. Here was someone who would be sympathetic with the iconoclastic rebel Ross. In reality this would have been unlikely, even during Basset's Foxite phase from 1783 to 1793. It was entirely unbelievable after that point.

Despite some rather fierce and uncompromising political views, Basset was an affable host, welcoming guests to his house. James Boswell found him to be 'a genteel, smart little man, well-informed and lively' on his visit in 1792. Later, both the Liverpool banker Thomas Staniforth in 1800 and the landscape painter Joseph Farington in 1811 were duly impressed by the hospitality they received. Yet Basset was also extremely prickly, quick to detect insult or take offence and not averse to public disputes with his neighbours. In the early 1780s he feuded with George Boscawen of Tregothnan. The key issue at stake was control of Truro Corporation and the town's two Members of Parliament. Ultimately, an accommodation was reached between the pair in 1786. In 1810 he fought a duel with Sir Christopher Hawkins near London. This had been precipitated by some obscure argument over boroughmongering, of which more in the final chapter.

'rode without a greatcoat, and was much wet'

Francis Basset had been born a year before George Evelyn Boscawen. Basset was never slow to point out to visitors that the Boscawens, in contrast to his own 'ancient family', had only 'recently' attained their exalted position through trading as Truro merchants in Tudor times and a series of strategic marriages to heiresses. George Boscawen was the only surviving son of Admiral Edward Boscawen, famed as 'Old Dreadnought', the heroic naval commander of the mid-eighteenth century. George also embarked on a military career, but unlike his father, entered the army rather than navy, becoming a colonel in 1795. He spent much of his time in court circles, where he was appointed a privy councillor to George III. Boscawen is portrayed in the *Poldark* books as a rather remote figure, in comparison with the ever-active Basset. This may have been the case, although, given the time he had to spend in London, George Boscawen appears to have been as fully involved in the political and social life of Cornwall as might be expected. Moreover, Boswell, who had known Boscawen at Edinburgh, described him as 'having the reputation of a good bottle companion'.

A third Cornish landlord, Christopher Hawkins, is also mentioned by name in the *Poldark* saga. Boswell reported in 1792 that he was 'said to be exceedingly rich', but 'he lives on a very economical plan, and very retired'. When meeting Boswell at Penzance during heavy rain, Hawkins 'rode without a greatcoat, and was much wet'. His house at Trewithen was described as 'on a bleak eminence, without much shelter except that of some plantations of Scotch firs'. It contrasted with his other, older house at Trewinnard, near St Erth, 'a collection of strange rooms huddled together with a number of inconvenient passages and narrow staircases', but with 'an air of antiquity and cultivation' attached to it, according to Boswell. Hawkins had been born a year after Basset and, like him, was an MP. In fact, buying, owning and controlling parliamentary boroughs was one of the main sources of his wealth, along with some lucrative mining ventures found on his property. A long career in Parliament was relatively undistinguished, to say the least. Hawkins spoke just four times in almost 40 years and then he was reported as being 'inaudible'. Nonetheless, as a loyal Tory supporter of Pitt, he was rewarded by being created a baronet in 1791.

Like Basset, Hawkins took an interest in the industrial achievements of his compatriots, supporting Richard Trevithick at one stage and commissioning a steam threshing machine from him in 1812. He remained unmarried with a reputation for being a miser. His biographer cites a squib supposedly written about his house at Trewithen:

A large house and no cheer,
A large park and no deer,
A large cellar and no beer
Sir Christopher Hawkins lives here.

'the representative of which is now a parish pauper'

These three men were not the only major landowners in Cornwall. The Lanhydrock estate was as large as any and, like most Cornish estates, possessed land scattered across the region. The Roberts family, Truro merchants like the Boscawens, had bought the estate (and a peerage) in the seventeenth century and built the house while altering their surname to the much more exclusive Robartes. That did not prevent the direct line from dying out. By the 1780s the estate had passed on to the Hunt family, who spent most of their time in London. In 1804 Anna Hunt married James Agar, son of an Irish peer. Agar's son later added the name Robartes to his own.

Other more locally based landlords included the Edgcumbes of Mount Edgcumbe in the far south-east of Cornwall. The Edgcumbes had originally been based at Cotehele, up the Tamar valley. They were an old family and could trace their lineage back to the 1300s, moving to their new house at Mount Edgcumbe, opposite the growing town of Plymouth Dock or Devonport, in the mid-1500s. They lived not far from the Eliots at St Germans and the Pole-Carews at Antony. A scattering of other gentry of various levels of wealth and lengths of lineage were found in Cornwall. By the 1790s these were being joined by those newly wealthy families who had made their money from mining, smelting and banking. The Lemons had led the way, followed by the Williamses and the Bolithos.

As some families rose, others fell. The Lysons' *History of Cornwall* of 1814 noted 'George Rescorla, the representative of this reduced family, is a day-labourer at Roche'. Meanwhile, another 'reduced family' of former landowners were the Wadges of Lewannick, near Launceston, 'the representative of which is now a parish pauper'. Landowning families were not immune from the ups and downs of the broader economy, although most managed to avoid a drastic slide on the scale of the Rescorlas or Wadges.

While individual families could rise or fall, direct lines of succession be broken by a lack of heirs and new families muscle in, the landed gentry as a distinct group or class securely maintained its hold over society in this period, in Cornwall as elsewhere. This only came under challenge in the 1790s and then fleetingly. A combination of some draconian laws, blizzards of tracts from moralists, an outpouring of preaching from evangelists and a strong dose of bullish patriotism produced by the long wars with France kept the lid on mutterings of discontent and muted calls for reform, at least for one more generation.

'good husbandry'

The ultimate basis of the gentry's power was wealth. Possession of land was central to that wealth, with the bulk of their income coming from the rents extracted from farmers, businesses and the other tenants who occupied their land for shorter or longer periods of time. Rental incomes rose in the 1790s and 1800s as a result of wartime inflation and a temporary boom in agriculture. But in Cornwall farm rents were supplemented by the income from mining. Sometimes landed families bought shares in mines, but more often than not their involvement was less risky, limited to receiving the royalties from owning the mineral rights. As we have seen, these entitled them to a proportion of the value of all the ore raised, irrespective of whether the mine was profitable or not. As long as the mine continued to produce, this was a risk-free income.

For some families, money from mining was a lot more important than that from farm rentals. The Bassets of Tehidy were the obvious case, their mining profits in the eighteenth century being two or three times that of renting out land. But it also applied in varying degrees to many landed families. It was estimated that the Enys family, based near Penryn, received 40 per cent of their income from mining in the early 1700s. Even estates that were distant from the mining districts could benefit, given the scattered nature of their holdings. For the Lanhydrock estate in 1805 mineral royalties accounted for almost as much income as did rents, even though Lanhydrock House was miles away from the nearest mine.

Occasionally, the Cornish gentry engaged more directly in trade, taking shares in mining and smelting ventures. As the boundaries between 'old' and 'new' money became eroded by the new merchant families who had prospered from industry, families like the Lemons, it became more acceptable for other landowners to invest in business. Banking was an amenable pursuit for a gentleman, although banking, like other businesses, brought its dangers. Edward Stackhouse, who had inherited Pendarves near Camborne and changed his name to Pendarves, was a partner in the North Cornwall Bank from 1812. Unfortunately for him, the bank failed in 1822, leaving Edward in debt to a number of creditors. He 'at once reduced his establishment, gave up his carriage and horses and allowed himself only £500 a year (around £63,000 nowadays) until everyone was paid in full'. Pendarves escaped the bankruptcy court and went on to become an MP.

Although rents and royalties, whether from farming or mining, continued to provide the majority of the income for landed families while their direct involvement in trade remained marginal, landowners were often to the fore in encouraging innovation and improvement. We saw in Chapter 2 how Sir Francis Basset was closely involved in infrastructure investments, in harbours, tramways and drainage projects that were of benefit to the mining industry. He was also among those who were encouraging other landowners to follow his example and let out smallholdings on 'unimproved' land to labouring families. When Joseph Farington visited Tehidy in 1811 he reported Basset dining with some principal farmers, who were judging a competition for the best kept smallholdings on Basset lands. By these means and others, 'good husbandry' and the latest techniques were fostered. Cornish landowners also showed considerable interest in the work of inventors like Trevithick. Richard Trevithick even roped in Lady de Dunstanville along with Davies Gilbert, to help him demonstrate a model of his high-pressure steam engine in his kitchen around 1800.

'one of the handsomest and most commodious mansions'

Landowners like the Bassets had a considerable income, but they also spent a large amount of it. Some of this was unavoidable, such as taxes. The main tax which landowners paid was the land tax, but a Parliament dominated by the landed gentry had worked hard during the 1700s to keep the land tax low, transferring government taxation to customs and excise duties instead. These fell on the population more generally, including the poor. However, the costs of the war in 1799 led Pitt to introduce a temporary income tax, which remained in place until 1816 and added to the costs of the gentry during these years. Other necessary spending would have involved repairs and upkeep of buildings and the costs of managing the estate and maintaining the household.

Then there was more avoidable spending, for example on the house and its furnishings and the gardens and park in which it was situated. The 1790s was a peak decade for country house building and many Cornish landowners spent heavily on improving their houses around this time. Building new houses from scratch was unusual although in 1808 Sir Colman Rashleigh had an entirely new house built at a distance from his existing sixteenth century manor house at Luxulyan. More common were major rebuilds. Heligan House, home of the Tremaynes, was almost wholly rebuilt in the decade before 1809, becoming 'one of the handsomest and most commodious mansions of the county'. The Earl of Falmouth's Tregothnan was described by Thomas Staniforth in 1800 as 'very indifferent', but it was largely rebuilt in 1816-18, the new Gothic style house encasing some of the old. Other houses were also expanded and remodelled in the fashionable Gothic style, such as Pentillie, the home of the Corytons in the far east of Cornwall overlooking the Tamar river. This was altered in 1810-15.

Extensions were common, such as the east front at Trelowarren or additions, such as a dining room at Tehidy added by the Bassets in the 1810s. Libraries and chapels were also sought-after extras, often requiring new wings. Even the miserly Sir Christopher Hawkins felt he had to rebuild the south front of his Trewithen House. In the early 1800s many country houses in Cornwall would have echoed to the sounds of builders demolishing, adding and rebuilding parts of the house. This must have given employment to several hundred masons, carpenters and other craftsmen at the time.

New extensions and additions demanded the most up to date furnishings and more money would be spent on completing the interior in the latest style and purchasing works of art to decorate the walls. Francis Basset was particularly keen on keeping up with the latest fashion, replacing candles with oil lamps at Tehidy in the 1780s, buying the latest four-poster beds and mahogany furniture and 'Turkey mode' carpets. He also installed the first water closet in 1790, which must have made the housemaids' work more pleasant, even if, given the lack of a sewage system, the effluent probably ended up in the same cesspit or river.

'decently dressed'

The gentry also spent a lot of money in this period on the parks and gardens around the houses. This was an age of new ideas in landscaping. Walks, streams, temples and follies appeared, with an abundance of trees. It was a turn away from geometrically rigid and classical French-inspired design to a more 'natural' view from the house. But this was a very unnatural 'nature'. There were no people in it; instead it was populated by some aesthetically pleasing clumps of trees and neatly positioned cattle and sheep, the trees emphasising the solidity and permanence of the estate and its family.

Humphrey Repton, the prominent landscape designer, could command five guineas a day (or ten times the weekly wage of a labourer) plus expenses for his advice. But money was no object and Repton was commissioned to produce several of his 'Red Books' of designs for Cornish parks, including Port Eliot in 1792 and Pentillie in 1809. Some of his designs were put into practice, others appeared decades after he produced them and some never saw the light of day. However, the influence of Repton and other designers was felt in the growing use of terraces around the house, conservatories, as at Port Eliot, and flowerbeds. At Mount Edgcumbe, an orangery was added to the gardens in 1785 and a fountain in 1800. These accompanied a triumphal arch which had been put in place after the visit of George III in 1789. New walls emphasised the boundaries of parks, as at Clowance. Here the St Aubyns had a substantial stone wall built in the 1790s enclosing its parkland and preserving it from prying eyes.

While landscaping their parks, removing inconvenient cottages and planting thousands of trees, landlords would sometimes see it as their duty to open up those parks at times to the general public. At Tehidy in 1810 there were 'public days' when people were invited to stroll through the grounds, safe in the knowledge that they would not be chased off by the gamekeeper. This was more organised at Mount Edgcumbe at the other end of Cornwall. There, the Earl in 1809 was allowing the park gates to be opened to the inhabitants of Plymouth across the water every Monday, as long as they were 'decently dressed'. They had to enter their names in a book and on one Monday in June there had been 905 visitors of a suitable sartorial standard.

'charities to sundry poor people in the course of the year'
Another expense that would have been regarded as unavoidable was the cost of charity. Charitable provision was of two kinds. First, the landowner would be expected to subscribe to the many schemes that were emerging at the turn of the new century to 'improve' society. The hospital, a 'county' library, the major literary institutions that came in the 1800s and 1810s all had subscription lists headed by the great and the good. There was a certain social cachet in appearing high up the list of subscribers, ranked by the amount given. Any self-respecting gentleman would not want to be missing from such subscription lists. Similarly, at times of food shortages and hardship the gentry were expected to pitch in and help fund soup kitchens or contribute to funds to buy in grain from elsewhere.

The second type of charity was more regular and directed at the tenants and inhabitants of the landlord's own estate. Sometimes this involved one-off payments to those in need. For example, in 1805 the Lanhydrock estate accounts include a guinea given to 'Coombes, the man that had his home robbed.' More regular payments included the £1, 17 shillings and sixpence to pay for 'three quarters of a year schooling for poor children [at] Lanhydrock.' Down at Redruth the amount of 'charities to sundry poor people in the course of the year' doled out by the local Lanhydrock estate steward came to £5 and three shillings. However, to put that in perspective, this amounted to only just over one per cent of the stewards' costs for the year, almost half of which (£200) was his annual salary. At Lanhydrock the £21 which paid the poor rates for the parish was more significant, although this still amounted to only just over three per cent of the general outgoings.

Charity was as much about ceremony as cash. At vital events – christenings, weddings, funerals, birthdays – and at Christmas, there would be charitable presentations, dutifully reported in the press. For instance, in 1810 on the marriage of Viscount Falmouth to Miss Bankes of Dorset, a suit of clothes was given to every poor person in St Michael Penkivel, the parish effectively owned by the Viscount. Even the new gentry, perhaps especially the new gentry, honoured what was seen as their obligation to give the occasional hand-out to the poor. On William Lemon attaining his 21st birthday in 1795, even though he 'was not in the county', the tradesmen and labourers who worked for the family were 'hospitably entertained' at their country house at Carclew, while 'considerable quantities of provisions, bedding and clothes were distributed to a very numerous poor'. The *Sherborne Mercury* did not ask why there were so many poor in the first place.

'I will never raise wages'

Yet another necessary expense was managing the household and estate. The day to day running of the estate was delegated to stewards or land agents, or sometimes lawyers. They would consult with and give advice to the landowner when necessary but would be directly responsible for letting the farms and houses, surveying and maintaining boundaries, overseeing any building work, collecting rents and payments, keeping accounts and sifting the many requests for charity and donations that flowed in. This was a responsible job and stewards like William Jenkin at Redruth, who managed the local interests of the Lanhydrock estate, were well-paid in consequence.

The steward on the home estate would also superintend the servants, although there could be considerable leeway for some of them. At Trelowarren in 1820 the butler was in overall authority over the indoor male servants and the stable men and was expected to 'report their conduct when necessary'. All the female servants were under the management of the housekeeper, 'with the exception of the cook'. She could hire and fire them 'without applying' to the landlord, Sir Richard Vyvyan, or his steward. She also had the power to 'attend to the poor and distribute small charities', although 'nothing to be given to vagrants'.

Unfortunately, the wages paid to the butler and housekeeper at Trelowarren were not stated but they probably amounted to £50 or more a year plus board. (A sum of £50 then would equal almost £5,000 now, while the annual earnings of a labourer would have been around £20-25 a year at the time.) At Tehidy in 1793 the cook was paid £40 plus board and the gardener £30. There would be others on a pay similar to the cook, such as the head gamekeeper. They were tasked at Trelowarren to watch the woods 'for wood stealers and depredators' as well as poachers. The pay of coachmen and grooms would be somewhat less than that of the gardener. The gardener at Rashleigh's Menabilly in the 1830s received as much as 60 guineas a year, plus a cottage with an allowance of vegetables, fuel and milk and a 'present of five guineas at the end of every year, after the first', provided he gave satisfaction, 'as I will never raise wages'. But at Menabilly the gardener had more than the usual responsibilities, living in and 'taking charge of Menabilly House during the winter months when [the family is] resident in London'.

Female servants were paid less. At Tehidy, laundrymaids were paid 18 guineas a year, the lady's maids 12 guineas and a general housemaid 10 guineas a year. By the end of the century, the servants at Tehidy had been given uniforms, their provision in 1778 establishing Francis Basset as Cornwall's most progressive landowner, at least in his own eyes. The servants at Tehidy were also from that date summoned by bells. In the second *Poldark* book Demelza summoned Jinny Carter by pulling on a tassel in 1788. This would have been unusual for small landowners like the Poldarks, who would be more likely to shout to get their servants' attention. Whether shouted at or not, loyal servants could sometimes be rewarded when their employer died. Sir Vyell Vyvyan in his will of 1815 gave a year's wages to 'my old servants John Smith, James Sander and William Holegrove' and five guineas to his servant Avis Tregunno. Avis received a year's wages in addition, as did 'each of my other servants who have lived in my service five years'.

Spending on the house and its management and on charitable donations were unavoidable outgoings for the gentry, while improvements to the grounds were seen as essential to keep up with the neighbours. On occasion, over-enthusiastic building projects could turn out to be more costly than predicted, as did the Trevanions' ambitious reconstruction of Caerhays Castle in the early 1800s. Problems were more likely to arise when less necessary spending on sport, hospitality, gambling or politics got out of hand. Francis Poldark threw away a lot his wealth gambling at cards. Most Cornish landed families were able to avoid his fate, any problems being more likely to arise from unwise investments, over-extended finances or excessive borrowing. That said, debts were commonplace, the gentry being able to raise money fairly easily, usually from known acquaintances with a high degree of trust, on the collateral of their estates.

'entertainment was handsome'

But what did they do when they were not checking their accounts, handing out charitable donations or planning the next fashionable improvement? When not managing their estates or their servants, landed families engaged in an endless, peripatetic social round, visiting each other's houses and dining together. Invitations to visit were issued freely. However, in the age before the telephone, the precise time or even day was left open. Given the mobility of some of the gentry the first task was to find them at home. In 1800 the Liverpool banker Thomas Staniforth and his wife, whose daughter had married John Hext of Restormel, near Lostwithiel, came to stay for three or four months while their daughter was expecting a child. One day they decided to act on an invitation from Sir Christopher Hawkins to visit his house at Trewithen. They sent a servant on ahead 'to inform Sir Christopher of our intention of dining with him'. But when they arrived they found he had gone to a meeting about a school at Helston. They left cards and continued on to Truro. On the way there they 'met him on the road but I [Staniforth] did not recollect him till he was past'.

Sometimes, even if the landowner was not at home, the visitor could be shown around the house. At Boconnoc the steward provided tea and showed the Staniforths the collection of china, the orangery and the greenhouses. The visitors were luckier at Tehidy, where they stayed for three nights. 'Our reception was friendly and hospitable by his Lordship' while the 'entertainment was handsome'. A decade earlier James Boswell had also visited Tehidy. There he:

> found life in a seat of ancient family, the ground
> prettily worked by rising and falling; a great deal of
> wood; a large and splendid house; table, servants
> everything in style. Lady Basset was a charming little
> woman with that elegance of look, manner and address
> which is very rare.

All this was very much to the taste of this insufferable snob. Even more so was the astounding variety of alcoholic beverages on offer during the dinner of two soups, a fish course, venison and other dishes with an 'admirable dessert'. Later, when staying at Boconnoc, Boswell was offered a 'supper of roast hare, roast chicken and partridge and other dishes' as well as the inevitable 'choice wines'. At this time, dinners usually began between four and five in the late afternoon. Joseph Farington, the landscape painter who visited Cornwall in 1810, never dined earlier than 3.30 or later than five during his stay. Dinners were the main occasion for conversation, although Farington reported Basset as saying he would not 'for social intercourse wish to see more than seven at table'. After dinner tea was taken around eight o'clock.

Evenings were classed as 'usual' by Farington if they involved 'tea, cards and books'. At Tehidy 'after tea the ladies were employed in music and in working at a social round table'. This 'work' would presumably have been embroidery of some kind. When Staniforth visited Tehidy, Francis Basset's daughter, an only child, played the piano 'while the ladies worked'. There was 'pleasant conversation' until around eleven when the ladies retired, the men following at midnight. Sometimes cards were played although Staniforth preferred to read Borlase's *History of Cornwall* while his son in law and the ladies played cards. Card games, usually whist, could be played for money, Boswell winning two guineas at whist (the equivalent of a month's salary for a labourer) while staying at Truro.

Conversation, reading, tea, music and cards were the staple evening's entertainment of the landed gentry. During the day, when not visiting other houses or viewing sites of interest (the Staniforths were taken to Roche Rock, the Cheesewring, sailed down the Fowey River and shown the new port of Charlestown during their stay), much time was spent by the men walking, shooting or fishing. While Thomas Staniforth preferred fishing, both the river and sea varieties, his son in law was out almost every morning shooting the wildlife on his estate. The life expectancy for woodcocks, partridges or rabbits was not long in the grounds and woods around Restormel House.

conversation, reading and playing music

Women also enjoyed the visiting and dining and the walks around the newly landscaped grounds of the country house, but the life of the women of the upper class was more restricted than that of their menfolk. Some would take an active role in managing the house, although this would often be devolved to housekeeper and cook, leaving the lady of the house little more than a supervisory role. Sewing and embroidery, the art of conversation, reading and playing music were supplemented by an expected involvement in charitable activity. When Farington visited Tehidy, he reported that Miss Basset was off to inspect a Sunday School she had established in the vicinity. Girls were expected to have the social graces and be accomplished in the arts. Sir Francis Basset had paid to have a tutor come down from London in the summer to give his daughter drawing lessons.

The ability to play the piano or draw added to girls' status in the marriage market. It was here that the mother would play the important role, arranging the round of country house visits and dinners in such a way as to include meeting with eligible young men or bachelors. As did Mrs Teague when she visited Ross Poldark with her daughter Ruth before Ross's marriage to Demelza. A lucky escape for him. Ross had met Ruth at a ball at the assembly rooms in Truro and such events also played a critical role in the match-making process. So did time spent in London, restricted to the wealthier section of provincial gentry and sometimes the families of MPs. Marriages were not exactly arranged, more a matter of negotiation once the couple had declared their compatibility.

At the marriage, the father of the bride had to provide what was called a 'portion', a lump sum which effectively became the property of the husband after marriage, as the law did not recognise that married women had any separate assets. In return, the groom would promise a 'jointure', an annual payment to the widow in the event of his dying first. Usually the annual jointure was around a tenth of the portion but sometimes, in order to attract a higher status match, a family might offer a higher portion for their daughter or a higher jointure for a son. In such a way new money could marry into old families, but only at a cost. Marriage portions controlled the entry of new blood into the elite.

Of course, there were some who avoided or flouted the conventions of the marriage market. In *Poldark*, Ross scandalised Cornish society by marrying the daughter of a miner. Such a gulf in social status was in reality very uncommon. Moreover, the story of Sir John St Aubyn suggests that Cornish 'society' could still be quite tolerant of those who ignored the accepted norms. Born in 1758, John succeeded in 1772 to the family estates at Clowance in west Cornwall and at Devonport. John dutifully served as Sheriff of Cornwall and then became a Member of Parliament. Over the years he represented Truro, Penryn and Helston. Not that his political career was marked by any great achievements, as he never actually bothered to speak in the Commons. He was also rarely found living on his Cornish estates, preferring the life of the Home Counties. Nonetheless, he was a patron of the arts, in particular befriending and sponsoring John Opie, the most prominent Cornish artist of the time.

This did not prevent him from pursuing a colourful private life. John was attracted to the opposite sex from an early age, forming 'a connection' with an Italian woman and having a child by her while spending three years in France on an extended Grand Tour. He then conducted long-distance relationships with not one, but two Cornish women. One was Martha Nicholls, daughter of a landscape gardener and the other Juliana Vinicombe of Marazion. Martha bore him seven illegitimate children and Juliana another eight, before he did the decent thing and married Juliana in 1822, aged 64. (She was 11 years younger.) Sir John eventually passed away in 1839 at a good age for the time of 81. He was one of the last of the more relaxed Cornish squirearchy who apparently cared little about reputation or gossip.

When they were not enjoying hospitality, gardens, illicit relationships or country sports, landowners involved themselves in running society more generally. Most of them, like Ross Poldark, took this seriously, out of a sense of responsibility, duty or obligation or more reluctantly as a necessary price to pay for their good fortune, or more cynically as a way of buttressing their power. This was the final call on their time. Moreover, at the end of the 1700s there were growing opportunities to involve themselves in planning, financing and organising the new institutions that were starting to appear. The casual approach of the eighteenth century was fading and a more serious attitude emerging in regard to what would later be called 'social problems'. This was fuelled partly by evangelical enthusiasm and partly by concerns about the more mobile, less controllable, populations being created by industrialisation and urbanisation. Landowners like Ross Poldark, with a strong sense of social responsibility, were centrally involved in the creation of the new institutions that anticipated the Victorian age and a more scientific, or at least rigorous, approach to social issues. We must therefore take a little time to visit some of the institutions that were beginning to make their appearance at this time.

10
The Prison

I f one of the 'rioters' we saw in action in chapter 8 was unlucky enough to be arrested, he or she may have been taken to the newly-built prison at Bodmin to await trial. This was the prison to which Ross Poldark dutifully reported the week before his trial for incitement to riot and felonious plundering of a ship. As a gentleman Ross would have been treated considerably more kindly than the more usual occupants.

Bodmin Jail was actually one of the first model prisons to be built in the British Isles. Hosting its first inmates in 1779 it was constructed along the principles proposed by John Howard, who had written a searing indictment of the state of prisons after a tour around them in the 1770s. The jail was purpose built, with 100 cells, each intended for just one occupant and with segregated areas for men and women. A rule of silence and a basic diet made conditions hard, but not intolerable. There was running water and the hard labour involved tasks like sawing wood and cutting gravestones for men and spinning and carding wool or washing and mending the clothing of inmates for women. A report in 1812 complimented the jailer, James Chapple. He was 'humane, active and intelligent', while the authors of the report were impressed that 'the floors of the day-rooms and cells are washed once a week in winter, twice in summer'.

'knocked down, cut, kicked and mangled ... in a most brutal manner'
Despite having one of the first modern prisons, Cornwall was in fact relatively crime-free in Poldark's days. That is if the ongoing smuggling business and the occasional technically illegal beach harvests are ignored. However, this does not mean that it was entirely peaceable. The regular food 'riots' could be supplemented by more informal fracas. For instance, two occurred in one year in 1804. In July at Newlyn there was what the *Times*

termed 'afflicting circumstances'. A fisherman, Samuel Jenkin, 'having drunk excessively at a public house, became very quarrelsome' and offered to fight anyone. His challenge was taken up by Thomas Richards, 'another fisherman, somewhat inebriated'. The pair were in the street preparing to beat each other black and blue when Joseph Strick, a mason and the neighbour of Richards, pitched in and tried to persuade Richards to come away. Richards was having none of it and 'gave Strick such violent blows on the face that so exasperated him as to throw Richards from his arms'. He (Strick) then gave him 'two or three hard blows to the stomach on which he fell to rise no more'. The unfortunate Strick was committed to the assizes on a charge of manslaughter, a warning to others to take care when trying to stop a fight.

A few months later at Truro two soldiers who were stationed in the town arrived at the New Inn in Kenwyn Street at ten in the evening. They were already drunk and the landlord refused to serve them. They left but came back at midnight (there were no licensing hours in 1804). They demanded rum from a Mr Allen, a miller from Gwennap, who they mistook for the landlord. Allen retreated in alarm. The soldiers contented themselves with breaking some door panels and then left. They were pursued by the landlord and two others, who caught up with them near the Infirmary. There was a scuffle and the pub landlord, a man named Morris, took the cap of one of the soldiers for identification purposes. The soldiers followed Morris and his colleagues back to the inn. There the landlord shut and locked the door. But the soldiers 'began to cut and thrust at him through the broken panel with a sabre and a bayonet', before bursting open the door and attacking those inside. Allen received a cut to his hand while another, an innkeeper from Chacewater called Roberts, was stabbed in the thigh. Roberts then ran out and was chased to Calenick Street where he was 'knocked down, cut, kicked and mangled ... in a most brutal manner.'

after almost a year in the prison hulks

Commotions like these, while not everyday occurrences, were fairly commonplace. It is significant that both these cases involved drink. In a society where heavy drinking was not unknown violent affrays would be expected. More generally though, at the end of the 1700s Cornwall was not the lawless place that some later Methodists, keen to take the credit for its moral reformation, liked to paint it. For instance, at the summer assizes of 1789 only two people were on trial. One, John Burris, was accused of stealing two silver tablespoons and four silver teaspoons. For this heinous crime, he was sentenced to death. The number of such sentences had risen sharply during the 1700s as the 160 offences punishable by death in 1765 had become over 200 by 1800. Yet, as the severity of the law gradually tightened, the number of death sentences that were commuted also rose. In John Burris's case, his sentence was quickly reduced and, like around half of those receiving death sentences, he was reprieved.

Cornwall had Bodmin Jail as an alternative to the death sentence, although long periods of incarceration in prison were rare before the Victorian age. A second possibility that was increasingly resorted to was transportation. Before the 1780s this had been to North America, but the American Revolution had put paid to that option. In the mid-1780s an alternative became available in the new colony of Australia. Some of those sentenced to fixed periods of transportation, such as Robert Lenderyou, who received seven years transportation in 1794 for stealing cotton from a shop at Redruth, may never have been transported anywhere. Instead, they were kept in fever-ridden prison hulks, out of commission navy vessels anchored at Portsmouth, Plymouth or London, for the duration of their sentence.

Normally, the plan was for the convicted felon to spend a few months in these hulks before being taken on a convict ship to the other side of the world. One of those sentenced to transportation at this time was Mary Bryant, born Mary Broad, of Fowey. In 1785, aged 20, Mary was part of a gang of three who robbed a woman on the road to Plymouth, making off with 11 guineas and her silk bonnet. They were caught and sentenced to death. Mary's sentence was then reduced to seven years transportation. Almost a year was spent languishing in the prison hulks, before she was included in the first convoy of 11 convict ships carrying colonists to New South Wales in Australia.

After a long voyage via South Africa, the convoy landed at present-day Sydney and the 1,500 people on board, half of them sentenced convicts, began to establish their settlement. Things did not go well, to say the least. Disease cut a swathe through the settlers, plants brought from Europe failed to thrive, farm animals perished, and hunger became their constant companion. To that we must add the harsh punishment meted out to anyone who complained too loudly.

Mary had married her Cornish husband Will Bryant and had a child on the way out and she had another while at Sydney. But this didn't stop her joining with other malcontents who were fed up with conditions and began plotting a way out. Over a year or so, they carefully prepared their escape. By March 1791 they were ready. Stealing the governor's cutter, Mary, Will, their two children and seven others set off northwards along the coasts of New South Wales and Queensland. On reaching the northernmost point of the continent, they headed out to open sea and, two months later, landed at the Dutch colony of Timor in the East Indies.

Once there, they claimed to be survivors of a shipwreck. Their story was at first accepted. But then the local authorities at Timor discovered the truth, reportedly when Will Bryant got drunk and began boasting of their exploits. Unwilling to alienate the British, the Dutch promptly handed the group over to be shipped back to England. Conditions on board were clearly not of the best. During the journey, Will, both their children and three other companions all died.

In 1792 Mary was tried again at the Old Bailey and sentenced to serve the remaining year or so of her sentence in Newgate Jail in London. But by then, her story was being publicised in the press. Supported by James Boswell, a campaign was launched for her release. This did not succeed in getting her out early but when her sentence expired in 1793, she received a free pardon and, more importantly, a pension of £10 a year from Boswell. Unfortunately, however, he died two years after this, and the pension ceased. Mary returned to Cornwall but what happened to her after that remains a mystery.

'behaved in the most riotous and disorderly manner'

Most women who found themselves on the wrong side of the law at this time remained a lot less well-known than Mary Bryant. One such was Jane Carleen. Jane was a servant who, like many others, had a child by her master in 1803. This particular employer, John Tremayne of St Keverne, had turned her out and her child was born in the local workhouse. After the birth, Jane left with her child, but a few days later an unattended baby was found some distance away in a cart near Marazion, with injuries to its side. The child died of its injuries 17 days later. It proved to be Jane's unnamed baby. She was committed to the assizes where the judge told her she was lucky the child was found alive or the charge would have been murder. As it was, she was found guilty of 'misdemeanour', sentenced to two years in prison and a fine of £20. The judge had been minded to send her to the pillory but feared that 'the indignation of the populace might endanger her life'. John Tremayne was to appear at the next assizes, also charged with misdemeanour. It is not known whether he paid her £20 fine, a considerable sum amounting to about £2,000 these days.

Not all women were passive victims, as was Jane. The bold Margaret who propositioned Ross Poldark in a pub was not an exceptional part of Truro life. There were several reports of 'riotous and disorderly women' in the town in the 1790s. For example, Honor Humphrey had 'frequently occasioned riotous noise in the streets.' In 1796 Elizabeth Pill claimed that Honor Rawe, a widow, had come to her house 'in a state of intoxication and behaved in the most riotous and disorderly manner'. Women appeared regularly at the quarter sessions. Mary and Susanna Grey were up before the magistrates in Bodmin in 1792 for 'lewd and disorderly' behaviour, a description usually reserved for prostitutes. In 1819 at the Cornwall quarter sessions held in Truro, Grace Johns was accused of assault on the governor of Maker workhouse and his wife, while Jane Varcoe had to answer for being 'lewd and disorderly and keeping a house of ill-fame' at St Stephen in Brannel. All these women were discharged.

When they were punished it was usually by the summary form of being whipped or put in the stocks or pillory. The stocks, where the offender was seated, was used most often for drunks. Pillories held the offender in an uncomfortable standing position. Such summary justice sometimes concluded with a public flogging. The usual punishment for petty thieving was to be stripped and receive 30 or 36 lashes on the bare back, this being doled out to men and women alike. Floggings could be in addition to prison terms. At Helston in 1784 Mary Hext, who had stolen a leather purse containing eleven shillings, was sentenced to be 'whipped and committed to the house of correction ... for one year'. At Launceston in 1811 Jonathan Barnes was publicly whipped for stealing oats while at Truro there was a regular flogging route which took the captive around the Middle Row at Boscawen Street before the row was demolished.

'the keeper began shovelling away the dirt'

Those sentenced to short terms in prison of a few days or a week or two were more likely to spend time in a local prison than in the new model prison at Bodmin. Even there, overcrowding meant that by 1820 prisoners were still being transferred to the older county jail at Launceston Castle. This was the jail from which Ross and Dwight Enys had freed Jim Carter. The actual conditions there were, if anything, even worse than those painted by Winston Graham in his book. The jail was not large, consisting of three dungeons in a building, now long gone, in 'a large yard belonging to the old ruinous castle'. John Howard visited it in 1775. He found that there were two small dungeons for men and another for women. Each was around six to seven foot deep and varied in width from five to nine feet. It was 'very offensive, no chimney, no drains, no water, damp earth floors'. 'I once found the prisoners - there were six to eleven usually housed there – chained two or three together. Their provision is put down to them through a hole in the floor above (used as a chapel)'. On his first visit Howard found the jail keeper, his assistant and all the prisoners to be sick with fever, while a previous keeper and his wife were reported to have both died of fever in the same night. Local lock-ups, used for petty criminals, were little better. The town jails at Penzance and Falmouth had no water, although the prison at Truro had been rebuilt in the 1770s and consisted of 'four convenient rooms.' The debtors' prison at Lostwithiel had also been 'lately improved and whitewashed'.

Probably the worst prison visited by Howard in Cornwall was the privately owned debtors' prison for the Hundred of Penwith, at Penzance. This comprised two rooms in the keeper's stable yard. The one for men was eleven foot square with one small window and a 'very damp' earth floor.

> The door had not been opened for four weeks when I went in, and then the keeper began shovelling away the dirt. There was only one debtor, who seemed to have been robust, but was grown pale by ten weeks close confinement, with little food, which he had from a brother, who is poor and has a family. He said the dampness of the prison, with but little straw, had obliged him ... to send for the bed on which some of his children lay.

Two of his children had died during the ten weeks he had been in prison and 'they were almost starving'. Later, he wrote again to Howard, reporting that he now had a companion, 'as miserable as himself'.

'eight poor widows of this parish and borough'

The number of debtors in Cornwall's prisons in the 1770s appears to have been almost as many as the number of convicts. As debtors pondered on how they or someone else might clear their debts, the poor more generally might be offered aid in poorhouses or workhouses, which were becoming more numerous by the end of the eighteenth century. At this period however, the workhouse was not the sole, or even the main, resort in times of hardship. Poor relief involved a mix of the official poor law and charity. The source of the charitable help could be the church, which tended to direct its aid towards the temporarily destitute, injured and disabled soldiers, shipwrecked sailors and the like who had been cast up on the shores of coastal parishes or were passing through. Help for those on the move might also be obtained from borough authorities. The corporation at Penzance gave ten shillings and six pence to a 'Turkish gentleman in distress' in 1792 as well as a shilling for a 'poor woman passed from Southampton to Scilly' and 'some distressed sailors from Genoa passed from Falmouth'. These latter cases would presumably have possessed passes issued to them at their previous place of stay vouching for their genuine need. Help could also of course be given to permanent residents. Stephen Phillips received two shillings at Penzance after 'he lost his boat in a gale of wind', which doesn't sound an over generous recompense.

The local gentry were active in providing charity in similar circumstances or on regular occasions, sealing their link with their local community. In 1812 Francis Enys gave bread to the poor of Gerrans parish for example, following the 'usual custom'. Each of 34 men and women received at least six pence worth of bread. William Jenkin, acting on behalf of the Lanhydrock estate in 1799, informed his new employer that he was in the habit of dropping 'a small matter into the hands of poor distressed families which lie within the neighbourhood of Tincroft Mine as their distress happens to come to my knowledge'. The Lanhydrock estate owned the mineral rights to this mine and was following the practice of their rivals, the locally-based Bassets who provided 'liberal donations to poor families' in their home parish of Illogan. This bounty was not just one way though. In return for these 'liberal donations', the Bassets pressed Illogan's parochial authorities not to apply the poor rate to mineral royalties, as happened in most other parishes. This worked until 1799 when the parish vestry at Illogan decided that more money could be raised by adding the mineral royalties to the assessed poor rate than relying on uncertain donations at the whim of the landowner. It is not known whether the charitable donations continued after this or at what level.

In the boroughs there were often small charitable trusts. These supplied charity to specific groups. In 1788 Mrs Hannah Bedford, the widow of a clergyman at Launceston, established a trust of £50, the interest from which would go to 'eight poor widows of this parish and borough'. In 1801 in the same town Mrs Mary Bedford gave £50 'in trust for as many poor persons of this borough as may be considered the greatest objects of charity'. At Redruth in 1816 there was a charitable club for poor aged widows and pregnant women, providing linen, woollens and coats. Similar trusts funded almshouses for the poor, usually widows and the elderly, in places such as Tregony and Truro, where the residents also received two shillings a week allowance. These were supplemented by emergency aid at times of exceptional distress. As we saw in the account of food rioting, subscriptions were collected, usually headed by the most prominent local landowners, at times of food shortages or when there was a likelihood of rioting. The money was used to buy food such as salted pilchards to make up for the deficit in grain or the high price of bread. In crisis times soup kitchens were the equivalent of our food banks, offering the poor free soup. In 1801 the soup at Illogan, where 36 gallons was being consumed daily, was made from bullocks' heads, peas, rice, onions and turnips.

'petty bullying'

If the gastronomic delights of the free soup were not enough and charities insufficient, the poor could always turn to the official poor relief provided by the state since Elizabethan times. This was managed by the local parish or borough authorities and answerable to the justices of the peace. Each authority had to provide poor law overseers, an unpaid position usually lasting a year. The overseer's job was to collect a poor rate levied annually on local property owners and distribute the proceeds to any qualified poor person who applied for relief. In a rural parish around a quarter of households would pay the poor rate. By the 1790s growing complaints were being heard from this minority as the cost of the poor rate began to rise.

From the late 1600s, in order to qualify and receive relief a person had to prove that they had a 'settlement' in the parish. To keep families together, settlement was not automatically gained by being born in a parish, unless it were an illegitimate birth. Instead, the child would gain the settlement of his or her father. However, there were a number of other ways it could be acquired. If a woman married, she would gain the settlement of her husband. Working for a year in a parish, being an apprentice there for more than 40 days, or renting a house or land for a year also gained a settlement. To receive relief an applicant was examined to prove they had a settlement by one of these means. For example, at Helston in 1815 Samuel Eva, aged 67, was examined. He had been born in neighbouring Wendron parish but left at 17 to work as a granite stonemason, then went to Devonport for 30 years. He returned to Helston for a short period when ill and was given aid in the local workhouse for six weeks. On recovering, he went back to Plymouth for another seven years. Finally, back in Helston again, his settlement in

Helston was eventually proven by his having been employed by 'Richard Johns, deceased'.

If an applicant for poor relief could not prove their settlement a removal order was made against them and they would be taken to the parish where they had a presumed settlement. As can be imagined, this left a considerable degree of room for disputes between parish overseers as to which parish was responsible for paying for a particular pauper. It led to a lot of 'petty bullying', as one historian has termed it, with overseers pushing potential paupers out of the parish before they could qualify for poor relief. This was particularly harsh for any unmarried woman who was unfortunate enough to get pregnant. Her child would automatically receive a settlement but was likely to cost the authorities money, so strenuous efforts were made to remove such women from the parish and dump them somewhere else.

Removals and such legal measures as that of 1697 that required paupers to wear a badge on their shoulders with a letter 'P' and the initial of the parish make the poor law of the time look exceedingly harsh. Indeed, a meeting of the 'principal inhabitants' of Redruth in 1813 proposed to badge the town's paupers in this way. However, this also implies that hitherto it was not in place and in fact badging was rarely adopted in practice. The system was harshest on 'vagabonds' and strangers found begging. Such people were more likely to find themselves subject to summary justice. In 1819 vagrants at Bodmin were convicted of begging and flogged through the streets. On the other hand, if a pauper was elderly and well-known to the overseers, their treatment by the poor law in Poldark's times could be quite humane. Small payments of money or sometimes in kind were regularly doled out to people in their homes. This could include help with funeral costs, clothing, tools or medicines. For example, at St Erme in 1776 Honor Plint received two shillings a week poor relief for 32 weeks. In addition, she was given wood, shoes and stockings, coal, an apron, half a pound of candles and even 'liquor' to the value of nine pence. Four week's payment for nursing her while sick and her funeral charges suggest the overseer was making Honor's last days as comfortable as possible.

'as shall be fit and convenient for persons in their degree'
There was considerable flexibility in the system. In some places upcountry the poor rate was used to supplement labourers' wages from the 1790s. There were only a few examples of that in Cornwall, where wages were higher, although unemployed labourers were often paid a shilling or so a day to mend the roads, as at Gwinear and Phillack in 1816, or dig up the soil

of unimproved crofts. At the same time there was concern that if the 'able-bodied', those able to work, became dependent on poor relief they would become idle and be a burden on the ratepayer. One 'solution', increasingly turned to in the 1700s, was the 'workhouse'. There were already poorhouses, places where the poor who were unable to rent a cottage or look after themselves were housed at the expense of the parish. But these did not necessarily demand that their inmates do any work. Workhouses were different in that support would be offered, but only in return for work. The problem was how to cope simultaneously with those who were too young, too disabled or too old to work on the one hand and the 'able-bodied' poor on the other. Reserving the workhouse solely for the 'able-bodied' while continuing to grant other paupers relief in their own homes or, if they did not have their own home, in a separate poorhouse was the obvious recourse.

In practice, it was too expensive to maintain separate poorhouses for these folk. If the parish relied on a workhouse then it had also to serve as a place of refuge for the aged poor, too old or infirm to live independently, or for the unmarried mother unable to find accommodation and her child, too young to work. Usually, the workhouse housed the least likely workforce imaginable – the old, the sick, the very young. Even the able-bodied population of workhouses would have included a fair proportion of semi-criminal workshy vagrants, those with learning difficulties and the mentally disturbed. And what work could they do that would not undermine the labour market outside the workhouse? At Redruth in 1799 woollen manufacture was proposed, as it had been in the newly built workhouse at Truro 20 years earlier, although there the rider 'for the few that can work' may be significant. Later, the brain-numbing task of oakum picking, teasing the fibres out of old ropes to seal the timber hulls of ships or make matting, became the preferred employment for workhouse inmates.

Workhouses had first appeared in the 1600s and were being encouraged by the Government from the 1720s. Not every parish bothered to build one, however. In Cornwall they tended to be confined to the more populous places. Legislation in 1782 encouraged parishes to band together to share the cost of workhouse provision and this led to some sending their poor to workhouses elsewhere. In 1795 Gerrans parish on the Roseland, which already possessed a poorhouse, capable of housing up to a dozen elderly folk, decided to send some paupers to Padstow workhouse, 35 miles away on the opposite coast. The parish would provide 'for each person wearing apparel, bedding and medicines as shall be fit and convenient for persons in their degree' and if the pauper earned any money for their work it would be refunded to the parish. Padstow appears to have been quite entrepreneurial, making agreements with 32 parishes in the 1790s, from Kilkhampton in the far north to Callington in the east and as far west as Perranzabuloe and Probus. However, it does not seem to have been much of a success, the workhouse being temporarily shut down soon after 1800. In 1811 George Worgan, investigating the state of Cornish farming, found that only 35 of Cornwall's over 200 parishes had a workhouse. Moreover, in Cornwall the poor may have been numerous, but the proportion of the population receiving out-relief (that is aid while living at home) was lower than the average for England and Wales. Consequently, the wailing of the ratepayers was less noisy.

'it would render them indolent and insolent to their superiors'

At least ratepayers did not have to grumble about the cost of education. Schooling at this period was entirely privately financed. Some still questioned the wisdom of any education for the poor. Rather surprisingly, given his consistent encouragement of science and technological innovation, one of those opposing the provision of schools for the poor was Davies Gilbert. In 1807 he stated that it would be:

> prejudicial to their morals and happiness; it would
> teach them to despise their lot in life, instead of
> making them good servants in agriculture and other
> laborious employments to which their rank in society
> had destined them; instead of teaching them
> subordination, it would render them factious and
> refractory ... it would enable them to read seditious
> pamphlets ... it would render them indolent and
> insolent to their superiors.

Davies Gilbert and his colleagues seriously underestimated the possibility that mass education could in fact reinforce the existing social order, justify inequality, instil discipline and help to produce the very subordination he lauded.

Nonetheless, even girls were sometimes receiving some schooling by the 1790s. For example, at Redruth a charity school had been set up to teach 'ten little girls' twice a week, although the emphasis was on practical skills such as 'sewing, spinning, knitting etc.' as much as reading. Girls were not, however, admitted into the grammar schools that were found in Cornwall's larger market towns. Some of these, such as those at Truro, Helston or Launceston could trace their history well back into the eighteenth century. Truro Grammar School, where Ross and Francis Poldark from the less exalted landowning class rubbed shoulders with the sons of newly rich merchants such as George Warleggan, was the most prestigious school in Cornwall at this time. Boys were sent to it from all over Cornwall, although sometimes, as in the case of Edward Pellew, their stays were quite short. Pellew ran away from the school to escape the flogging, which was no doubt thought to be a necessary ingredient of a boy's education.

Other grammar schools were providing some competition by the 1800s. Redruth Grammar School was founded in 1801 and attracted around 60 boys, sons of local tradesmen and professional families. They paid fees of £2 (around £200 now) for a term's education, which included stationery and coal. In return the boys were taught the normal grammar school curriculum of Greek, Latin, French, drawing, maths and geography. The headmaster in 1805 was also 'at great pains to correct the provincial dialect of his pupils'. For this he was paid £90 a year (around £8,000 now), while the second master received £60. By 1807 the school had grown to a capacity of 200 boys, including ten boarders who paid £25 a year plus one guinea entrance fee. Day scholars were charged four guineas a year, which suggests a price fall since 1801. Indeed, in 1804 an 'infant seminary' for girls at Redruth was just as expensive as the Grammar School.

While provision for the middle classes was clearly expanding in this period, the vast majority of families were unable to afford the cost of such education. Sometimes, there was an alternative available in charity schools, established at an earlier period and intended to offer free education for the children of the poor. In 1797 the charity school at Redruth was 'very large and duly attended'. But the provision of charity schools was patchy and by the 1800s, with the ravages of wartime inflation, many charity school trustees were being forced to prioritise the payment of the teachers' salary or the upkeep of the buildings. With little left over to provide free teaching, some sort of fee had to be paid by the pupils. For example, at St Anthony in Meneage on the Lizard a charity school had been endowed in the 1740s, receiving a sum amounting to £4 a year. Any surplus after paying the regular costs of the school was 'applied to the purchasing of spelling books and shoes for the children'. Each child was charged a penny and a half a week for reading and threepence for writing. Only a small minority of parishes possessed such schools. Others were sometimes supported by a local landowner. Sir Christopher Hawkins for instance paid for a school in Grampound Town Hall in the 1810s, attended by 30 boys and 30 girls.

After 1811 a few new schools began to appear, following the principles of the National Society for Promoting Religious Education, to provide elementary education for the children of the poor in accordance with the teaching of the Church of England. These, known as National Schools, employed a supposedly more scientific monitorial system which rested largely on drilling discipline into the children who spent much time learning by rote. There were not too many in Cornwall before 1820, although later they became the basis of the English system of mass education. One National School was found at St Neot in 1818, teaching 50 or 60 children. The master received a salary of £22 a year, while another £2 was spent buying books. The money was raised through a subscription organised by the curate of the local church.

The majority of schooling was not supplied by charitable subscription or the Church but by private ventures. Some of these mimicked the grammar schools, with their focus on the classics, and appealed to the better-off. Others aimed lower and offered a basic education to the children of the poor at a modest price. A large parish such as St Austell contained as many as 18 such schools in 1818, educating at that time 353 children 'who are in great want of books'. These included the so-called 'dame schools', although some of those in the mining districts were run not by women but by men injured in the mines. In agricultural St Clether, in north Cornwall, a dame school was 'kept by an old woman, containing from eight to 16 children'. In Grampound in 1818 there were three such schools, teaching 'about 40' children, who each paid two to four pence a week for the privilege. This suggests the total income of the three women who ran them was around ten shillings a month, about the equivalent of one farm labourer's weekly wage.

Finally, a new type of schooling was being offered by Sunday Schools. These had begun to appear in the early 1790s, the *Sherborne Mercury* reporting in 1792 that 'several Sunday schools have lately been established in Cornwall, the beneficial effects of which are already very perceivable'. The growth of Sunday schools accelerated after 1800. In the towns there might be several by 1818, with each denomination offering its own school. For example, at Redruth there were three, one provided by the Church of England, a second by the Baptists and the third (and largest) by the Methodists. Altogether 400 children were attending, possibly as many as a third of the children in the parish. At Falmouth there were as many as five Sunday schools, run by Anglicans, Baptists, Independents, Methodists and

Quakers. This last provided a secular education with none of the religious indoctrination that marked the others. Sunday schools could even be started at the mines. One began in 1811 at Wheal Alfred mine, between Helston and Camborne, attracting 250 sons and daughters of the miners. While such schools might have taught a basic literacy, little effort was put into writing skills and the quality of the education was limited, learning by heart verses from psalms for example.

'physic is half of it humbug'

If schooling was rough and ready so was medical practice. Physicians had risen in social status during the eighteenth century and joined the ranks of lawyers as a respected profession. But the technique of many doctors at this time could not be said to be much of an improvement on the customary medical knowledge passed on by women from one generation to the next. In the *Poldark* universe Verity was right to wonder whether Dr Choake knew any more than the old women at the fair. For instance, the slow replacement of female midwives by male doctors had no discernible impact on the death rate of women in childbirth, which remained around one to one and a half per cent for each confinement. Richard Polwhele, as late as the 1820s, was noting some of the herbal remedies widely employed 'by some church-town crony [who] will sometimes cure a disease which had been given up by her betters as irremediable'. Each everyday infection had its corresponding herbal cure. Mugwort tea with camomile was taken for colds, elderflower for fevers, mint for coughs and camomile again for stomach upsets. Meanwhile, the bite of an adder was tackled by a mixture of plantain and salad oil.

Many swore that such remedies were 'better than doctor's trade'. The bleeding, purges and leeches that seem to have been the first resort of Dr Choake were not unusual. The treatment advised at Penzance in 1809 for a man aged 54 suffering from a strangulated hernia was manipulation, bleeding, a tobacco enema, and a warm bath. The result was duly noted - 'died'. At Penzance also, the dispensary accounts included 'drugs, leeches, laudanum and beer'. There were some, like the keen young Dr Enys, who had new-fangled ideas based more on scientific experiment than tradition. At Truro Dr John Wolcot, the writer and satirist who took John Opie under his wing, was notably scathing about the pretensions of his peers. For example, he encouraged patients with fever to drink water, something routinely denied them by other doctors, who deemed such rashness to be inevitably fatal. Wolcot wrote that 'physic is half of it humbug ... the patient's pockets are often picked by it ... A physician can do little than watch nature and, if he sees her inclined to go right, give her a shove in the back'.

Meanwhile, dentistry remained primitive, with the routine treatment being extraction, often performed by someone like the local blacksmith, another family member, or the sufferer themselves. An increasing consumption of sugar in tea during the 1700s probably caused a deterioration in the state of people's teeth. Gaps, ill-fitting false teeth or, as in Aunt Agatha's case, toothless jaws, were the fate of the majority as old age beckoned. Yet, like doctors, specialised dentists were beginning to sell their services more aggressively. In 1811 a notice appeared in Truro advertising a husband and wife dentistry practice. They would 'render the teeth white and beautiful, though ever so tarnished, without impairing the enamel; such as are loose they fasten, they also fix real and artificial teeth ... they engraft teeth also on old stumps ... the most dangerous stumps drawn, without the use of a surgeon's implement'.

'mitigate the sufferings of the poor in seasons of sickness'

With no form of anaesthesia other than alcohol available until the 1850s, dentistry and much surgery was a difficult task. Nowadays, surgery is confined to hospitals, but in Poldark's days hospitals were few and far between. In some places upcountry charitable foundations had been founding hospitals from the early 1700s. These hospitals were not for the wealthy, who would at this time be treated at home. Instead, they were places where the sick poor could be healed. Not that the poor were especially eager to enter them. There was some suspicion that hospitals were used by surgeons to practice their black arts on the poor with no fear of repercussions. When Dwight Enys visited Bodmin in the winter of 1790/91 he went to the hospital to see this new institution. In fact, there was no such place in Bodmin or anywhere else in Cornwall that early. Although one of the first places to get a purpose-built prison, Cornwall was slow to obtain its hospital. There had been much talk of building a hospital - a meeting in 1790 had agreed that a hospital for a the 'sick and lame poor' was a jolly good idea - but the infirmary at Truro did not appear until 1799.

When the Cornwall Infirmary was finally opened it had 20 beds. No patients with infectious diseases were admitted although those with chronic illnesses could sometimes stay in the hospital for a considerable length of time. Around 1810 Mary Cornish from Helston had been 'taken ill and put in Truro Infirmary where she remained for 13 months.' Patients would be recommended by doctors or others for a stay in the hospital. For instance, Thomas Tregedeon, aged 25, was one of the first patients, recommended by William Jenkin, the Lanhydrock estate agent at Redruth. The patient's sponsors would pay their fees and those of the doctor who would visit them in the hospital. In 1812 the *West Briton* reported that there was 'no bed vacant' at the Infirmary, but this was unusual. In normal times around seven or eight were empty.

More day to day medical treatment was provided by the local dispensaries which began to be set up after the turn of the century. The Penzance Public Dispensary and Humane Society was established in 1809 with the aim 'to remove or to mitigate the sufferings of the poor in seasons of sickness.' It paid for a physician, a surgeon, a dispensing chemist and a nurse and was an early example of a pharmacy. Other towns such as Helston and Truro also had their dispensaries which offered a range of services, from vaccinations against smallpox to saving persons from death by drowning to distributing coal to the sick in addition to handing out medicines. In the meantime, miners could obtain support at times of accidents or illness from the sick clubs that had been set up at most of the larger mines by the 1800s. A few pence was paid by the miner every month, in return for which a physician would attend them for a specified period of time when they were ill. The problem was that when mines closed, as they invariably did after a time, the sick club assets disappeared with them. This is why miners by 1800 were also among the most likely occupational group to be members of an independent friendly society to insure themselves to some extent against periods of reduced pay through illness or accidents.

While medical provision for the poor and medical knowledge more generally was beginning to improve by the early 1800s, the final area that cried out for reform was the treatment of the mentally ill. In the eighteenth century, insanity was still regarded by some as the result of evil spirits rather than an illness. It was therefore the responsibility of the church rather than doctors. While the deranged member of a landowner's family could be safely hidden away at home, most of the insane or mentally ill were dealt with in the 1700s by being cast into any convenient poorhouse. Even those who suggested remedies were not that enlightened. John Wesley for example suggested that a cure for madness was to 'set the patient with his head under a great waterfall, as long as his strength will bear it'. If waterboarding did not have the desired effect then he 'should eat only apples for a month'.

Sometimes the insane were chained up if they were a danger to themselves or others. Conditions were often grim. A visitor to Bodmin workhouse in 1804 found:

> a room where a poor lunatic was confined. He lay stretched on a little short and dirty straw at the further end with a few rags, but no shirt upon him. He held a book in one hand, at arms length, on which his eyes were intently fixed ... The floor of this room was earth and literally a puddle of water and dirt more than one inch deep. It was with difficulty I could step into it without treading on his excrement which lay everywhere about the floor and, from the appearance of what was in the fireplace, must have been there a fortnight or more. The keeper had, most unmercifully beat the poor fellow and given him two black eyes.

That was a particularly bad example, but at Liskeard a survey in 1807 found two women chained to a damp stone floor in filthy conditions. In 1819 Philippa May, a woman chained up in the workhouse at Padstow, broke out of her constraints and strangled to death another woman who was with her in the same room.

It was because of scandals like these that moves began to be made to build an asylum at Bodmin for the insane poor. Enabled by the County Asylum Act of 1808, this took its first patients in 1820, at the end of the Poldark period. Even then, it took some time for the mentally ill to be transferred to Bodmin as parishes had to pay the cost of their upkeep while there. That cost was considerably higher than placing them in the local workhouse, even though the diet at Bodmin was similar to that of a workhouse. It was not until the New Poor Law of 1834 that the practice of locking up the mentally ill in local poorhouses or workhouses ceased.

'keeping guard over a sailor at St Erme Green one night'
The day to day management of law and order and the poor law was in the hands of an army of unpaid overseers, churchwardens and constables. There was no full-time police force in Poldark's time. In times of need the response was to swear in more special constables or call in the military or turn to the Volunteers after 1794. In the towns the constables were appointed by and answerable to the corporation or town council. In the countryside constables

would receive their orders direct from the magistrates. For example, at St Stephens by Saltash in 1805 the constables were told by a magistrate 'to apprehend George Rowling, labourer, for stealing potatoes from a field belonging to Samuel Bews'. Once successfully apprehended, the constable or constables would then have to escort the prisoner to the county jail at Bodmin to await trial. In less serious cases the constable would ensure miscreants were safely penned up in a local jail or another suitable place. At St Erme in 1795 the constables paid three shillings to John Boson and William Rickard for 'keeping guard over a sailor at St Erme Green one night by order of Edward Collins', Collins being a magistrate.

Magistrates, or justices of the peace, had to be men of property, owning land with a rentable value of at least £100 a year. Dissenters and Catholics were excluded, while the eighteenth century saw a rise in the proportion of clergymen on the bench. Once there, magistrates would have considerable powers over such things as the regulation of wages and prices, apprenticeships, the licensing of alehouses, overseeing highway and bridge repairs, checking the administration of the poor law and collecting taxes. These matters were reviewed and discussed at the Quarter Sessions, where the magistrates also acted as judges in the criminal cases brought before them. These were relatively mild offences, serious cases being reserved for the assizes, held every six months alternately at Launceston and Bodmin.

The cases heard at Bodmin Quarter Sessions in 1792 included Mary Dennis, who had claimed she was pregnant when she was not and Thomas Moyle, brought before the magistrates for disorderly behaviour in Wendron and threatening the life of Joan Dowah. Both Mary and Thomas were sent for one month's hard labour. The other cases, of being lewd and disorderly, being idle and disorderly in St Austell workhouse and of two men found wandering and begging in Egloshayle and at Linkinhorne, were all discharged.

Magistrates were appointed by and answerable to the Lord Lieutenant. This position had from the 1500s taken over from the sheriff as the most important in local government. Only the wealthiest landowners figured as lords lieutenant. In Poldark's time in Cornwall the position was monopolised by the Edgcumbes of Mount Edgcumbe in south-east Cornwall. George Edgcumbe, the first Earl, was Lord Lieutenant until 1795, followed by his son Richard, Lord Lieutenant from 1795 to 1839. In the meantime, the status of sheriff had declined and had become a time consuming and quite expensive job dealing more with the day to day issues of local government.

The power of the County Bench and its justices of the peace only went as far as the boundaries of the Cornish boroughs. The boroughs had their own magistrates and were run by their corporations. These included places such as Truro, Launceston, Liskeard and Helston, but not relatively new towns such as Redruth or St Austell, places that were as big or bigger by 1800. By the 1780s and 90s most of the old borough corporations had become self-perpetuating. Corporations selected their own replacements and chose the mayor. Not that this prevented conflict. In Truro between 1780 and 1784 there was a vicious struggle on the town council between supporters of the Boscawens, who throughout the eighteenth century had acted as Truro's patrons, and new merchant money represented by Henry Rosewarne. Sir Francis Basset, who was at the time feuding with the Boscawens, saw an opportunity and threw his weight behind the insurgents. They temporarily won control of the council in 1780 and of the two MPs it elected. However, the Boscawens were only dislodged for a short period. A year after their client Captain Edward Pellew had turned up at the Town hall in 1784, armed and ready to challenge a councillor to a duel, the Boscawens took back control and Basset retired from the fray.

Even in the towns therefore, it was difficult, if not impossible, to escape the influence of the landed gentry, who made up Cornwall's magistracy. But their power did not stop there as they also monopolised Cornwall's parliamentary representation. Control of Parliament may have appeared remote to most people in Poldark's Cornwall, but it meant that landowners could combine their control of the local magistracy with the making of laws to protect their wealth and status.

For the average cottager the power of the landed class was at this time most visible in the game laws. These laws protected the sole right of landowners to kill deer, pheasants, partridges, hares and rabbits on their land. Various legislation had been passed in the eighteenth century to protect and strengthen landowners' hunting rights. These built on the game laws of the seventeenth century which first restricted killing game to landowners of a certain wealth and authorised them to appoint gamekeepers to protect those rights. Laws to ensure the strict preservation of game were passed and poaching became a criminal offence later punishable by transportation. The landowning class's obsession with killing wild animals as a pastime meant that other country dwellers were denied the opportunity of killing them for food, even if they were hungry. In Poldark, Jim Carter's attempt to put food on the table resulted in his arrest and eventual death from a fever caught while in jail.

The game laws were probably the major factor causing friction between the classes in the countryside. But Members of Parliament defended them staunchly as essential for social order. In theory, those MPs were answerable to those who had elected them as their representatives. But by Poldark's time the number of voters who sent MPs to London was fewer than it had been a century or so earlier, even while the population in general was much greater. While the House of Lords speaks for itself, a large proportion of the seats in the Commons were by this time also basically owned by landowners who possessed sufficient property in a town to control its representation. With 44 MPs in the 1790s, almost a tenth of the total, Cornish landowners were uniquely placed to supplement their income by buying and selling parliamentary boroughs. In fact, given the number of parliamentary seats in Cornwall, politics and boroughmongering were of much more importance than in other places. Indeed, it was stated that Cornish families owed their status either to the mine or to the borough, as we shall find out in the final chapter.

11
The Borough

On a chill morning one day in March 1810, the dawn chorus on an out of the way heath near London was disturbed by the sounds of horsemen. Two parties of men arrived separately and, after a little discussion, calmly began preparing to fight a duel. Detaching themselves from their companions, two of them, one from each party, stood back to back and then paced out the requisite number of steps. They turned. Shots were exchanged but whether by design or bad aim neither hit their target. The two men, by then in their fifties, were Francis Basset, Lord de Dunstanville, and Sir Christopher Hawkins. The account of the duel laconically stated that 'the boroughs were the cause'. Disagreements and disputes over the control of the boroughs and the election of borough MPs were at the heart of the feuding between gentry families in Poldark's time, although rarely going as far as duelling.

In the sixth book of the *Poldark* saga Ross is persuaded by Lord Falmouth to become a Member of Parliament for Truro. After some hesitation and flirting with the ideologically more sympathetic Francis Basset, Ross agrees. Although in the book the outcome is uncertain, in reality there was little need to worry about the actual election. This was because Truro was essentially a pocket borough, in the pocket of the local landowner who was Lord Falmouth. He told the town's corporation, who selected the voters, what to do and they did it. Although Ross was sympathetic to the newer ideas of reform, Lord Falmouth was totally opposed to any such notions. However, it was not unusual for an MP to hold different opinions from his patron, although he would be expected to support the Government if his patron had pledged to do so.

Most of Ross's fictional parliamentary activities were based on fact. In Ross's days, Cornwall had 21 parliamentary boroughs, each returning two

MPs. There were another two who represented the 'county', which including all those towns, villages and rural areas outside the 21 boroughs. The less accurate aspect of the fiction concerned the supposed ideological rift between Basset and Boscawen, Lord de Dunstanville and Lord Falmouth. In the real world, there was no such difference between them. In 1792 in a parliamentary debate Basset 'expressed himself strongly against all such [reforming] societies as those alluded to. Men attempting thus to ride the whirlwind knew not where the tempest might end'. George Boscawen would have heartily agreed. Both detested anything remotely resembling democracy and both were opposed to parliamentary reform. In this their views were typical of almost all the older landed families of Cornwall. The one exception before 1800 was the aggressive borough-monger, Sir Christopher Hawkins, who paradoxically expressed some lukewarm support for parliamentary reform in the 1780s and 1790s.

'frequently corrupt, often expensive, and in few elections were there genuine contests'

A parliamentary borough was not the same as any old borough. Parliamentary boroughs had the right, sometimes going back as far as the late 1200s, to send two representatives to Westminster. In Cornwall's case, the number with that right was increased sharply in Tudor times when several new parliamentary seats were added to its medieval boroughs. In consequence, Cornwall's 44 MPs meant that it was grossly over-represented. With just over one per cent of the population of Great Britain, Cornwall returned almost ten per cent of the House of Commons. The whole of Scotland after the Act of Union in 1707 only had 45 MPs while the precociously growing industrial cities of northern England were often left with no direct representation. Manchester and Leeds for example had no MPs. In contrast places in Cornwall which were little more than villages – such as Tregony, Mitchell, St Mawes and Bossiney – each had their two MPs. Looe had four MPs, two for East Looe and two for West. Newport in the valley below Launceston had two MPs as well as Launceston itself. Even within Cornwall the fastest growing towns around 1800 – Camborne, Redruth, St Austell - and two of the biggest - Falmouth and Penzance - had no MPs whereas tiny St Germans did.

Borough politics in the 1780s were 'frequently corrupt, often expensive, and in few elections were there genuine contests.' This was mainly due to two factors. The first was the nature of the franchise, which had arisen haphazardly and varied in detail from place to place, although generally giving greater weight to property than to persons. The second factor that gave landowners considerable opportunity to control a borough was the low number of voters. Camelford only had 20 electors in 1816 as did St Germans, while at Bossiney in 1784 various disqualifications among the usual ten or so voters left just one person – the local vicar – as the sole voter electing two MPs.

To understand how the patrons controlled the boroughs we need to understand who could vote in Poldark's days. There were, very broadly, three types of parliamentary borough. In the first, known as householder boroughs, in theory all male residents could vote as long as they were householders and not in receipt of poor relief. Sometimes this led to relatively large numbers of voters, as at Penryn, Tregony, Grampound and St Ives. Such boroughs were unstable and difficult to control. They were therefore the most likely places where patrons had to turn to outright bribery to maintain or secure their control. If there were smaller numbers of householders, as at Callington, it was easier for a landowner to gain control by buying up a lot of property. He could then put pressure on his tenants to vote the way he wanted them to. That could be guaranteed because at this time there was no secret ballot. Someone's vote was public knowledge.

Householder boroughs shaded into the second type, which were burgage boroughs. In places such as Newport, Saltash or West Looe the vote was tied to particular properties rather than to people. If a landowner could buy up these properties, he could increase his influence; if he could demolish them he could reduce the number of voters. The final type of borough was the corporation borough, where only the town council or burgesses selected by the town council had the right to vote. The older Cornish boroughs tended to be of this type, places such as Lostwithiel, Bodmin, Launceston, Helston and Liskeard. Here, councillors, who were themselves self-selected rather than subject to election, would pledge their vote and if necessary, the votes of any misnamed 'freemen' they had selected, to a dominant landowner. In return that landowner would be expected to provide charity, maintain schools and sometimes, as at Helston, pay the poor rate for the town. If the corporation felt they were not getting value for money, they could sometimes look for a new patron. Helston Town Council did this in 1804 when for a short time it swapped the usual patronage of the absentee Duke of Leeds, who had inherited the Godolphin estate, for that of Hawkins.

In order to possess a parliamentary borough a patron had to have an 'interest' in it. Fundamentally, this meant owning land and property in the borough. Through this, pressure could be exerted on tenants. In the bigger towns it would not be easy to own sufficient property. Boroughs with only a few voters were the easiest (and cheapest) to control, which is why in this period there was a tendency for the number of voters to fall, even as population more generally was rising. During the Poldark period there was a steady reduction of voters in many Cornish boroughs. The number at Launceston in 1796 was 23; by 1816 it was 15. By that year there were just 25 voters in Truro, 21 at East Looe, 12 at West Looe and a mere seven at St Germans. Each of these places sent two MPs to the House of Commons. At Bossiney, anyone with the status of freeman could vote, but this status was hereditary. As a result, by 1816 there were only nine voters, eight of whom were from the same family. Such pocket boroughs with tiny numbers of voters tended to go under the radar. In contrast, boroughs with more voters required more open bribery to persuade the voters to sell their votes. It cost Christopher Hawkins £13,000 (around £1.4 million now) in 1796 to ensure the seats at Tregony and Grampound went to his nominees. At Penryn, the going rate for a vote was openly recognised, and elections were welcomed by the voters as a useful boost to their incomes.

'a disgrace to the office ... you are a broomstick'

Occasionally, there would be attempts to throw off landowner influence. These usually occurred in the corporation boroughs. At Liskeard in 1802 opponents of the Eliot interest that controlled the borough put up a candidate in the 'independent interest'. Many of those who voted for the independent candidate were then promptly disqualified by the mayor, who was the returning officer. There were disputed returns and a petition to the Commons, 'complaining of an undue return for the said borough'. Meanwhile, a riot broke out connected with the election. Even in householder boroughs, discontents could surface. At Tregony in 1812 the voters 'showed symptoms of deserting the old interest and voting against the proprietor of the borough'. They had invited others to stand but kept it secret 'lest they should be turned out before the dissolution [of parliament]'.

These rebellions of the townsfolk tended to become more frequent after 1805, when a mood of reform began to grip some of the lesser gentry in the countryside, spreading during the 1810s to the farmers. This echoed a growing sense of self-confidence among the professional classes and tradespeople of the towns, newly respectable and often driven by a self-righteous dissenting evangelism at odds with the tradition-bound deference to the local, or sometimes not so local, landlord who owned their borough. In 1818 there was another challenge at Truro led by the local middle class who accused their long-established patrons, the Boscawens of Tregothnan, of foisting MPs on them with little or no regard for their wishes. The Boscawens had faced down a similar revolt in the early 1780s, but this time they lost control and Lord Falmouth had to demur to the demands of the townsfolk. If Ross had still been MP for Truro he would have been out on his ear. At Liskeard the unsuccessful challenge of 1802 to 1804 was followed up by another effort in 1818-19 to oust the Eliots as patrons, although here it was again unsuccessful.

These incidents notwithstanding, in most of the 'closed' boroughs of Cornwall there was a 'profound repose' at election time. As the reformers' newspaper the *West Briton* observed in 1812, 'when the day of election comes, the freemen will be informed whom it is that their patrons "favourably recommend" for the honour of their votes' and perform their duty obediently and diligently. Political conflict did not usually occur during elections but between them as the gentry manoeuvred and squabbled between themselves over control of the boroughs and the status and influence this brought with it.

This was a golden age for lawyers as claims and counterclaims swirled around the right to vote in a context of some ambiguity about who exactly held that right. Local disputes were a small echo of the wider battles between the gentry over control of the boroughs. After the St Ives election of 1819 a dispute between the town clerk and the mayor over the election return reached the courts. There were claims the mayor had provoked the town clerk by saying he would not have been town clerk if it were not for the action of the mayor and his friends on the council. The mayor countered by claiming the clerk had accused him of being 'a disgrace to the office ... you are a broomstick etc.'. The case was dismissed with the judge concluding that the conduct of both parties was 'bad'.

Why was so much energy and money spent by the gentry on controlling Cornwall's parliamentary seats? The answer is threefold – money, status and power. Once control was secure, patrons could make a profit by selling the seats to aspiring candidates or to the government at elections where they needed to bolster their support. In this way control over a parliamentary seat was a form of property, an asset that could be bought and sold on the market. Second, by using their MPs to support the government of the time, a landowner might hope for reward in the shape of a baronetcy or even a peerage. Basset duly received his from Pitt, while Hawkins received a baronetcy in 1791. Finally, control of the boroughs seems to have served as a surrogate for conflict between gentry families as they struggled for prestige and status. The power obtained through control over MPs gave the gentry a direct connection to the parliament in London. This was then reflected back into Cornwall, their London connections adding to their local power and setting them above those whose ambitions were limited to a Cornish stage.

'the haughtiness of his temper [which] keeps pace with his ambition'

In the early 1780s when Ross returned from America the main borough owners in Cornwall were, in the west, the Boscawens and in east Cornwall the Edgcumbes and Eliots. Between them, these families controlled 16 of Cornwall's 42 borough seats. The Boscawens had Truro and Mitchell and could count on one seat in Tregony and at St Mawes. The Eliots held Liskeard and St Germans and split Grampound with the Edgcumbes, who in turn controlled Lostwithiel and had a half interest in Fowey and Bossiney. Two new boroughmongers then appeared on the scene in the shape of Francis Basset and Christopher Hawkins. These two then aggressively challenged the older families by attempting to extend their borough patronage at their expense.

Basset was first in the field, opposing the Boscawen interest in 1780 most spectacularly in Truro. This opportunity arose because Henry Rosewarne, a merchant based at Bosvigo on the town's outskirts, was challenging the Boscawens for control of the town council and therefore its two MPs. Rosewarne had wide ranging interests in the coal, timber and wine trades, an involvement in tin smelting and was vice-warden of the Stannaries. In 1780 he succeeded in convincing the rest of the town council to elect him and his nominee as MPs in the place of the Boscawen candidates. Francis Basset enthusiastically supported this campaign and threw his weight behind Rosewarne.

Differences between Basset and Boscawen were exacerbated by personal antipathies between them and Basset's notional support of Charles Stuart Fox and the Whigs, in opposition to William Pitt, in the 1780s and early 1790s. We have already seen how James Boswell, when visiting Tehidy, expressed some surprise at the contradiction between Basset's opinions and his attachment to Fox. Ed Jaggard, the historian of Cornish politics in this era, argues that the rivalries between patrons resulted more from family squabbles and personal competitiveness as a new generation of young men born between 1757 and 1761 came of age and inherited their estates. Cousin networks then came into play as they marshalled their forces in a quest for more power and control. Basset, who seems to have suffered from chronic insecurity, over-compensated by stressing the ancient lineage of his family at every opportunity (even though its riches rested on eighteenth century copper mining) and pushed for greater rewards commensurate with his new wealth. One of his aims was to secure a peerage, which he achieved in 1796 after switching sides and supporting Pitt once war with France broke out in 1793.

Basset also tried to extend his influence at Penryn at the expense of the absentee landlord the Duke of Leeds and also the Edgcumbes, who had some local influence there. Moreover, he spent money buying up property at Mitchell in the hope of dislodging the Boscawens from that place too. These machinations were successful. By the late 1780s Basset controlled a seat at Mitchell and had managed to obtain Tregony and, with more difficulty, Penryn. In the meantime, although regaining Truro in 1785, the Boscawens had lost their interest at Tregony, St Mawes and Mitchell and instead of six seats now just had three.

This was the high point of Francis Basset's political intervention before he over-reached himself in the 1790 'county' election and alienated many of Cornwall's other landed families. Basset had already in 1784 broken the unspoken convention that those who manipulated borough politics should stay out of the relatively freer county elections. In that year he had openly worked for the election of his cousin Sir John Molesworth to one of the county seats. When Molesworth abruptly retired in 1790 Basset then pushed forward another cousin, Sir John St Aubyn, for the vacant seat. He succeeded only in stirring up the non-committed voters. His opponents were quick to castigate 'the haughtiness of his temper [which] keeps pace with his ambition, and his want of judgement is equal to both'. The *Times* reported that 'the contest is warm, and chaises and four are flying all over the county with voters.' The majority of these did not support St Aubyn and in the event Basset's plans collapsed. Thereafter, he steered clear of county politics. While the aggressive efforts to increase his influence waned somewhat after this setback, Basset continued to be involved in borough politics. He installed Davies Gilbert as MP for Bodmin and in 1815 was buying property at Camelford to forestall Lord Falmouth who was trying to expand his interest in that borough.

Meanwhile, a second Cornish boroughmonger had emerged in turn to challenge Basset. Christopher Hawkins was first elected for Mitchell in the Boscawen interest in 1784. By 1796 he had bought out Basset's interest at Mitchell and also controlled Grampound. With these seats as his base he then began assaults on Penryn, Helston, Tregony and St Ives. By 1816 he controlled six seats – at Grampound, Penryn, Mitchell and St Ives, and had briefly held Helston. The unpredictable, retiring bachelor Hawkins contrasted with the showy aggression of Francis Basset, who was never slow in pushing himself forward in everything he was involved with. Hawkins in contrast appears to have indulged in boroughmongering with an 'element of prank playing', less interested in the political outcome than the fun of the chase. His duel with Basset in 1810 could hardly have been entirely unpredictable or shocking for contemporaries.

This pair had between them expanded their interests at the expense of the established parliamentary dabblers - the Boscawens, Eliots and Edgcumbes – although the latter were never pushed out entirely, merely retreating to their core seats. In doing so, they tended to stay away from those parliamentary boroughs where control was contested or less secure. These were places where the number of electors was larger and in consequence more difficult to keep in line. The largest electorate in Cornwall was at Penryn, while Tregony and Grampound also presented some difficulties at times. In those boroughs, bribery was a necessary resort for the ambitious borough owner in order to keep the voters content. It was that element of open corruption that ultimately led to the demise of the unreformed system. The equally corrupt but commonplace practice of controlling a borough and nominating MPs with no reference to the actual voters went on undisturbed in the background and was accepted as normal by all but the minority who supported various measures of parliamentary reform.

'profited in the school of corruption'

In 1813 the campaigner William Cobbett reported that a parliamentary committee had found that the Duke of Leeds had violated the law at Helston by making use of bribes. When Christopher Hawkins lost influence there, the town's corporation had turned back to the Duke of Leeds, inviting him to resume his patronage. In return they demanded he pay the town's poor rates, as was the previous practice. This amounted to around £1,600 a year (equal to £110,000 these days). It was not this however that got the Duke into trouble but the open sale of the town's two seats. These were found to have been offered to aspiring parliamentarians for 5,000 guineas apiece. Cobbett recounted how the vote was managed by the corporation on behalf of their patron. He asked 'and by whom was this system of cunning and corruption arranged and conducted? Why, chiefly by clergymen. Wherever bribery, corruption, treating, intimidation or political persecution, or any species of undue influence or dirty work was to be managed, the clergy ... were the most active and prominent agents'. He went on to cite the example of Tregony, where 'a clergyman was among the foremost in delinquency'.

Although Cobbett did not name him, that clergyman was the Reverend Richard Gurney, Vicar of Cuby. Gurney was at the centre of Tregony's borough politics throughout the Poldark years. In 1792 he had been implicated in encouraging 'mob uproar'. Three effigies representing gentlemen of Tregony who opposed the Reverend's party were carried through the borough and back to his house. His 'lady appeared with a brandy bottle and wine glass in her hand, and in the presence of her husband distributed the contents of it to the mob, and [the Reverend] and his lady appeared extremely pleased with what they had done'.

Later, in 1803, hot feelings between different parties at Tregony were still apparent. In that year Gurney brought a prosecution against five residents that reached the King's Bench in London. He claimed the accused had 'erected on a vacant piece of ground opposite to Mr Gurney's house an effigy, meaning to represent the prosecutor, and that these people had committed several acts of violence, had broken some of Mr Gurney's windows and had violently assaulted the peace officers.' However, his case was dismissed by the judge because of his previous behaviour. In 1817 Gurney came to the notice of Court of King's Bench yet again. This time the court had moved for information against Gurney, who was a magistrate, as well as a fellow magistrate, William Moorman. The two of them had been accused of refusing to licence an inn (the Queen's Head) from corrupt motives, due to their dislike of the Earl of Darlington, who was trying to increase his influence in the borough. Insufficient grounds were found to prosecute Gurney although moves were made against Moorman.

There was a postscript to this a year or so later. A letter had been published in the *West Briton* in 1817 alleging that the vice warden of the Devon Stannary Court had been removed 'in order to make room for Mr R.Gurney, son of the Reverend R. Gurney of electioneering notoriety'. Not content with the income from 'two considerable benefices', the correspondent, writing under the pseudonym 'an enemy to corruption', claimed the Gurneys had obtained a promise that the salary for the vice warden post would be increased eight-fold. The Gurneys then brought a prosecution for criminal libel against the author of the letter. The case was heard at the Bodmin summer assizes of 1818. What created extra interest was the revelation that the author of the letter was a woman, Mary Anne Tucker of Plymouth. Mary, the sister of a Plymouth solicitor, spurned legal representation and forcibly defended herself. 'I could mention many anecdotes', she said, 'showing how Mr Richard Gurney and his son have profited in the school of corruption'. Despite the judge expressing 'his decided opinion that the publication ... was libellous in the highest degree' the jury found Mary Tucker not guilty.

'the tumult became so great that the Mayor adjourned the poll'

A year after this, a trial of five men from Tregony and Grampound found them guilty of travelling to London to procure MPs for unnamed patrons at a price of £3,500 a seat (equivalent to £300,000 nowadays). Such cases clamping down on the open buying and selling of parliamentary seats and the bribery of electors were on the increase in the 1810s. Cornish boroughs such as Tregony, Penryn and Grampound were becoming notorious for the blatant bribery that occurred there as patrons struggled to maintain their hold. It was claimed in 1813 that at Penryn the former practice had been to give each voter 20 guineas (around £1,500) at elections, although that amount had decreased as there were now too many voters (at 400) for even the deepest pocket to sustain. In the 1818 general election, after 'an arduous and unexampled struggle of three weeks duration', Sir Christopher Hawkins and his nominee Henry Swann were declared to have been elected. After a petition was received from his opponents at Penryn, Swann was then thrown out of the Commons on bribery charges. It was found that £20 was still the going rate for a vote. This was paid in instalments, £5 down and £5 after the vote was recorded, with the other £10 made up by Hawkins. Sir Christopher himself, despite being implicated directly, managed to escape expulsion from Parliament in 1819. He had been even luckier in 1807 when he was brought to trial also charged with bribery and corruption at Penryn. Although acquitted, this dashed any lingering hopes he had of obtaining a peerage.

At the 1818 general election the traditional bribery that was rife at Penryn was not restricted to that place alone. At Camelford and Fowey there were petitions after the election disputing the return of the MPs. At Grampound, one of the voters, a Mr Allen of Truro, had demanded every elector should have to take the bribery oath before casting their vote. At this 'the tumult became so great that the Mayor adjourned the poll until the next morning.' The inevitable election petition followed challenging the result. In 1819, after a prolonged debate in Parliament, it was moved that Grampound should be disenfranchised for 'gross and notorious corruption'.

This was of great symbolic importance as it established a precedent that Parliament could reform the system of representation.

But Grampound was unlucky, being no worse than Penryn, Camelford or Fowey, all of which were mentioned at one time as possible candidates to lose their seats. Grampound's misfortune, according to the *West Briton*, lay in the fact that its electors 'went to market with their franchises, without the intervention of a borough broker; they have no patron and, therefore, there is no probability that the visitation due to their transgressions will be averted by the interruption of noble influence, either in the lower or upper House of Parliament'. Poor Grampound was merely a convenient scapegoat for a rotten system and its avaricious ruling class.

In the end only one Cornish borough lost its MPs in the Poldark years. Most of the rest followed Grampound into the curiosity shop of history with the Reform Act of 1832. However, that did not end corruption or the undue influence of the landed class over local politics and elections. Demands for political change were maintained, although shifting to the working classes rather than the small gentry and farmers who had come together to demand reform in the 1810s. These early reformers had profited from revelations of corruption in high places, such as the news in 1815 that the Admiralty had been overpaying private contractors for ships that turned out to be useless. When the mistress of the King's brother, the Duke of York, was found to have sold commissions in 1809, calls for reform from the middle classes were long and loud.

In Cornwall John Colman Rashleigh of Killiow near Truro led a growing reform movement. In 1811 as many as 14 Cornishmen attended a meeting of the Friends of Reform in London and in 1813 they began a successful campaign to open up 'county' meetings to all the male inhabitants of Cornwall. Men like Francis Basset were appalled by this. Later, in 1825, when it looked likely that a reformer would be elected to a county seat, Basset's opinion was typically acerbic: 'it will be a disgrace to have a member forced upon the county by a party chiefly composed of the lower orders'. But the tide was beginning to turn against the reactionary views of Basset. They had swung during the 1810s to be more in tune with the reformers, principled men, liberal in their views, who wanted to see a moderate reform of an indefensible system and who were sympathetic to the plight of the poor and keen to represent their woes on their behalf. Indeed, men of the same ilk as Ross Poldark.

But for every Ross Poldark we have to remember there was a George Warleggan, equally keen to defend their new-found wealth and status by joining the landed class and adopting their ways. They were able to do so, being incorporated by the old, landed families as long as they accepted the latter's rules of behaviour. By these means, despite the fears of some, 'society', either in Cornwall or anywhere else in the UK, did not collapse but staggered on pragmatically. A cloak of modernity, buttressed by pomp, ceremony and ritual, was thrown over the stale traditionalism that endured and festered underneath, ready to re-emerge once the times were more propitious.

Conclusion and reflections

W e've now reached the end of our journey through the Cornwall of *Poldark*. In doing so, we discovered that Winston Graham in his books placed the trials and tribulations of the Poldarks in a historically recognisable context. What is striking is how often the comments of the observers of those times are echoed in Graham's books. Clearly, he borrowed heavily from actual historical incidents and contemporary accounts, sometimes changing the location and timing, at other times embellishing and dramatising, but never to the point where all credibility was entirely lost. The later TV series, in particular the final season, may prove irritating to insiders, with its constant genuflection towards the tourist gaze, but Winston Graham himself was broadly faithful to the Cornwall of the period from 1783 to 1820.

In 1997 Nickianne Moody suggested that *Poldark* satisfied a nostalgic longing for an 'idealised social contract' when it first appeared in 1945. It was a 'fantasy of class reconciliation' at a time of class conflict. That may understate the descriptions of class conflict, or at least of stark differences between rich and poor, the powerful and the powerless that pepper the pages of Graham's books. Moreover, while we live in uncertain times and seek solace in nostalgia, so did previous generations in Cornwall's industrialising period. It's just that the uncertainties they faced were different in those days, less globalised, more local.

Reading *Poldark* leads to some reflection on a few ironies. First, our present uncertainties revolve around the urgent requirement to 'transition' away from fossil-fuelled capitalist industrialisation, one that our Cornish predecessors were to the fore in initiating. Second, instead of being at the centre of global maritime communications, as it was at the end of the 1700s, Cornwall has now been relegated to the end of the line, more 'remote' than it was over 200 years ago despite reaching a point of tourist overcapacity and unsustainable overcrowding. Finally, Cornwall is now being changed in the interests of others rather than, as it was in Poldark's times, transforming itself in its own interests. This occurs despite such tokens as the meaningless designation of the Cornish as a 'national minority' in 2014, a status comprehensively ignored by local and central government and media alike since that time.

In many ways Cornwall was a relatively go-ahead, even progressive, place in the 1810s. Falmouth was one of the most multicultural towns in the British Isles, the first place to get the news from around the globe, its packet boats a critical element in Britain's communications with the rest of the world, the naval squadron based there playing a key role in the early days of the wars of the 1790s. Furthermore, Cornish gentry were at the forefront of calls for parliamentary reform and an end to 'old corruption', even as most of its oldest and wealthiest families clung on to the system that had oiled their accumulation of fortunes. Yet even that comfortable oligarchy had been forced to adapt and open its doors to the close-knit inter-married merchant elite that was shaking up Cornish landed society in the later years of the eighteenth century.

New money and the new families it propelled forward was underpinned by the phenomenal rise of copper mining during the 1700s. This had created an intense, concentrated island of commerce and industry in west Cornwall which, in the early 1800s, began to break its bonds and extend its influence eastwards. Here was the beating heart of Cornish society, entrepreneurial, questing and inventive - the society that had bred the unpredictable genius of Trevithick and Opie and the more solid achievements of people like Humphry Davy and Davies Gilbert.

The traditional landed class might have continued to pull the strings both locally and in their control of parliamentary representation, as we saw in the final chapter, but even that was by the 1820s being challenged by others. Underneath this was the bubbling cauldron of social change. A young population steadily growing in numbers, new villages and a more ambitious and self-confident class of mine captains, tradesmen and merchants all added a new instability. Even the humble were experiencing changes on a previously unknown scale as they toiled through the drudgery of their everyday lives.

Not all of their time was spent in quiet desperation however, as they gathered together in their community life. No longer was the old Cornish language heard on their lips, tethering them to their Celtic past. Instead of gaping at the mystery plays, they were now flocking to wrestling tournaments. Feast days and wrestling were surviving the onslaught of condemnation that showered down from moralising evangelists on the one hand and over-serious Methodists on the other. Yet other old ways, such as hurling and animal baiting were on their way out. Meanwhile, the more boisterous elements of traditional festivals, the mock mayors, the guise dancing, the Christmas plays and the drunken liberties that had accompanied them were beginning to fade under the stern gaze of a newly respectable urban middle class.

Those who now looked askance at the old undisciplined ways were soon being joined by an equally respectable working-class element, as Methodism was embraced wholeheartedly by the common people. At first appealing most deeply to women, the two great revivals of 1799 and 1814 sealed Methodism's place as the principal devotion of the Cornish people. By 1820 the old ways were being joined by the new mass folk culture of Methodism, one of tea treats and hymn singing, that was to colour Cornwall in the nineteenth century.

Yet Methodism had not destroyed the old culture, merely stitched itself onto the old ways, moderating and mitigating them. For instance, food riots remained a part of the Cornish repertoire, an essential resort when grain was short and bread prices soared. Indeed, by the 1790s they had been honed to a high state of perfection and efficiency, prising charity from the better-off even as the latter deployed new weapons, particularly the mounted Volunteers, against them.

Condemnation from on high had also failed to dent the people's willingness to engage in beach-harvesting or wrecking, or their active support for, or at least tacit toleration of, the gangs of smugglers who supplied them with cheap alcohol and consumer goods. A harsh penal code that relied on the threat of the death penalty or transportation or, for lesser crimes, incarceration in foul prisons or public floggings, didn't do much to deter theft and misdemeanours. Moreover, many of these last seem to have been driven as much by necessity as greed.

Cornwall at the turn of the eighteenth century was a society of contrasts: stunning wealth and abject poverty, country houses and overcrowded, stinking cottages, ramshackle and corrupt institutions yet calls for reform, brutal punishments coupled with a growing humanitarian impulse. In short it was a classic laboratory for the interaction of the new and the traditional. It had been one of the first regions in Europe to chart a path to an industrial society. Because that had occurred so early, its society blended the familiar and the novel in a pattern rarely encountered elsewhere.

While Cornwall was a kaleidoscope of contrasts around 1800, the Cornwall of that period might also productively be contrasted with our Cornwall 200 or more years later. The most glaring contrast is that the Cornish of Poldark's days believed they were in control of their own destiny. The Cornish of our days do not. Cornwall is now acted upon rather than acting for itself. In those earlier times, a native merchant class was pointing the way towards a new society while the communities of that society were led by an innovative, confident and optimistic middle class. It was a Cornwall that, buoyed up by its mineral riches, was able and willing to punch far above its weight. Its elite overcame the economic depression of the 1780s, its engineers greatly improved on Boulton and Watt's steam engine, its smugglers fended off the Government's revenue men, while its reformers· were over-represented in the growing clamour for change that accompanied the late 1810s.

It's time therefore to leave Ross and Demelza to their own devices while we remember the real heroes (and villains) of the time - the Cornish people.

Further reading and sources

The examples in this book come from various primary sources and newspapers quarried over several years teaching and writing on the history of this period. But the following books also provided examples and/or offer further reading on this period.

Peter Beacham and Nikolaus Pevsner, *Cornwall*, London, 2014.

Allan Buckley, *The Cornish Mining Industry: A Brief History*, Penryn, 1988.

Allen Buckley, *Princes of the Working Valley: The Day and Night Book of two Dolcoath Mine Captains 1822-23*, Truro, 2007.

Bernard Deacon, *Cornwall: A Concise History*, Cardiff, 2007, chapters 4 and 5.

Bernard Deacon, *Industrial Celts: Making the Modern Cornish Identity 1750-1870*, Redruth, 2017.

Ed Jaggard, *Cornwall Politics in the Age of Reform 1790-1885*, Woodbridge, 1999, *chapters 1-3.*

A.K. Hamilton Jenkin, *News from Cornwall, with a memoir of William Jenkin*, London, 1951.

A.K. Hamilton Jenkin, *The Cornish Miner*, London, 1927.

A.K. Hamilton Jenkin, *Cornwall and its People*, London, 1945.

Jean Hext (ed.), *The Staniforth Diary: A Visit to Cornwall in 1800*, Truro, 1965.

Viv Hendra, *The Cornish Wonder: A Portrait of John Opie*, Truro, 2007.

Alan Kent, *The Literature of Cornwall*, Bristol, 2000, chapter 2

Alan Kent, *The Festivals of Cornwall: Ritual. Revival. Reinvention*, Bristol 2018.

Richard McGrady, *Music and Musicians in Early Nineteenth Century Cornwall*, Exeter, 1991.

June Palmer, *Truro in the Eighteenth Century*, Truro, no date.

Philip Payton, *Cornwall; A History*, 1996, 2004 and 2017, Exeter, chapters 8 and 9.

Cathryn Pearce, *Cornish Wrecking 1700-1860: Reality and Popular Myth*, Woodbridge, 2010.

John Rowe, *Cornwall in the Age of the Industrial Revolution*, Liverpool, 1953 and St Austell, 1993.

John Rule, *Cornish Cases: Essays in Eighteenth and Nineteenth Century Social History*, Southampton, 2006.

F.W.L. Stockdale, *Excursions through Cornwall 1824*, Truro, 1972.

Michael Tangye, *Tehidy and the Bassets: The Rise and Fall of a Great Cornish Family*, Redruth, 1984.

H.Spencer Toy, *The Cornish Pocket Borough*, Penzance, 1968.

James Whetter, *Cornish People in the 18th Century*, Gorran, 2000

James Whetter, *Cornwall from the Newspapers, 1781-93*, Gorran, 2000.

Some academic articles and PhD theses have been particularly helpful or relevant, notably

John Dirring, 'The organisation and practice of banking in Cornwall, 1771-1922', unpublished PhD thesis, University of Exeter, 2015.

Hannah Greig, '"The new Downton Abbey?": Poldark and the presentation and perception of an eighteenth century past', *Journal of British Cinema and Television* 16 (2019), 94-113.

David Luker, 'Cornish Methodism, Revivalism and popular belief, c.1780-18670', unpublished DPhil thesis, University of Oxford, 1987.

Nickianne Moody, 'Poldark country and national culture', in Ella Westland (ed.), *Cornwall: The Cultural Construction of Place*, Penzance, 1997, 129-136.

Rachel Moseley, '"It's a wild country. Wild ... passionate ... strange": Poldark and the place-image of Cornwall', *Visual Culture in Britain* 14 (2013), 218-237.

John Rule, 'The labouring miner in Cornwall, c.1740-1870', unpublished PhD thesis, University of Warwick, 1971.

Mike Tripp, 'Persistence of difference: A history of Cornish wrestling, unpublished PhD thesis, University of Exeter, 2009.

Printed in France by Amazon
Brétigny-sur-Orge, FR

15088667R00114